Communities

ADVENTURES IN TIME AND PLACE

James A. Banks

Barry K. Beyer

Gloria Contreras

Jean Craven

Gloria Ladson-Billings

Mary A. McFarland

Walter C. Parker

NATIONAL GEOGRAPHIC SOCIETY

THIS SNOW GLOBE WAS MADE
BY AN ARTIST NAMED BRENDA
PEPPER. IT SHOWS HOW
PEOPLE LIVE AND TRAVEL
IN A COMMUNITY.

THE PRINCETON REVIEW

McGraw-Hill

New York   Farmington

PROGRAM AUTHORS

Dr. James A. Banks
Professor of Education and
Director of the Center for
Multicultural Education
University of Washington
Seattle, Washington

Dr. Barry K. Beyer
Professor Emeritus, Graduate
School of Education
George Mason University
Fairfax, Virginia

Dr. Gloria Contreras
Professor of Education
University of North Texas
Denton, Texas

Jean Craven
District Coordinator of
Curriculum Development
Albuquerque Public Schools
Albuquerque, New Mexico

Dr. Gloria Ladson-Billings
Professor of Education
University of Wisconsin
Madison, Wisconsin

Dr. Mary A. McFarland
Instructional Coordinator of
Social Studies, K–12, and
Director of Staff Development
Parkway School District
Chesterfield, Missouri

Dr. Walter C. Parker
Professor and Program Chair for
Social Studies Education
University of Washington
Seattle, Washington

NATIONAL
GEOGRAPHIC
SOCIETY

Washington, D.C.

**CONSULTANTS FOR
TEST PREPARATION**

THE
PRINCETON
REVIEW

The Princeton Review is not affiliated
with Princeton University or ETS.

HISTORIANS/SCHOLARS

Dr. Carlos E. Cortés
Professor Emeritus of History
University of California
Riverside, California

Dr. John Bodnar
Professor of History
Indiana University
Bloomington, Indiana

Dr. Sheilah Clark-Ekong
Professor, Department of Anthropology
University of Missouri, St. Louis
St. Louis, Missouri

Dr. Darlene Clark Hine
John A. Hannah Professor of History
Michigan State University
East Lansing, Michigan

Council on Islamic Education
Fountain Valley, California

Dr. John L. Esposito
Professor of Religion and
International Affairs
Georgetown University
Washington, D.C.

Dr. Gary Mason
Department of Geography
Michigan State University
East Lansing, Michigan

Dr. Juan Mora-Torres
Professor of Latin American History
University of Texas at San Antonio
San Antonio, Texas

Dr. Valerie Ooka Pang
Professor, School of Teacher Education
San Diego State University
San Diego, California

Dr. Curtis C. Roseman
Professor of Geography
University of Southern California
Los Angeles, California

Dr. Joseph Rosenbloom
Professor, Classics Department
Washington University
St. Louis, Missouri

Dr. Robert Seltzer
Professor of Jewish History
Hunter College
City University of New York
New York, New York

Dr. Robert M. Senkewicz
Professor of History
Santa Clara University
Santa Clara, California

Dr. Peter Stearns
Dean, College of Humanities and
Social Studies
Carnegie Mellon University
Pittsburgh, Pennsylvania

**CALIFORNIA PROGRAM
CONSULTANTS**

Diane Bowers
Former Assistant Director of
Education for the Yurok Tribe
Klamath, California

Dr. Karen Nakai
Lecturer of History-Social Science
Department of Education
University of California
Irvine, California

Shelly Osborne
Teacher-Literacy Mentor
Franklin School
Alameda, California

Lyn Reese
Director, Women in History Project
Berkeley, California

Evelyn Staton
Librarian
San Francisco School District
Member, Multiethnic Literature Forum
for San Francisco
San Francisco, California

CONSULTING AUTHORS

Dr. James Flood
Professor of Teacher Education,
Reading and Language Development
San Diego State University
San Diego, California

Dr. Diane Lapp
Professor of Teacher Education,
Reading and Language Development
San Diego State University
San Diego, California

**GRADE-LEVEL
CONSULTANTS**

Rob Allen
Elementary School Teacher
Two Mile Prairie Elementary School
Columbia, Missouri

Elaine Culton Braucher
Third Grade Teacher
North Side Elementary School
Harrisburg, Pennsylvania

Astrid Delaney
Third Grade Teacher
Alcott Elementary School
Pomona, California

Glenda S. LaFavers
Third Grade Teacher
Windsor Elementary School
Amarillo, Texas

Linda Lee
Third Grade Teacher
Chabot Elementary School
Oakland, California

Akida Lewis
Instructional Advisor
Los Angeles Unified School District
Los Angeles, California

Mary Ann McGrath, Ph.D.
Third Grade Teacher
Lyman Elementary School
Lyman, South Carolina

Vicki Mirabal
Elementary School Teacher
Chelwood Elementary School
Albuquerque, New Mexico

Donna Yamada
Elementary School Teacher
Booksin Elementary School
San Jose, California

**CONTRIBUTING
WRITERS**

Karen C. Baicker
Maplewood, New Jersey

Matthew Goodman
Brooklyn, New York

Linda Scher
Raleigh, North Carolina

Acknowledgments
The publisher gratefully acknowledges permission to reprint the following copyrighted material: From "The Channel Tunnel" by Adam Westgarth from **Connexions** by Adam Westgarth and others. Reprinted by permission. From "Coyote Gets Turkey Up a Tree" from **And It Is Still That Way** by Tina Naiche, collected by Byrd Baylor. Reprinted by permission. From "The Express Train" **More Sounds We Found**. Copyright 1988 by Wide World Music, Inc. (ASCAP), a division of Shawnee Press, Inc. International. Copyright Secured. All rights reserved. Reprinted by permission. From "The Light at the End of the Chunnel" reprinted by permission of National Geographic Society. From **Uncle Jed's Barbershop**. Reprinted with permission of Simon & Schuster Books for Young Readers from UNCLE JED'S BARBERSHOP by Margaree King Mitchell, illustrated by James Ransome. Text copyright ©1993 by Margaree King Mitchell. Illustrations copyright ©1993 James Ransome. "Open Range" (Poem) from **Cowboys and Indians** by Kathryn and Bryon Jackson. Copyright 1948 by Simon & Schuster, Inc. and Artists and Writers Guild. From **Ben Franklin of Old Philadelphia** by Margaret Cousins. Copyright 1952 by Margaret Cousins, renewed 1980. Random House. From **New Letters of Abigail Adams** edited with an introduction by Stewart Mitchell. Copyright 1947 by the American Antiquarian Society. Greenwood Press Publishers, a division of Williamhouse-Regency, Inc. **The Great Migration**. Copyright 1993 by the Museum of Modern Art, New York and the Phillips Collection. "Harvest" from **Slave Songs of the Georgia Sea Islands** by Lydia Parrish. Copyright 1942 by Lydia Parrish, renewed 1969 by Maxfield Parish, Jr. Reprinted by permission of Farrar, Straus & Giroux, Inc. From **No Star Nights** by Anne Egan Smucker. Text copyright 1989 by Anne Egan Smucker. Illustrations copyright 1989 by Steve Johnson. Reprinted by permission of Alfred A. Knopf. World Book Encyclopedia. Copyright ©1996 World Book, Inc. By permission of the publisher. *(continued on page R40)*

McGraw-Hill School Division 🔭

A Division of The McGraw·Hill Companies

McGraw-Hill School Division
Two Penn Plaza
New York, New York 10121

Printed in the United States of America

ISBN 0-02-149135-6

1 2 3 4 5 6 7 8 9 071/046 04 03 02 01 00

Handbook for Reading Social Studies

One important thing you will do this year is to read this textbook. In order to understand important facts and ideas it is necessary to read in a certain way. This Reading Handbook will show you some helpful ways to read social studies.

Main Idea and Supporting Details

As you read, look for the **main idea** and **supporting details**. The main idea is what the paragraph is mostly about. The details support or add to the main idea. Keeping track of the main idea and supporting details will help you remember what you read.

TiP!

- The first sentence or two of a paragraph often—but not always—contains the main idea.

- Use titles and subheads as a guide in identifying the main idea of a selection.

To Find the Main Idea
Ask yourself:

• What is this paragraph mostly about?

To Find the Supporting Details
Ask yourself:

• What words give more information about the main idea?

In this book, you will read about immigrants. Immigrants are people who come to live in a new country. Read this paragraph and notice the main idea and supporting details.

Most immigrants worked very hard. Often they did several jobs to make a living. "My father was a glazier (window-maker) and a religious leader," said Mr. Selinfreund. "He even drove a taxi and became a button-maker."

from page 221

The Main Idea is that immigrants worked hard.

The Supporting Details are the jobs one immigrant held.

TRY IT!

Read this paragraph about immigrants. Copy and complete the chart below.

Many women and children worked, too. Some worked in factories. Children sold pencils, candy, or newspapers. But life was not all work for children. The streets were also their playgrounds. They played tag and stickball. Instead of a baseball bat, they used a broomstick. But everything stopped when the soda man came by selling cold sodas.

from page 221

Main Idea | Immigrants worked, but they also played.

Details

| Children sold pencils. | Children played tag and stickball. | |

• How did you find the main idea and details?

Keep in Mind...

For more help in reading social studies, try these strategies:

☑ **Reread**
Review each sentence carefully. Make sure you understand what each sentence is about before you read further.

☑ **Form a mental picture**
As you read, think about what you are reading. How would it look?

☑ **Look up unknown words**
Use a dictionary or the glossary in your book to find the meanings of any words you do not know.

Practice Activities

1 **READ** Read "A Country of Immigrants" on page 222. What is the main idea?

2 **WRITE** Write about a job you would like. Be sure to use a main idea and supporting details.

Context Clues

As you read your book, you may find a word that you do not know. One way to find the meaning of a new word is to look for **context clues**. Context clues are the words and sentences around the new word. Using context clues helps you become a better reader.

- Have you heard this word before? How was it used?

- Write down the context clues you used to find the meaning of the new word.

- Use the new word in a sentence of your own to help you remember it.

To Use Context Clues
Ask yourself:

- **What word is new to me?**

- **What might the word mean?**

- **What other words, phrases, and sentences help me figure out the meaning of the new word?**

- **What information do these other words, phrases, and sentences give to me?**

In your book you will read about the weather in different parts of our country. Read this paragraph about San Francisco Bay and notice the context clues for the word *fog*.

If you ever visit San Francisco Bay, you might hear the sound of loud foghorns blowing over the bay. These horns help ship captains safely move their ships through the fog. San Francisco is famous for its thick, white fog. Warm winds blow in from the east, and cool ocean winds blow in from the west. When these winds meet, fog is made.

from page 120

Context Clue:
foghorns

Context Clue:
safely move their ships through

Context Clues:
thick, white

TRY IT!

Natural resources are things found in nature that people use. Read this paragraph from your book. Make a context clues chart like the one below. Write the context clues that help you learn the meaning of the term *boom towns*.

Earth's resources provide jobs for many people. Sometimes "boom towns" grow when a resource is discovered. Many people move quickly to these towns to try to make money mining gold, oil, or other resources. Once the resource runs out, the jobs disappear.

from page 311

• How did you find the meaning of *boom towns*?

Practice Activities

1 READ Read the second paragraph under "Communicating Long Ago" on page 250. What context clues help you discover the meaning of *town crier*?

2 WRITE Look up *desert* in a dictionary. Write a paragraph about a desert using context clues to help define the word.

Keep in Mind...

For more help in reading social studies strategies, try these:

☑ **Reread**
Review each sentence carefully. Make sure you understand what each sentence means before reading further.

☑ **Form the big picture**
As you read, think about the topic and the most important information in each paragraph or section.

☑ **Summarize**
In your own words, tell about what you are reading.

Sequencing

As you read your book, look for the order in which things happen. **Sequencing** is putting events in the order in which they happened. This helps you understand and remember what you read. Sequencing organizes your information.

- Look for words like *first*, *next*, *then*, *finally*, *last*, *before*, and *after* to find the order of events.

- Look for dates that tell when events happened.

- Use chapter time lines to help you remember the sequence of events.

To Use Sequencing

Ask yourself:

- **What event happened first?**

- **What event happened next?**

- **What order of these events makes sense?**

Read this paragraph about life on a farm, and notice the sequence of events.

By mid-June, the wheat has turned from dark green to light green, and then to a golden color. The wheat is ready to be gathered. Farmers use a machine called a combine to cut the wheat, clean it, and put it in a holding tank. From there, trucks haul the wheat to storage tanks. Finally it is sold to companies that grind the wheat into flour. The flour is then made into bread, cakes, pasta, and other foods. These foods are then sold all over the world.

from page 302

First Step:
Gathering, cutting and cleaning the wheat with a combine

Second Step:
Hauling the wheat to a storage tank

Third Step:
Selling wheat to be ground into flour

Fourth Step:
Making food from the flour

Fifth Step:
Selling foods

TRY IT!

Read this paragraph. Copy the chart below and record the sequence of events.

> Many people other than farmers help make the food you see at your table. Some people process the food. To process is to change something into a different form. People process wheat to make bread and oranges to make orange juice. People at factories put the food into packages. Truckers drive the packages to stores. Stores sell the products to consumers.
>
> *from page 305*

People process food in factories.

People in factories put food into packages.

Stores sell the products to customers.

- How did you find what happened first, next, and last?

Practice Activities

1 **READ** Read "California Becomes a State" on page 127. State the sequence of events.

2 **WRITE** Write a paragraph about some important events in your life. Use the correct sequence.

Keep in Mind...

For more help in reading social studies, try these strategies:

☑ **Look up unknown words**
Use a dictionary or the glossary in your book to find the meanings of any words you do not know.

☑ **Reread**
Review each sentence carefully. Make sure you understand what each sentence means before you read further.

☑ **Form the big picture**
As you read, think about the topic and the most important information of the paragraph or section.

☑ **Summarize**
In your own words, tell about what you are reading.

Make Predictions

As you read a paragraph or section in your book, think about what might come next. Thinking about what happens next is to **make predictions**. A prediction does not have a correct or incorrect answer. Making predictions helps you to carefully think about what you are reading.

- Think about other things you know that will help you make a good guess.

- Test your predictions: read further to see if they were correct.

- Revise your predictions: read further to see if more information changes your prediction.

To Make a Prediction
Ask yourself:

- **What is being described?**

- **What information do I already know about the topic?**

- **What similar things do I know?**

- **What do I think might happen next?**

The lessons in this book begin with a Read Aloud. These sections of your book are sometimes poems or quotations that will give you an idea of the subject of each lesson. Read the following Read Aloud and prediction.

Background Information:
I know that San Francisco is a hilly city.

A hilly city
with water on three sides,
a steep street
with eight curves,
cool, foggy summers
and warm winters, …
What City is this?

Prediction:
This lesson will be about San Francisco.

Background Information:
I know that San Francisco is foggy.

Text Information:
The words hilly, steep, and warm winters are clues about the city.

from page 118

TRY IT!

Read this section introduction. Copy and complete the chart.

"Fog in Channel. Continent Cut Off." These words appeared in a newspaper headline in England long ago. It describes what happened when fog prevented ships from sailing across the English Channel.

But thanks to technology, things have changed. Today people do not have to rely on ships and planes to cross the English Channel.

from page 256

Text Information:

Fog kept ships from sailing in the Channel. Now technology has changed that.

Background Information:

My Prediction:

• What steps did you take to make your prediction?

Keep in Mind...

For more help in reading social studies, try these strategies:

☑ **Sequencing**
As you read, think about the order in which events happened.

☑ **Form the big picture**
As you read, think about the topic and the most important information of the paragraph or section.

☑ **Relate to personal experience**
Think about how what you are reading about relates to your own life.

Practice Activities

1 **READ** Read the section of your book titled "All Aboard!" on page 259. Predict how the tunnel might affect people. To test your prediction, read "A Big Change" on page 260.

2 **WRITE** Write a paragraph predicting tomorrow's weather. What information did you use?

Compare and Contrast

This book often **compares** and **contrasts** people and events. To compare is to see how things are alike. To contrast things is to see how they are different. Comparing and contrasting helps you understand the relationships between things you read about.

- To compare, look for clue words such as: *like*, *similar*, *in common*, *same*, and *resemble*.

- To contrast, look for clue words such as: *before*, *after*, *different from*, *unlike*, and *by contrast*.

To Compare

Ask yourself:

- How are two or more things alike?

To Contrast

Ask yourself:

- How are two or more things different?

In your book you will read about different communities. Read this paragraph about Sacramento and Los Angeles. Notice what is alike and different about the cities.

Sacramento, California, has about 375,000 people. It is the capital of the state of California. It is the seventh largest city in the state. Los Angeles is the largest city in the state. It has about 3.5 million people!

from page 9

Compare:
Both cities are in California.

Contrast:
Sacramento has fewer people than Los Angeles. Sacramento is the capital of the state.

TRY IT!

Read these paragraphs about bodies of water. Compare and contrast oceans with rivers and lakes. Record your responses in the chart below.

> Oceans are the largest bodies of water. The Atlantic Ocean and the Pacific Ocean are very large. They border the east and west sides of the United States. Oceans are made of salt water.
>
> Rivers and lakes are also bodies of water. They are mostly made of fresh water. Sometimes they are very large.
>
> *from page 37*

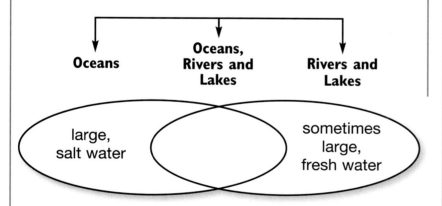

Oceans → large, salt water

Oceans, Rivers and Lakes

Rivers and Lakes → sometimes large, fresh water

Keep in Mind...

For more help in reading social studies, try these strategies:

☑ **Look up unknown words**
Use a dictionary or the glossary in your book to find the meanings of any unfamiliar words.

☑ **Sequencing**
As you read, think about the order in which things happened.

☑ **Form the big picture**
As you read, think about the most important information in the paragraph or section.

☑ **Summarize**
Briefly describe what your reading is about.

Practice Activities

1 **READ** Read the letter about Rochester, Indiana at the top of page 19. Compare and contrast Rochester with your own community.

2 **WRITE** Write a paragraph about two foods. How are they alike? How are they different?

Summarize

After you read a paragraph or section of this book, you can **summarize** what you have read. In a **summary**, you briefly tell in your own words about the most important information in the section. Summarizing is a way to help you understand what you read.

- Look for titles, headings, and key words that identify important information.

- Organize the information in a clear way.

- Keep your summary brief.

- Don't include information and facts that are not important.

To Summarize

Ask yourself:

- What is this paragraph or section about?

- What information is most important?

In this book you will read about a community named Shapleigh. Read this paragraph and the sample summary.

Mr. Jim Brown teaches sixth graders in Shapleigh. A few years ago his students decided that <u>some land in Shapleigh was going to waste</u>. When the yearly town meeting was about to happen, Mr. Brown's <u>students decided to take action</u>. They studied and planned. Then they <u>convinced people at the town meeting that they could build a park</u> on the land. And the result, a beautiful park, has improved their community!

from page 188

Summary:
Students convinced their town to build a new park.

The underlined phrases show the most important information.

TRY IT!

Read these paragraphs. Copy and complete the summary chart below.

Taking part in the town meeting was important for Mr. Brown's students. "I was surprised," said Adam Pierce. "We made a difference in how people thought about the park. We changed their opinions."

"It felt good that Shapleigh was getting something out of our hard work," said Wendy. "I know it would be nice to have a park for people to enjoy." A vote by citizens at the town meeting showed that they agreed with Mr. Brown's students.

from page 189

Important Information

The citizens agreed with the students.

Students changed the citizens' opinions.

Summary

The students affected the vote.

• How did you pick facts for your summary?

Practice Activities

1 **READ** Read the first paragraph on page 133. Summarize this section in your own words.

2 **WRITE** On a separate sheet of paper, write a paragraph that summarizes a favorite book.

Use Visuals

One way to learn from your reading is to use **visuals**. Visuals are the graphs, charts, pictures, and maps in your book. Visuals provide information in a clear and useful way.

■ Read the caption and labels for information they give.

■ Look for objects in the picture that might give more information.

■ When looking at graphs, maps, or charts, be sure to read the key to find the meanings of special symbols.

To Use Visuals

Look closely at the visual. Ask yourself:

• What does the graph, chart, picture, or map show?

• How does it help me to understand what I have read?

• How does it add to the information I have read?

• What information do the visual's caption or labels provide?

In your book you will study the Lower East Side, a community in New York City, as it was about a hundred years ago. Study this photo and read the caption.

Notice what the people are doing and how they are dressed.

The caption tells us where this photograph was taken.

The Lower East Side was a community alive with very crowded apartments and busy streets.

TRY IT!

Study this photo of the Lower East Side and read the caption. Copy the chart on a separate sheet of paper. Think about the information given in the picture and caption and fill in the chart.

Life was both difficult and fun. Children often worked to earn money to help their families. But there was also time to play street games like stickball.

from page 221

Visual information:
This appears to be a city scene.

Caption information:
This is a street game called stickball.

Visual:
Children playing stickball

Visual information:

Visual information:
Children are wearing old fashioned clothes.

Keep in Mind...

For more help in using visuals in social studies, try these strategies:

☑ **Study the pictures**
Look at the pictures of people and events to help you understand the reading. Read the labels on the pictures that tell what they are about.

☑ **Study the map**
The maps in your book show you places where events happened.

☑ **Study the chapter openers**
The first page of a chapter often summarizes what you will read about and also may contain useful maps and time lines.

Practice Activities

1 **READ** Read the captions and study the pictures on page 7 of your book. How do the pictures help you understand the captions?

2 **WRITE** Find a picture or drawing that interests you. Write a caption to help explain the picture.

CONTENTS

v

UNIT FOUR

204

Communities on the Move

REFERENCE SECTION

STANDARDIZED TEST SUPPORT

FEATURES

SKILLS

Geography Skills

Thinking Skills

Study Skills

CITIZENSHIP

Making a Difference

Viewpoints

LEGACIES

CHARTS, GRAPHS, & DIAGRAMS

TIME LINES

MAPS

YOUR TEXTBOOK at a glance

Your book is *Communities: Adventures in Time and Place*. It has twelve chapters and a special section, as well as many other parts to study and enjoy.

NATIONAL GEOGRAPHIC

Look at Your World

How do people travel from one place to another?

What are some things that help make the Southwest special?

Special pages from National Geographic bring you ideas and Adventures in geography.

MANY VOICES
MUSIC

America

Good citizens care about their community and their country. When people sing the song "America," they show pride about living in the United States. In what ways do you show pride in our country?

My coun-try,
lib- er- ty,
fa- thers died,
From ev'- ry—

Links to CURRENT EVENTS

Catch of the Day!

What are new ways people use natural resources?

Virginia's waters have long provided people with food. Today fish and shellfish are not only found in the water, but also on land! They are now raised in tanks on fish farms in Virginia.

Where do the foods you eat come from? Keep a list. Then compare your list with others from your class.

Living with the Environment

In the last chapter you read about how the Anasazi used natural resources to survive in the dry environment of Mesa Verde. But the Powhatan's environment around Jamestown was different. There was plenty of rain for plants and trees. The area around Jamestown is a coastal plain. A coastal plain is flat land along the coast. It was good for farming. The Powhatan grew corn, beans, and squash. They also hunted deer and other animals.

The English also liked Jamestown's environment. They saw the location as a good place to build a community. Their boats had a good port in the deep waters of Chesapeake Bay. The waters, which surrounded the English on three sides, helped to protect the English against attack. The Native Americans and the Spanish often used land routes for attack.

LESSON 1

Ben Franklin and Philadelphia

Focus Activity

READ TO LEARN

How did Ben Franklin make a difference in Philadelphia?

VOCABULARY
- almanac
- tax
- American Revolution
- Declaration of Independence

PEOPLE
- Benjamin Franklin
- Thomas Jefferson

PLACES
- Philadelphia, Pennsylvania

146

Read Aloud
"Most of the shop fronts were painted red, blue, green, or yellow, and the big swinging signs in front of them were brilliant with paint. . . . The people of Philadelphia wore bright colors and had a taste for fine clothes."

Welcome to Philadelphia!

These are the words of a writer named Margaret Cousins. She describes what life was like in the city of Philadelphia, Pennsylvania in the early 1700s. At that time there were 13 English colonies in America. The colonies had many cities. The biggest, busiest city of all was Philadelphia. About 38,000 people lived there, more people than in Boston and New York City put together.

Philadelphia became one of the most important communities in our country's history. Many things happened there that led the colonies to become the United States of America. Let's take a look at what Philadelphia was like back in colonial days.

Some lessons have Links or Did You Know—activities and facts to share. You will also see Many Voices—songs, writing, and art by many people.

Look at the special lessons and features shown at right. They build your **Skills** and bring you interesting subjects from the past and present. ▶

Legacy
LINKING PAST AND PRESENT
Our
Country's

Geography Skills

Reading Grid Maps

Infographic   interNET CONNECTION Visit our website: www.mhschool.com

A Day with the Anasazi
Pretend you are standing across from the cliff house where Little Rabbit and his family lived long ago. What might you see?

Meet Ben Franklin

Everyone in Philadelphia was talking about one person—Benjamin Franklin. He seemed to be everywhere, doing just about everything.

Ben Franklin grew up in Boston, Massachusetts, in a family of 17 children. When he was 12, his father sent him to live and work with his older brother James, a printer. Ben quickly learned a lot about printing. But he did not get along with his brother. When he was 17, he left for Philadelphia.

When he arrived in Philadelphia in 1723, Ben found an exciting city. He talked to everyone and soon made many friends. He loved his new city, and he set out to make it even better.

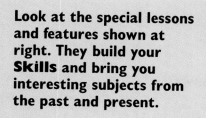

PENNSYLVANIA
Philadelphia

As a young man, Ben Franklin learned to use the printing press.

147

Your book has a **Reference Section** at the end. Use it to look up words, people, and places as you study them. ▼

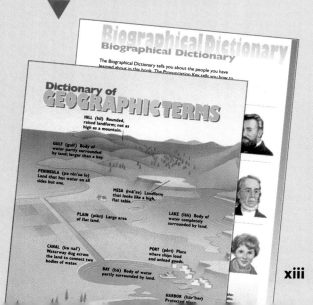

Biographical Dictionary

The Biographical Dictionary tells you about the people you have learned about in this book. The Pronunciation Key tells you how to...

Dictionary of GEOGRAPHIC TERMS

HILL (hil) Rounded, raised landform; not as high as a mountain.

GULF (gulf) Body of water partly surrounded by land; larger than a bay.

PENINSULA (pe nin'se le) Land that has water on all sides but one.

MESA (mā'sə) Landform that looks like a high, flat table.

PLAIN (plān) Large area of flat land.

LAKE (lāk) Body of water completely surrounded by land.

CANAL (kə nal') Waterway dug across the land to connect two bodies of water.

PORT (pôrt) Place where ships load and unload goods.

BAY (bā) Body of water partly surrounded by land.

HARBOR (här'bər) Protected place...

▲ Each lesson begins with a **Read Aloud** selection. A **Read to Learn** question and a list of important words, people, and places will guide your reading.

xiii

NATIONAL GEOGRAPHIC

Look at Your World

How do people travel from one place to another?

What are some things that help make the Southwest special?

What makes this place different from other places?

How does mail get to exactly the right place?

What foods do people get from trees?

GEOGRAPHY SKILLS

PART 1
Using Globes

VOCABULARY
North Pole
South Pole
equator

What are globes?

- A globe is a small model, or copy, of Earth.

- Find the North Pole and the South Pole on the globe. The North Pole is the farthest place north on Earth. The South Pole is the farthest place south on Earth.

- Find the equator on the globe. The equator is an imaginary line circling Earth, halfway between the North Pole and the South Pole. On a globe the equator is shown as a real line. The equator divides Earth in half. At the top is the northern half. What half is at the bottom?

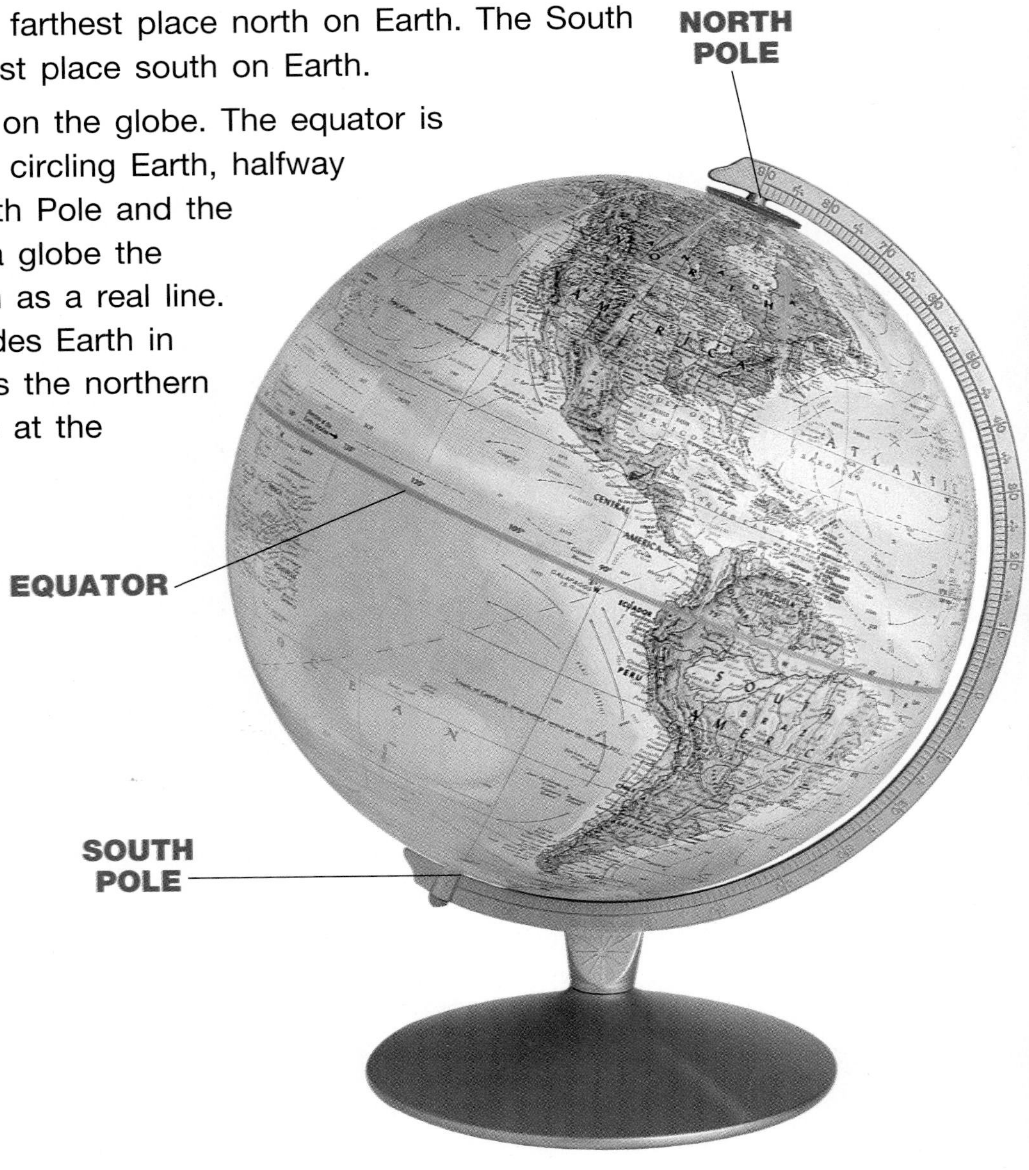

NORTH POLE

EQUATOR

SOUTH POLE

G4

PART 2
Using Maps

VOCABULARY

continent	map key	locator
ocean	cardinal directions	
symbol	compass rose	

What are maps?

● A map is a flat drawing of a place. This map shows Earth's seven continents. A continent is a very large body of land. Find the continents on the map. What are they called?

● The map also shows Earth's four oceans. An ocean is a very large body of salt water. Find and name the oceans.

More Practice

There are other maps that show continents and oceans in this book. For examples, see pages 58, 59, and R10-R11.

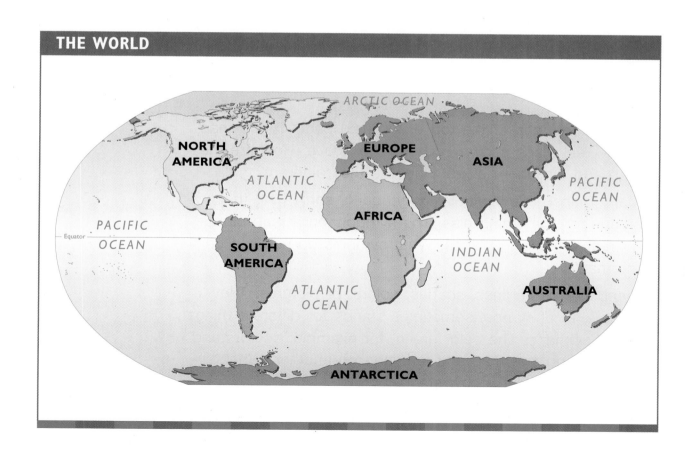

THE WORLD

ARCTIC OCEAN

NORTH AMERICA

EUROPE

ASIA

ATLANTIC OCEAN

PACIFIC OCEAN

PACIFIC OCEAN

AFRICA

Equator

SOUTH AMERICA

INDIAN OCEAN

ATLANTIC OCEAN

AUSTRALIA

ANTARCTICA

Why do maps use symbols?

● Look at the map at the top of the next page. It is a map of the real place shown in the photo above. How are the map and the photo alike? How are they different?

● Many maps have symbols. A symbol is something that stands for something else. The symbols on a map stand for real things and places. What symbols do you see on the map?

● Symbols can be lines, shapes, colors, or pictures. The same kind of symbol sometimes stands for different things on other maps. The color green, for example, could stand for parks on one map and farmland on another. What might a picture of a cow stand for?

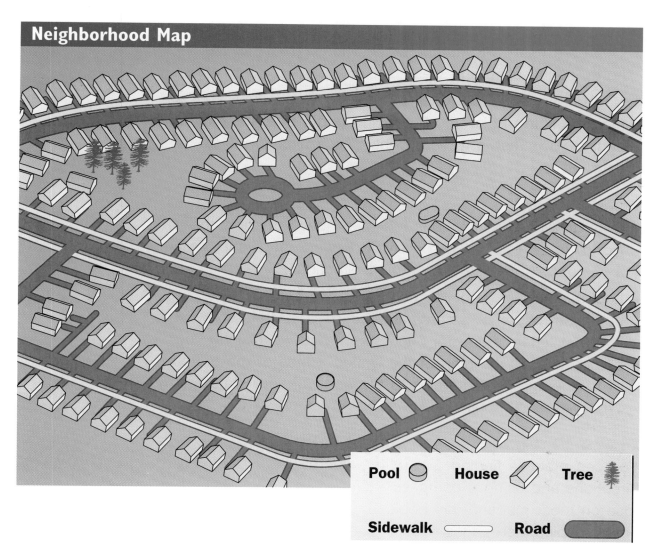

Neighborhood Map

Pool ⊖	House ▱	Tree 🌲
Sidewalk ⊂⎯⎯⊃	Road ⬭	

Why read a map title and map key?

- A map title tells you what the map shows. What is the title of this map?

- To find out what symbols on a map mean, you can look at a map key. A map key tells what the symbols on a map stand for. Look at the map on this page. What does the blue circle stand for? What symbol means tree?

More Practice

You can practice working with symbols and map keys on many maps in this book. For examples, see pages 25, 249, and 302.

What are cardinal directions?

● There are four cardinal directions. These directions are north, south, east, and west.

● North is the direction toward the North Pole. When you face the North Pole, you are facing north. South is directly behind you. East is to your right. Which direction is to your left?

What is a compass rose?

● How do you find directions if a map does not show the North Pole? You can use a small drawing on a map, called a compass rose, to help you find directions.

● Look at the picture of the compass rose below. The compass rose shows cardinal directions. North is shown by **N**. What letters stand for east, south, and west? Find your home state on the map of the United States at the bottom of the next page. What lies to the north of your state? What lies east, south, and west?

More Practice

You can practice finding directions and using a compass rose on most maps in this book. For examples, see pages 119, 243, and 257.

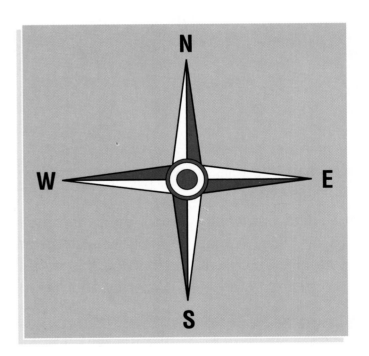

What is a locator?

- A **locator** is a small map included on a bigger, or main, map. A locator shows where the area in the main map is located. The area of the main map is shown in red on the locator. Find the locator on the map below.

- Study the locator. What does it show? Find the red area on the locator. On which continent is the red area? What country does the red area show? Now look at the main map. What does it show?

More Practice

There are other maps with locators in this book. For examples, see pages 53, 79, and 293.

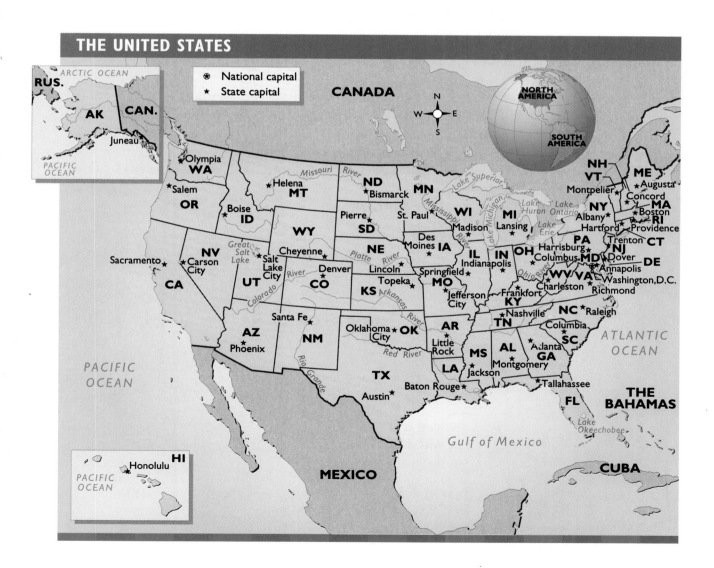

THE UNITED STATES

PART 3
Different Kinds of Maps

VOCABULARY
landform map
grid map

What is a landform map?

● The map below is a landform map. This kind of map shows the different landforms on Earth. Many landform maps use different colors to show the different kinds of land. Look at the map key. What color shows mountains? What other landforms are shown?

More Practice

There is another landform map in this book. See pages 40-41.

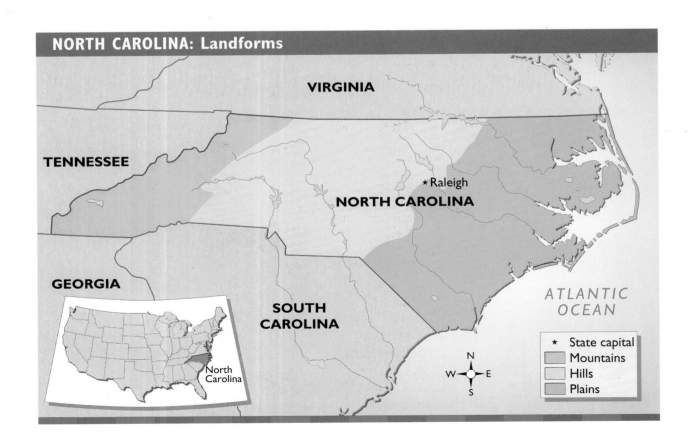

NORTH CAROLINA: Landforms

VIRGINIA

TENNESSEE

★Raleigh
NORTH CAROLINA

GEORGIA

SOUTH
CAROLINA

ATLANTIC
OCEAN

North
Carolina

N
W   E
S

★ State capital
Mountains
Hills
Plains

What is a grid map?

- When you visit a new place, a **grid map** can help you find your way around. A grid map uses a set of boxes, or grid, to locate places.

- Look at the grid map below. The boxes on a grid map have letters and numbers. All the boxes in the first row across are As. All the boxes in the first row down are 1s. So the first box to the left in the top row is A1. What is the second box in the second row? What place is located in C3?

More Practice

There are other grid maps shown in this book. For examples, see pages 176–177 and 179.

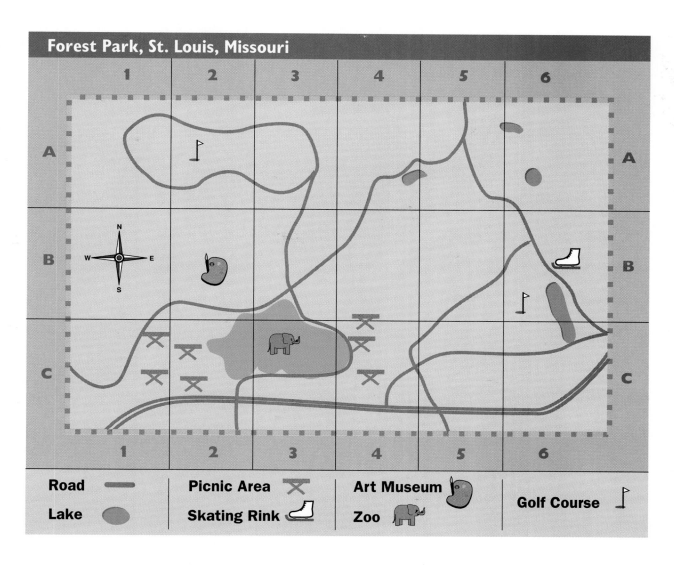

Forest Park, St. Louis, Missouri

| Road — | Picnic Area | Art Museum | |
| Lake | Skating Rink | Zoo | Golf Course |

Living in Communities

Why Does it Matter?

How would you describe where you live to someone who has never been there?

You could describe your family, your friends, your street, and the land and water nearby. In doing so, you are describing your community.

Your community is special. In this unit you will find out about communities across the country and around the world. Some may be like your community, and some may be very different. All are shaped by where they are located. And in their own ways, all communities are special.

FIND OUT MORE!
Visit our website:
www.mhschool.com

*inter*NET
CONNECTION

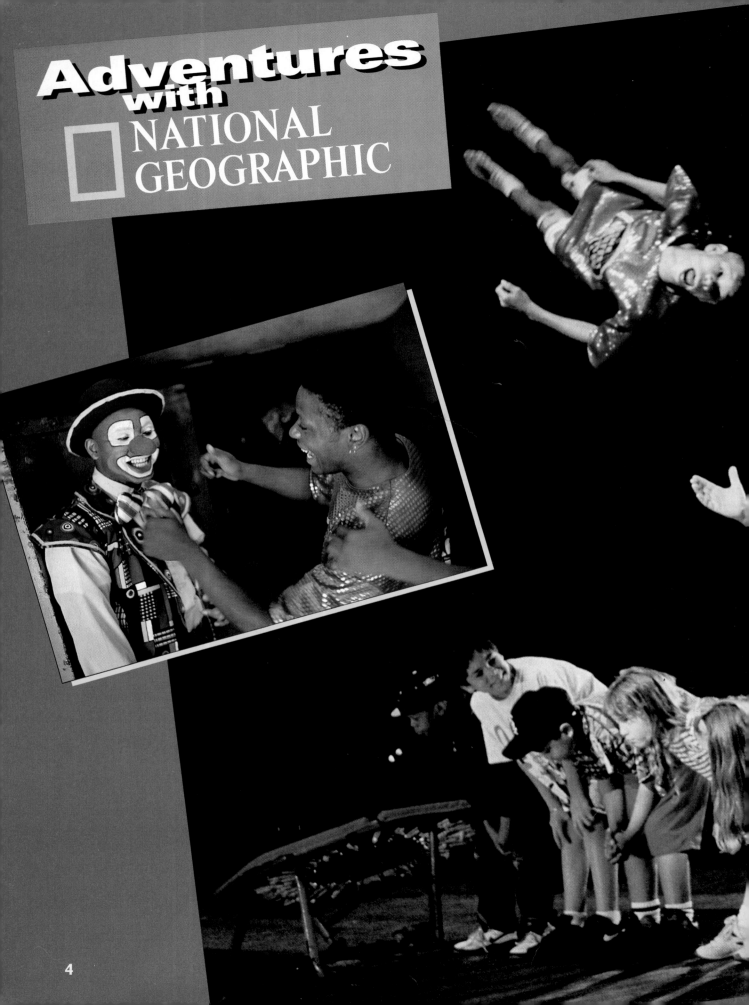

Adventures with
NATIONAL GEOGRAPHIC

4

CIRCUS SCHOOL

You'd flip for a chance to go to this school! It's for kids who perform with the Ringling Bros. and Barnum & Bailey Circus. These kids are part of a tumbling troupe that travels all over our country with the circus. Since they can't go to a regular school, they study in a trailer called the "Little Red Schoolhouse." And yes—even circus performers have to do homework.

GEO JOURNAL

The circus school is part of a community. Write about a special place in your own community.

Understanding Communities

THINKING ABOUT GEOGRAPHY AND CULTURE

What is special about your community's people? Perhaps they live on farms or maybe they work in tall skyscrapers. To find the locations of the communities shown, match the colored triangles on the map with the triangles by the pictures.

In Chapter 1 you will see several different types of communities. One of them might even be like yours.

Anaconda Range, Montana

Chicago, Illinois

Boca Raton, Florida

This rural community is located in Montana.

Chicago, Illinois, is an urban community.

Boca Raton, Florida, is a suburban community.

7

Looking at A Community

Focus Activity

READ TO LEARN

What is a community?

VOCABULARY

- community
- citizen
- pollution
- volunteer

PLACES

- Sacramento, California

People and Places

Before writing their postcards, Mrs. Roy's class discussed life in their community. "What is a community?" asked Mrs. Roy.

Max said a community is a special place. It is made up of many neighborhoods where people live. Karen said it is a place where friends and family have fun. And Marcus said a community has libraries, schools, and businesses.

"In a way each of you is right," said Mrs. Roy. "A community is usually made up of several neighborhoods. It is a place where different people live, work, and have fun together. What makes each community special are the people, today and long ago, who have worked to make it a better place for all to live in."

Living Together

"We have a lot of different types of people living here in our community," said Karen. "With so many different people, our community is very big."

"That depends," Mrs. Roy said. "What community are you comparing it with? Suppose you lived in a big city like Los Angeles. Sacramento would then seem very small. But if you lived in a small town, Sacramento might appear very big."

Sacramento, California, has about 375,000 people. It is the capital of the state of California. It is the seventh largest city in the state. Los Angeles is the largest city in the state. It has about 3.5 million people!

Still, no matter its size, every community is special. Think about your own community. What is special about it?

Mrs. Roy's class learns about communities.

A community is:

a place
people
neighborhoods
families
schools

houses of worship
working together
friends
helping each other
having fun

Working Together

One thing that makes each community special is the way people can make a living there. Sacramento is the state's capital. Many people in the city have jobs in government.

Some people work to make laws. Others decide how the state will spend money for highways and schools.

Other people in government may work at jobs like making sure there is enough water for communities. Water is important to people. How do people work together to provide water for your community?

Look at the map below. There are many museums and parks in Sacramento. Some people have jobs taking care of these places.

Do you like computers? There are many businesses in Sacramento that help to build computers and design software. People also work on farms near Sacramento.

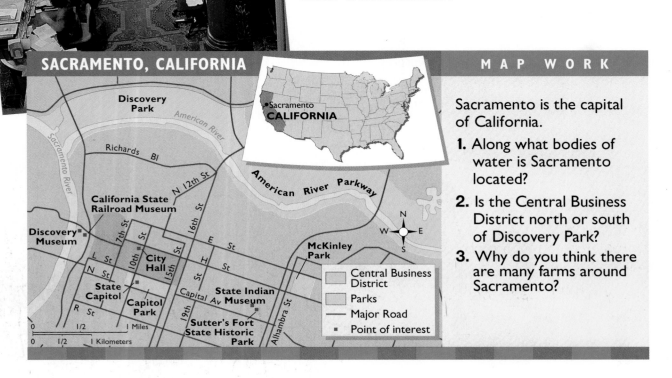

SACRAMENTO, CALIFORNIA

Discovery Park

American River

Richards Bl

Sacramento River

California State Railroad Museum

N 12th St

Discovery Museum

7th St

9th St

10th St

City Hall

L St

N St

State Capitol

15th St

16th St

E St

H St

American River Parkway

McKinley Park

Capitol Park

R St

Capital Av

19th St

State Indian Museum

Sutter's Fort State Historic Park

Alhambra St

•Sacramento
CALIFORNIA

0   1/2   1 Miles
0   1/2   1 Kilometers

Central Business District
Parks
Major Road
Point of interest

MAP WORK

Sacramento is the capital of California.

1. Along what bodies of water is Sacramento located?

2. Is the Central Business District north or south of Discovery Park?

3. Why do you think there are many farms around Sacramento?

Helping Each Other

Like other cities in our country, Sacramento knows how to work through its problems. In 1986 Sacramento was hit by a terrible flood. Large rainstorms caused rivers and creeks to overflow. But the citizens of Sacramento refused to give up. A citizen is a member of a community or a country. Citizens worked together to repair homes and businesses.

Another problem in Sacramento is water pollution. Pollution is anything that spoils land, water, and air. Today, volunteers are helping to fight water pollution in Sacramento. A volunteer is someone who does something by choice, without pay.

In Sacramento pollution is caused by people pouring motor oil and other wastes into drains in the street. Then the wastes flow into nearby rivers and streams. This pollution kills fish and other wildlife.

Some volunteers help people and pets during floods (above). Other volunteers fight pollution by painting pictures of fish near sewer drains (below). The fish remind people that wastes poured into the street can kill wildlife.

Having Fun

Look at the map on page 10. Can you find a large park? The American River Parkway is more than twenty miles long! People hike and ride bicycles there. They roller-skate and jog. Along the river, people come to relax and swim and have picnics. They also pick wild blackberries.

In many communities the land and water help shape how people have fun. This is also true of Sacramento. For people in Sacramento and other communities, having fun also means spending time with friends and family. What are some ways you and your family have fun in your community?

Whether visiting Sutter's Fort (above) or enjoying the wildlife and rafting on rivers (below), there is much to see and do in Sacramento.

WHY IT MATTERS

By learning about Sacramento with Mrs. Roy's class, you now know what a community is. As you read this book, you will explore and learn how people in different communities in our country and around the world live and work together.

One way to see how people live and work together is to visit the main street of a community. Around the United States of America the main street is often the center of community life. Turn the page and you too can visit "Main Street."

The way people live in communities today will influence communities in the future.

✓// Reviewing Facts and Ideas

MAIN IDEAS

- A community is a place where different people live, work, and have fun together. There are usually several neighborhoods in a community.

- All communities have problems. People work together to solve these problems.

- Sacramento, California, is a place where people live and work together to take care of their community.

THINK ABOUT IT

1. Describe Sacramento's location. What are two ways location is important?

2. **FOCUS** What is a community?

3. **THINKING SKILL** How is your community _different_ from Sacramento? How is it _like_ Sacramento?

4. **WRITE** Suppose Mrs. Roy's students had written to your class. Write a postcard to them describing your community.

Main Street, U.S.A.

Where do you go to get a library book or to meet a friend? You might go to the main street of your community.

Many communities have a main street. In the past Main Street was often the center of a community. Today people still go there to shop and to meet each other.

Because the main street is part of a community's past and present, you can call it a **legacy** (LEG uh see). A legacy is something that we value in our lives today that is also a valued part of our past.

Madison Public Library, New Jersey

A main street in Madison, New Jersey, 1913

14

A dogsled race down a main street in Anchorage, Alaska

Main Street in Marshall, North Carolina

A community event along a main street in California.

Communities Across the United States

Focus Activity

READ TO LEARN

What types of communities does our country have?

VOCABULARY

- urban
- suburb
- rural
- transportation

PLACES

- New Orleans, Louisiana
- Bothell, Washington
- Rochester, Indiana

Read Aloud

Hello. We are a third-grade class in Sacramento, California. We want to know about your community. What is it like? What do you do for fun? Where do people work in your community?

Hello from Around Our Country

This postcard was written by Mrs. Roy's class. They sent it to different schools around the United States. A few weeks later they received responses from all over the country. The students were very excited. Let's see what they found out about communities around our country.

16

A Letter from New Orleans

The following letter and photos came from a third-grade class in New Orleans. It is a city located in the state of Louisiana. New Orleans is an urban community. An urban community includes the city and its surrounding areas. What does this letter tell you about urban life?

The French Quarter is a neighborhood in New Orleans known for its music.

New Orleans is a big city. People come from all over the world to hear our jazz music. We even have a park named for one of our famous musicians, Louis Armstrong.

Our sidewalks are full of people. We walk or take streetcars to get around the city. Sometimes it gets crowded. Over 500,000 people live here!

Some of us live in big buildings. Others live in houses that are close together. There are many tall office buildings here. But we have many beautiful old buildings, too.

P.S. What kind of music do you like?

Hello from Bothell

Another letter came from the community of Bothell (BAHTH ul), Washington. Bothell is near the city of Seattle. Communities like Bothell are called suburbs. A suburb is a community located near a city. What does this letter tell you about living in a suburb?

In suburbs like Bothell, many people work in large business parks (top), and relax at places like Bothell Landing (bottom).

Hello! Things change quickly here in Bothell. There used to be a lot of open spaces for playing. But now our suburb is growing. Houses are closer and closer together. Even our roads are more crowded with cars. It sure is a problem!

Bothell has many business areas, like the one in the picture above. People work together and live near each other. We make things like airplanes. We even make video games!

For fun we also like to go with our families to walk and relax at Bothell Landing.

P.S. Our teacher helped us write this!

18

Regards from Rochester

Have you ever seen a round barn? Well, near Rochester, Indiana, we have them.

Rochester is a farming community. Some of our families have farmed here for a long time. We still raise corn and cows. But it's getting harder to make a living. Land and farm equipment are becoming more expensive.

Our houses are far apart here. There are not many stores nearby. But these things are changing as urban areas grow our way.

Maybe one day you'll come and see us and our neat barns!

Bye-bye.

No matter what shape the barn is, farming requires hard work and long days.

You can see from this letter that Rochester, Indiana, is a rural community. A rural community is a place of farms or open country. Distances between places are far in rural communities. Can you think of other types of rural communities? A small town in the mountains and a fishing village on the ocean are two other examples of rural communities.

In Rochester cars and trucks are the main form of transportation. Transportation is the moving of people and products from place to place. On the next page you will find a song about another type of transportation.

The Express Train

Composed by Barbara Mariconda and Denise Puccio.

People use different types of transportation in communities. Have you ever been on a commuter train?

WHY IT MATTERS

The way we live depends on where we live. In the United States we live in different types of communities. We also have different types of houses, jobs, and transportation. We have different ways of having fun as well.

Some communities are near each other and some are far apart. As communities grow closer together, contact between people increases. To get along with each other, it is important for us to understand neighbors and communities other than our own.

Freight trains carry goods to and from communities across the United States.

✓/// Reviewing Facts and Ideas

MAIN IDEAS

- The United States has different kinds of communities.
- New Orleans, Louisiana, is an urban community.
- Bothell, Washington, is a suburban community.
- Rochester, Indiana, is a rural community.
- Transportation is the moving of people and products from place to place.

THINK ABOUT IT

1. What is a rural community? How is it different from an urban community?

2. **FOCUS** What types of communities does our country have?

3. **THINKING SKILL** In which _group_ would you place your community: urban, suburban, or rural? Why?

4. **GEOGRAPHY** Draw a map showing the route from your community to another one.

Using Map Scales

VOCABULARY
scale

WHY THE SKILL MATTERS

Say you want to visit Rochester, Indiana, and other communities in the state. You start in Rochester, and you want to learn how far it is to Indianapolis. One way to do this is to read the scale of a map. The scale helps to measure the real distance between places. It shows that a certain distance on the map stands for a certain distance on Earth.

USING A MAP SCALE

Look at Map A. The scale is the line with marks that stand for miles. It shows that one inch on Map A stands for 200 miles.

One way to use map scales is to make a scale out of a paper strip. Look at the scale below. Place the long edge of your strip along the top of the scale. Mark every 1/2 inch to show 100 miles. You have just made your own scale. Use it to measure distances on Map A. How far is it from Rochester to Indianapolis? To find out, place the strip so that the **0** is at the dot for Rochester. Now read the number closest to Indianapolis. The distance from Rochester to Indianapolis is about 100 miles.

USING DIFFERENT SCALES

Not all maps have the same scale. Maps have different scales because they show larger or smaller parts of Earth. Even though the scales are different, the real distances remain the same. The scale on Map B is different from the scale on Map A. How many miles are shown by one inch on Map B?

Make a new strip to match the scale on Map B. Now measure the distance from Rochester to Indianapolis on Map B. Once again, the distance is about 100 miles.

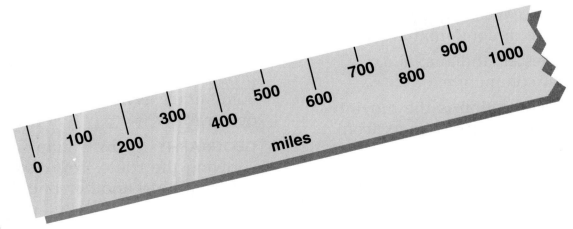

0   100   200   300   400   500   600   700   800   900   1000
miles

TRYING THE SKILL

As you continue to use map scales, look at the Helping Yourself box for reminders. Try measuring some other distances. Use your scale for Map A. Measure the distance from Uniontown to Indianapolis. Place the **0** on your strip at the dot for Uniontown. Line it up so that your strip reaches Indianapolis. How far apart are these two places? Now use your scale for Map B. About how far is it from Louisville to Cincinnati?

REVIEWING THE SKILL

Use Maps A and B to answer these questions.

1. What are map scales? How are they useful?

2. How many miles is it from Scotland to Indianapolis? How do you know?

3. Which map shows a larger area of Earth? Which scale shows more miles per inch?

4. Other than a paper strip, what could you use for a scale?

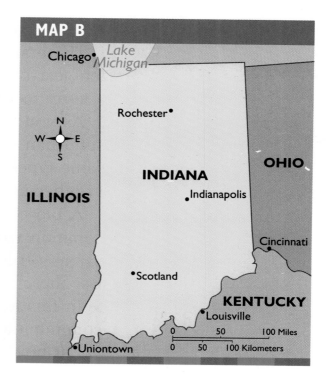

A Community in Mexico

Focus Activity

READ TO LEARN

What are communities like in Mexico?

VOCABULARY

- culture
- national park

PLACES

- Cuajimalpa, Mexico
- Mexico City, Mexico

Read Aloud

"I like living near Mexico City. There is so much to do and see here. There is a mixture of the very old and the very new. It's a special community to me."

"A mí me gusta vivir cerca de la Ciudad de México. Hay mucho que hacer y ver aquí. Hay una mezcla de lo viejo y de lo nuevo. Es una comunidad muy especial."

A World of Communities

These are the words of Ana Laura Flores, a ten-year-old girl who lives in Mexico. She wrote a letter to Mrs. Roy's class in Sacramento.

As you know, there are urban, rural, and suburban communities in our country. The same types of communities can also be found in other countries.

A big city in the United States has a lot in common with big cities in other countries. The same is true of farming communities as well. But there are also a lot of differences.

In this lesson you will read about some communities in Mexico. As you read, think about how they are the same and different from communities near you.

Living in Mexico City

Ana lives with her family in Cuajimalpa (kwah hee MAHL pah). It is a suburban community near Mexico City. Mexico City is the largest city in Mexico. In fact more people live in or near Mexico City than any other city in the world.

Mexico City has a lot in common with big cities in the United States. It is an exciting place. It has a rich past. Mexico City is the oldest city in North America.

Mexico City is also different from our cities. It has its own special culture. Culture is the way of life of a group of people.

Look at the map of Mexico City below. El Zócalo (el SOH kah loh) is the main square. What can you tell about the names on the map? Most of them are in Spanish. It is the main language of Mexico. Language is an important part of culture. In Mexico you may also hear people speaking many different native languages.

Built in the 1500s, La Catedral still is a popular place on El Zócalo.

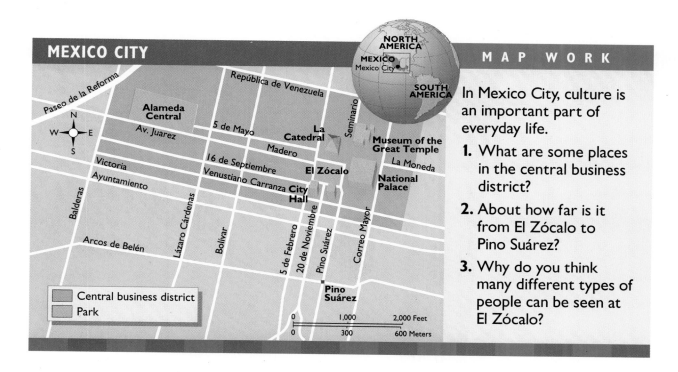

MEXICO CITY

Paseo de la Reforma
República de Venezuela
Alameda Central
5 de Mayo
Av. Juarez
La Catedral
Seminario
Madero
16 de Septiembre
El Zócalo
Museum of the Great Temple
La Moneda
Victoria
Ayuntamiento
Venustiano Carranza City Hall
National Palace
Balderas
Lázaro Cárdenas
Bolívar
Arcos de Belén
5 de Febrero
20 de Noviembre
Pino Suárez
Correo Mayor

Central business district
Park

Pino Suárez

0   1,000   2,000 Feet
0   300   600 Meters

NORTH AMERICA
MEXICO
Mexico City
SOUTH AMERICA

MAP WORK

In Mexico City, culture is an important part of everyday life.

1. What are some places in the central business district?

2. About how far is it from El Zócalo to Pino Suárez?

3. Why do you think many different types of people can be seen at El Zócalo?

Many Faces of Mexico City

What can a ride on the subway teach you? In Mexico City a trip on the subway will tell you a lot about Mexicans!

The city once built a subway station called Pino Suárez (PEE noh SWAH res). The remains of a very old Aztec Indian temple were discovered there. Today the station includes a display of an ancient stone. It was once used for religious ceremonies by the Aztecs.

What does this tell us about the people of Mexico City? It says they have a long, rich past of many different peoples and cultures.

Many people move to Mexico City every day. They come from different parts of Mexico. Like many cities in the United States and around the world, there are not enough jobs and homes for everyone. Some people in Mexico City live very well. Many are poor. People will have to work hard as they try to solve these problems.

Remains of an old Aztec temple were found while building the subway in Mexico City.

26

A Suburb Grows

Cuajimalpa is about 14 miles from downtown Mexico City. It used to be a rural village. Farmers, coal miners, and woodcutters lived there. Families like Ana's have lived and worked there for many years. But just as Mexico City has grown, new people have also moved to Cuajimalpa.

Slowly the community of Cuajimalpa is changing. New homes and buildings are being built on what used to be farms. People like Ana's father must find jobs in the city. Cuajimalpa is changing from a rural to a suburban community.

Mr. Flores works in Mexico City. He takes a bus to get there. The bus trip used to take him only 15 minutes. Now, because of increased traffic, the trip takes almost an hour.

Ana's mother takes care of her four children. She also works for a different family in another home nearby. Ana and her three sisters take a bus to school. During their free time they like to go to the town square to meet their friends.

As Cuajimalpa grows, Mr. Flores's bus ride to work takes longer and longer.

Communities Change

"What makes Cuajimalpa special," says Mr. Flores, "is the blend of the old and the new."

In the center of Cuajimalpa is an old marketplace. But the town also has modern supermarkets. While many new people now live in Cuajimalpa, most people have lived there for a long time.

Many people want to move to areas similar to Cuajimalpa. They like the beauty of the land. Near Cuajimalpa there is a large pine-tree forest. It is a national park. A national park is land that is set aside by a government for all people to enjoy. Making the pine forest a national park will protect it. The forest won't be "eaten up" by the growth of Mexico City.

As Cuajimalpa and Mexico City grow, people worry about air pollution. They are using their cars less often to help solve this problem. By working together, the people of Mexico are making their communities better places to live.

People can enjoy hiking in a national park near Cuajimalpa.

WHY IT MATTERS

Like communities in the United States, communities in Mexico are changing. Many urban and suburban areas are growing out toward rural areas. With this growth old ways of life change and cultures change.

All communities face problems as they grow and change. To solve these problems people must work together.

Outdoor markets are popular places in Mexico to buy food and other products.

Reviewing Facts and Ideas

MAIN IDEAS

- Communities in other countries have a lot in common with communities in the United States. They also have differences.

- Culture is an important part of what makes each community different. Mexico has a special culture.

- Cuajimalpa is a suburb of Mexico City. It used to be rural, but it has grown as Mexico City has spread out. Communities change.

THINK ABOUT IT

1. What are some special parts of Mexican culture?

2. **FOCUS** What are communities like in Mexico?

3. **THINKING SKILL** What do you *predict* will happen as urban areas continue to grow?

4. **GEOGRAPHY** Use the map on page 25 to measure the distance from Pino Suárez to the National Palace.

VIEWPOINTS

In Kenya, Africa, people can see animals in a type of zoo called a game park.

What do people think about zoos?

Around the world, people visit zoos to learn about animals. Many scientists believe zoos allow people to learn about wild animals and their natural environments. Some people like Khadashia King agree. She thinks zoos help people to learn about animals that are endangered. Endangered animals are animals that are in danger of dying out. But not everyone agrees. Charlotte Moore thinks the best place for animals is in the wild.

Still other people are not as certain. George Lujan thinks people can learn about wild animals at zoos. But he also thinks zoos are bad because they take animals away from their natural environment.

Read and think about the three different viewpoints on the next page. A viewpoint is what a person thinks about something. Then answer the questions that follow.

Three DIFFERENT Viewpoints

KHADASHIA KING
Third Grader, Manning, South Carolina
Excerpt from Interview, 1997

We should have zoos. Zoos give children an educational experience to see animals they wouldn't normally see. Zoos keep animals from dying out by giving them a safe environment, almost like a natural habitat. Lastly, zoos protect endangered species.

". . . zoos protect endangered species."

GEORGE LUJAN
Fourth Grader, Los Angeles, California
Excerpt from Interview, 1997

Zoos protect endangered animals and birds like the California condor. They keep them from dying out and help them to reproduce. You can learn a lot from visiting a zoo. You can read the signs on the cages which describe the animals. But one thing is bad about zoos—taking animals away from their families and the place they are used to living in.

"You can learn a lot from visiting a zoo."

CHARLOTTE MOORE
Fourth Grader, Virginia Beach, Virginia
Excerpt from Interview, 1997

The best place for animals is in the wild where they came from. In zoos, animals stay in cages all day and people watch them. They don't have any privacy. You can learn just as much from reading magazines and watching TV shows about animals as you can from watching them in zoos.

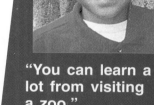

"The best place . . . is in the wild . . ."

BUILDING CITIZENSHIP

1. What is the viewpoint of each person? How does each person support his or her view?

2. How are these viewpoints alike? How are they different?

3. What other opinions might people have on this issue?

SHARING VIEWPOINTS

Discuss how you agree or disagree with these and other viewpoints. Make sure you give reasons to support your opinion. Then as a class write one statement that all of you can agree with.

CHAPTER 1 REVIEW

THINKING ABOUT VOCABULARY

Number a sheet of paper from 1 to 10. Beside each number write the word or term from the list below that matches the description.

citizen   national park
community   pollution
culture   suburb
rural   transportation
volunteer   urban

1. The way of life of a group of people
2. A member of a community or a country
3. A community located near a city
4. The moving of people and products from place to place
5. A place where different people live, work, and have fun together
6. Someone who does something by choice, without pay
7. A type of community with farms or open country
8. Land that is set aside by a government for all people to enjoy
9. Anything that spoils land, water, or air
10. A type of community that includes a city and its surrounding areas

THINKING ABOUT FACTS

1. Name three things that make up communities in our country.
2. How did the people of Sacramento help each other in 1986?
3. How has the community of Bothell, Washington, changed in the past few years? Why are these changes taking place?
4. Why do people in Rochester, Indiana, need cars to get from one place to another?
5. How are the communities of Cuajimalpa, Mexico, and Bothell, Washington, alike? How are they different?

THINK AND WRITE

WRITING A PARAGRAPH

Write a short paragraph describing how people in your community have come together to solve a problem.

WRITING ABOUT CHANGE

Think about a rural community where the drinking water makes everyone look young. Write a paragraph describing how this community might change if people from other communities learned of its water.

MAKING A LIST

In communities across the United States, Main Street is changing. Make a list of three stores or places in your community that were not around long ago. Write a sentence telling why you picked these places.

APPLYING GEOGRAPHY SKILLS

USING MAP SCALES

Answer the following questions to practice your skill of using map scales.

1. On the map scale at the right, one inch equals how many miles?

2. How many miles is Cincinnati from Uniontown?

3. What is the distance from St. Louis to Detroit?

4. Is Indianapolis closer to Louisville or to Rochester?

5. Why is it important to be able to read map scales?

INDIANA AND NEIGHBORING STATES

Summing Up the Chapter

Review the chapter before making a copy of the main idea pyramid below. The chapter theme is at the top of the pyramid. The main ideas are in the middle. Fill in the bottom with information that supports each main idea. Then describe how communities in both the United States and Mexico have changed in the past few years.

Communities are places where people live, work, and have fun together.

Communities are similar to each other.

Communities are different from each other.

Communities and Geography

THINKING ABOUT GEOGRAPHY AND CITIZENSHIP

In Chapter 2, you will see scenes of our country's natural beauty. You will also see the many ways people use the land and water around them.

Land and water are important to all communities. By working together to protect the environment, people will always be able to enjoy the natural wonders of our planet.

Grand Teton Mountains, Wyoming

Hartford, Connecticut

Florida Coast

People and animals enjoy the Atlantic Ocean along the coast of Florida.

In Hartford, Connecticut, and other communities, people recycle to help protect the environment.

The plains near the Grand Teton Mountains in Wyoming provide food for cows.

Our Country's Geography

Focus Activity

READ TO LEARN

What is geography?

VOCABULARY

- geography
- plain
- landform
- plateau
- climate

PLACES

- Atlantic Ocean
- Pacific Ocean
- Mississippi River
- Rocky Mountains

Read Aloud

It's a clear fall day. The mountain air is chilly. Inside her house, a woman puts on a jacket. She walks into the woods and hikes up the mountain. Along the way she picks up fallen branches. The leaves crunch under her feet. A squirrel runs away. The woman is cold and she thinks, "When I get home, I'll build a fire."

Geography Every Day

In this lesson you will read about everyday events like the ones above in a new way. Events like these are part of the story of geography. Geography is the study of Earth and the way people, plants, and animals live on and use it.

Take a look at the Infographic on pages 40–41. It shows some important features of our country's geography. You may find it helpful. You can refer to the Infographic as you read this lesson.

Splish, Splash, and Fish

What covers more of Earth than all the deserts, mountains, forests, cities, towns, and farms combined? The answer is water! How important is water? All plants, animals, and people need water to live.

Oceans are the largest bodies of water. The Atlantic Ocean and the Pacific Ocean are very large. They border the east and west sides of the United States. Oceans are made of salt water.

Rivers and lakes are also bodies of water. They are mostly made of fresh water. Sometimes they are very large. Use the Infographic to see which are the largest lakes in our country. Bodies of water can also be very small. A quiet pond or a wandering stream are smaller bodies of water.

People relate to bodies of water in many ways. Francis Akinsulie (ah kihn ZOO lee) is a student who lives in St. Louis, Missouri. Here's what he says about living along the mighty Mississippi River: "I like going to the river to see the boats going past carrying different things. I once saw someone catch a fish there and take it home in a bucket."

Compare the stream (above) with the Mississippi River at St. Louis (below), where Francis Akinsulie lives.

37

Skiing is one way people like Luis Garcia enjoy the Rocky Mountains.

Look at Those Landforms!

Did you ever notice that the land near your community may have different shapes? It can stretch out flat the way a plain does. A plain is a large area of flat land. Or land can also form a mountain, rising steeply to a point.

Mountains and plains are two kinds of landforms. A landform is the shape of the surface of the land. Two other landforms are hills and plateaus (pla TOHZ). A plateau is land that is raised above surrounding land. Plateaus are usually high and flat. Look at the Infographic. It shows a few of our country's many landforms. What kinds of landforms are near your community?

Luis Garcia lives in the community of Avon, Colorado. You can see from the Infographic that he lives in the Rocky Mountains. Luis says, "In the part of Mexico where I was born, it never snows. But here, with all the mountains, I get to go skiing and sledding. My whole class learned to ski together. Many people here have jobs that help people who come to ski."

Hot and Cold, Wet and Dry

Like the landforms in our country, the weather is also different in different communities. When we talk about the weather a place has over a long period of time, we are talking about climate.

How hot can it get? Take a July afternoon in Death Valley, California. Some people say you can cook an egg on the ground here before you can say "sunny side up." The climate here is hot and dry most of the year.

How cold can it get? Take a January day in Prospect Creek, Alaska. It's said that tears freeze here before they leave your eyes. Winters here are very cold.

How wet can it get? Take the island of Kauai (KOW i), Hawaii. It rains here about 460 inches every year. That's more rain than Death Valley gets in 400 years!

As you can see, our country has different kinds of climates. How would you describe the climate of your community?

In Death Valley (left) the climate is hot and dry. In Alaska (below) it is often very cold.

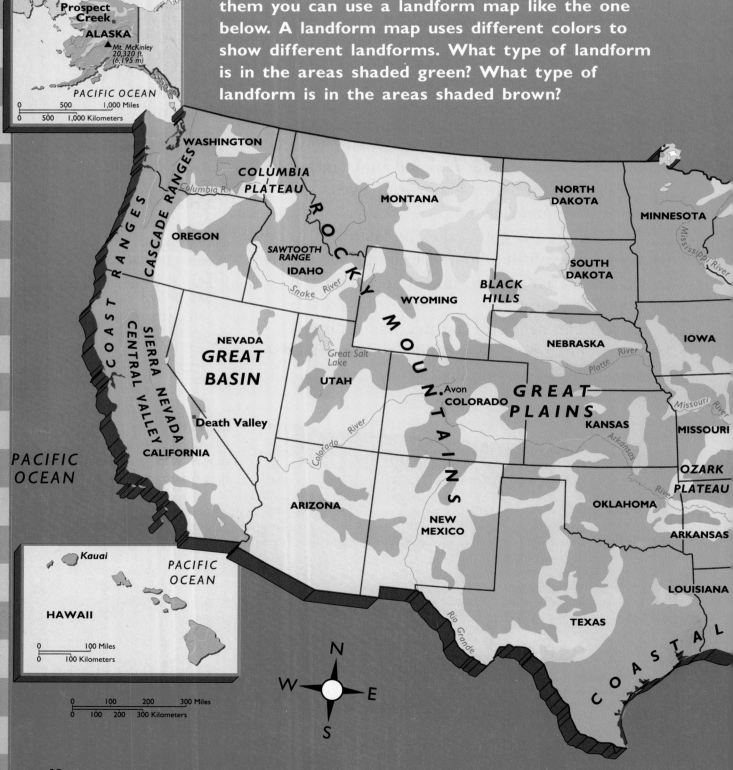

Infographic

interNET CONNECTION
Visit our website:
www.mhschool.com

Our Country's Landforms

You have just read that the United States has many
different types of landforms. To learn more about
them you can use a landform map like the one
below. A landform map uses different colors to
show different landforms. What type of landform
is in the areas shaded green? What type of
landform is in the areas shaded brown?

Prospect Creek
ALASKA
Mt. McKinley 20,320 ft. (6,195 m)
PACIFIC OCEAN
500 1,000 Miles
500 1,000 Kilometers

WASHINGTON
COLUMBIA PLATEAU
MONTANA
NORTH DAKOTA
MINNESOTA
CASCADE RANGES
Columbia R.
COAST RANGES
OREGON
SAWTOOTH RANGE
IDAHO
Snake River
ROCKY MOUNTAINS
WYOMING
BLACK HILLS
SOUTH DAKOTA
Mississippi River
SIERRA NEVADA
CENTRAL VALLEY
NEVADA
GREAT BASIN
Great Salt Lake
UTAH
NEBRASKA
IOWA
Platte River
Missouri River
Death Valley
CALIFORNIA
Colorado River
Avon
COLORADO
GREAT PLAINS
KANSAS
MISSOURI
OZARK PLATEAU
Arkansas River
PACIFIC OCEAN
ARIZONA
NEW MEXICO
OKLAHOMA
ARKANSAS
Kauai
PACIFIC OCEAN
HAWAII
100 Miles
100 Kilometers
LOUISIANA
Rio Grande
TEXAS
COASTAL

N
W   E
S

100 200 300 Miles
100 200 300 Kilometers

THE UNITED STATES: LANDFORMS

- Mountains
- Plateaus
- Hills
- Plains
- • City
- ■ Point of Interest

Sawtooth Mountains in Idaho

Hills in Virginia

Columbia Plateau in Oregon

Great Plains in Kansas

MAINE

VERMONT

NEW HAMPSHIRE

MASSACHUSETTS

NEW YORK

Lake Ontario

RHODE ISLAND

CONNECTICUT

NEW JERSEY

DELAWARE

MARYLAND

VIRGINIA

APPALACHIAN MOUNTAINS

PIEDMONT

COASTAL PLAIN

NORTH CAROLINA

SOUTH CAROLINA

PENNSYLVANIA

Lake Erie

OHIO

WEST VIRGINIA

KENTUCKY

TENNESSEE

Tennessee River

Ohio River

St. Louis

ILLINOIS

INDIANA

MICHIGAN

Lake Michigan

Lake Huron

Lake St. Clair

WISCONSIN

Lake Superior

ALABAMA

GEORGIA

MISSISSIPPI

P L A I N

FLORIDA

Gulf of Mexico

ATLANTIC OCEAN

41

A Poem Describes Geography

People live with landforms around them every day. Read the following poem. How many landforms can you find?

MANY VOICES
LITERATURE

OPEN RANGE

Prairie goes to the mountain,
　Mountain goes to the sky.
The sky sweeps across to the distant hills
And here, in the middle,
　Am I.

Hills crowd down to the river,
　River runs by the tree.
Tree throws its shadow on sunburnt grass
And here, in the shadow,
　Is me.

Shadows creep up the mountain,
　Mountain goes black on the sky,
The sky bursts out with a million stars
And here, by the campfire,
　Am I.

by Kathryn and Byron Jackson

range: open area of land
prairie: flat or rolling land covered with tall grasses

WHY IT MATTERS

What if someone told you that you would be studying geography this year? You might think you would be finding places on maps. But using maps is just one part of geography.

You have seen how geography is important to Francis Akinsulie, who lives near the Mississippi River. How else do you think geography makes a difference in people's lives? Luis Garcia's community is in the Rocky Mountains. Many people there rely on jobs that support skiing.

The location of a community has a lot to do with the jobs people do there. In forest areas many people work with wood from the trees. Where the climate is warm, people may work by providing help to sun-seeking visitors.

Geography makes a difference in people's lives. This difference can be seen every day in many communities throughout the world.

Geography **is important to the kinds of activities people enjoy in communities.**

✓ Reviewing Facts and Ideas

MAIN IDEAS

- Recognizing landforms is an important part of geography.
- Plains, mountains, hills, and plateaus are important landforms in our country.
- The climate in our country is very different in different areas.
- Geography is important to people's lives every day in different ways. It influences where people work and what they do for fun.

THINK ABOUT IT

1. What is a landform? Give three examples.
2. **FOCUS** What is geography?
3. **THINKING SKILL** If you lived near the water, what do you _predict_ you would do for fun?
4. **GEOGRAPHY** Look at the Infographic on pages 40–41. What plains are around the Arkansas River?

Fun with the Wind

People all over the world use the wind to fly kites. The first kites may have been flown in China more than 3,000 years ago.

Long ago kites were not only for fun. In some Asian countries they were used for fishing. More recently box kites have been used to carry weather instruments.

Today kites are used in many ways to explore the air and enjoy the wind.

Wherever you live, kites can be fun for you!

Pictured here are an old Polynesian fishing kite (left) and a modern box kite (above).

In 1752 Benjamin Franklin used a kite to show that lightning is one form of electricity.

Kites shaped like this come from the Asian country of Malaysia.

A boy in Egypt enjoys his kite. People all over the world have fun making and flying kites.

Caring for Our Natural Resources

Focus Activity

READ TO LEARN

Why are natural resources important?

VOCABULARY

- natural resource
- mineral
- environment
- recycling

A Wealth of Resources

This poem is called "Trees." It was written over 100 years ago by a poet named Sara Coleridge. She describes many different trees that grow on Earth. Do you have any of these trees in your community today?

Look around your classroom. Is there anything made from a tree? Perhaps your pencil or the paper in your book is made from trees. Trees are just one example of a natural resource. A natural resource is something found in nature that people use. In this lesson you will learn about other natural resources and why it is important to respect and care for them.

Land of Plenty

Look at the pictures on this page. They show some of our country's many natural resources. The United States is one of the richest countries in the world in natural resources.

Water is one of our most important natural resources. As you read in the previous lesson, the United States has many bodies of water, large and small. Plants need fresh water to grow. People and animals need fresh water to live. Boats travel on our oceans, rivers, and lakes. They carry people and goods.

Have you ever picked up a handful of soil? Did you know that you were holding another valuable resource? Soil is full of minerals to help plants grow. Minerals are things found in the earth that are not plants or animals. Iron, salt, and diamonds are all minerals.

You may live in the mountains, in the woods, near the ocean, or in the desert. But wherever you live, your community has many natural resources. Even the air you are breathing right now is a natural resource!

Natural resources include water and soil. People also use oil and metals from inside Earth.

Protecting the Environment

"Save the Whales." "Give a hoot . . . Don't pollute!" Have you ever noticed bumper stickers like these on a car? They show that people want to protect the environment. The environment is air, water, land, and the living things around us.

Protecting the environment and its resources takes a lot of work. Just putting a bumper sticker on a car is not enough. Every day you can take personal action to help protect the environment. Every time you use a bottle, can, or piece of paper, you can save it for recycling. Recycling is using something over again. Factories take used plastic, metal, and paper and recycle them.

There are other ways you can help protect the environment. A few years ago some eight-year-old girls in El Segundo, California, wanted to help their community fight air pollution. They knew that plants and trees improve the air. So they formed a group called the "Tree Musketeers." They then decided to plant trees and other plants around their community. Today their community is a more beautiful place to live. According to one Musketeer, Tara Church, "The trees help us keep the air in our community clean."

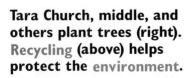

Tara Church, middle, and others plant trees (right). Recycling (above) helps protect the environment.

48

WHY IT MATTERS

Look around your classroom again. Now you may notice more natural resources than you did before. There is one more resource you may not have noticed: people! You, your teacher, your classmates, and everyone in your community are important resources. It is people who take the other resources around them and make them useful. It is people who will protect our natural resources for years to come.

A garden needs both natural and human resources.

Reviewing Facts and Ideas

MAIN IDEAS

- Our country is rich in natural resources including water, trees, soil, and the air we breathe.

- It is important to protect our environment. Everyone can take action to help make a difference.

- Recycling is one way to protect our environment.

- People are one of our most important resources.

THINK ABOUT IT

1. What are three examples of natural resources?

2. **FOCUS** Why are natural resources important?

3. **THINKING SKILL** How would you _sort_ materials from your home for recycling?

4. **WRITE** Write and design your own poster telling people to protect the environment. What will it say?

Using Intermediate Directions

VOCABULARY
intermediate directions

WHY THE SKILL MATTERS

El Segundo, the hometown of the "Tree Musketeers," is located near Los Angeles. To find where Los Angeles is located, you can look at a map of California. What if you wanted to travel from Los Angeles to Sacramento? Could you use the map to explain which direction to go?

You could if you knew how to use intermediate directions. An intermediate direction is halfway between two cardinal directions.

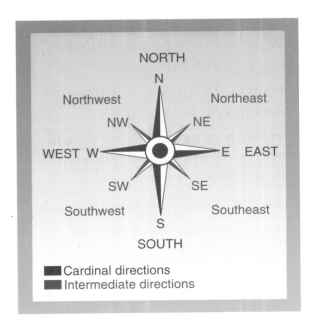

- Cardinal directions
- Intermediate directions

USING THE SKILL

You have already used a compass rose to find cardinal directions on a map. Look at the compass rose below. The cardinal directions are north, south, east, and west. North is shown by the letter **N**. What letters are used for east, south, and west?

Now look at the map on the next page. In which direction is Sacramento from Los Angeles? It is neither *exactly* north nor *exactly* west. Instead, it is northwest, which is between north and west. Northwest is an intermediate direction. Look again at the compass rose below and find northwest. It is shown by the letters **NW**. The other intermediate directions are northeast, southeast, and southwest. What letters does the compass rose show for them?

When you use intermediate directions, start by finding one place on the map. Then find the second place and describe the direction from the first place to the second. You may want to refer to the compass rose. If you start with Sacramento and go to Los Angeles, the direction is southeast.

TRYING THE SKILL

Now try describing directions between other places. Use the Helping Yourself box as you answer these questions.

Look at the map again. In which direction would you travel to go from Los Angeles to Denver, Colorado? In which direction would you go to get from Las Vegas, Nevada, to Los Angeles? How about Colorado Springs, Colorado, to Provo, Utah?

Helping yourself

- **Intermediate directions** are northeast, southeast, southwest, and northwest.

- **Find two places on the map. Use the compass rose to describe the direction from the first to the second.**

REVIEWING THE SKILL

1. What are intermediate directions?

2. If you were in Carson City, Nevada, in which direction would you travel to Tucson, Arizona? How can you tell?

3. In which direction is Salt Lake City, Utah, from Sacramento?

4. When is it helpful to know intermediate directions?

SOUTHWESTERN STATES

Sacramento ★ Carson City ★ · Salt Lake City ★ · Provo · Denver ★ Colorado Springs · NEVADA · UTAH · COLORADO · CALIFORNIA · Las Vegas · Los Angeles · Santa Fe ★ Albuquerque · ARIZONA · NEW MEXICO · Phoenix ★ Tucson · PACIFIC OCEAN

★ State capital
· Other city

0   100   200 Miles
0   100   200 Kilometers

A Fishing Community in Peru

Read Aloud

"I live by the sea. My community is filled with beautiful beaches. There are hundreds of fish and other sea animals. I am lucky to live here. My family has been here for almost 100 years. I want to live here forever. The land and water provide us with so many things for life."

Focus Activity

READ TO LEARN

How are natural resources important to people in Paracas, Peru?

VOCABULARY

- coast
- peninsula
- wildlife

PLACES

- Paracas, Peru

A Community by the Ocean

These are the words of a young boy. He lives with his family in the community of Paracas (pah RAH kahs) in the country of Peru. Peru is located along the Pacific Ocean. That's the same ocean that borders the west coast of the United States. A coast is land next to an ocean. But Peru is thousands of miles away from the United States. It is on the continent of South America.

For communities like Paracas the ocean is important to people's lives. The ocean provides them with many natural resources. In this lesson you will learn about these resources. You will also see that people are concerned about protecting them.

Living in Paracas

Do you know all the people in your community? Well, most people know each other in Paracas. There are only about 100 houses in this community. Many families have lived there for many years.

Fishing is important to many ocean communities around the world. Fishing is also a very important part of the culture of Paracas. Almost everyone in the community makes a living from fishing.

Look at the map below to locate Paracas. Paracas is a peninsula. A peninsula is land that has water on all sides but one. An island also has water around it. How is a peninsula different from an island?

For people in Paracas, being near the water is a lot of fun. Many children in Paracas play soccer. But they play on the beach instead of on grass. They watch sea lions. But instead of going to a zoo, they go to a nearby beach. There they can see hundreds of sea lions!

The sea lion is one of many animals that live along the coast of Peru.

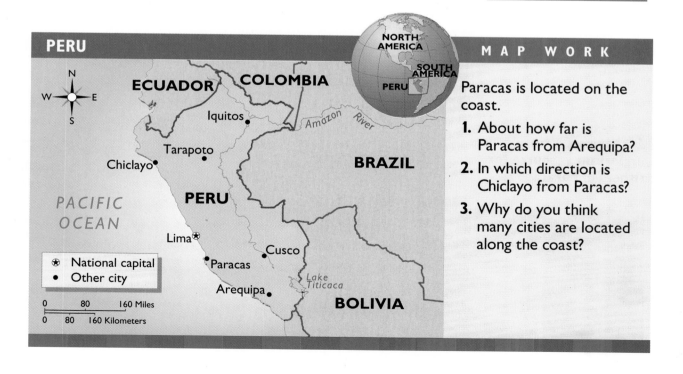

PERU

ECUADOR
COLOMBIA
Iquitos
Amazon River
Tarapoto
Chiclayo
BRAZIL
PACIFIC OCEAN
PERU
Lima
Cusco
Paracas
Lake Titicaca
National capital
Other city
Arequipa
BOLIVIA

0 80 160 Miles
0 80 160 Kilometers

NORTH AMERICA
SOUTH AMERICA
PERU

MAP WORK

Paracas is located on the coast.

1. About how far is Paracas from Arequipa?

2. In which direction is Chiclayo from Paracas?

3. Why do you think many cities are located along the coast?

A Rich Peninsula

An important natural resource in Paracas is its wildlife. Wildlife are animals that live naturally in an area. Fish are a kind of wildlife.

In Paracas anchovies (AN choh veez) are the most important fish. That's because many fishers make their living from anchovies. Every year millions of small fish are caught and shipped all over the world. The ocean here also has many whales, turtles, and crabs.

Paracas is one of the most important stopping points for birds. Birds are also wildlife. Many birds migrate, or travel, south to Paracas. During the winter they come from faraway places in the north. Some birds fly all the way to Paracas from Canada! The sanderling is one of these long-distance fliers.

These natural resources are important to Paracas for another reason. Visitors come from all over the world to see the wildlife. Some people in Paracas have jobs helping these visitors.

Anchovies are an important resource for fishers in Paracas.

Infographic

Endangered Animals Around the World

In Paracas and other communities, wildlife is a valuable natural resource. But sometimes people don't take care to protect resources. Look at the Infographic on this page. Which endangered species have you heard of?

The California condor is the largest flying bird in the United States. Hunting, pollution, and the destruction of open land areas have threatened their existence.

The black rhinoceros lives in Africa. Their horns are used for medicines.

Giant pandas come from China. The bamboo trees they need for food are being destroyed.

Saltwater crocodiles live in places such as Australia and Asia. Their skins are used to make shoes, wallets, and other products.

The sperm whale was hunted for food, oil, and bone around the world. Other types of whales are also endangered.

Caring for Resources

People in Peru care about their natural resources. Like many communities in the United States, Paracas is becoming polluted. Waste from nearby businesses is dumped into the ocean. Some fish are unsafe to eat.

But the pollution problem in Paracas is improving. People are keeping their beaches clean. Businesses are being more careful not to dump dangerous wastes into the ocean.

By taking care of natural resources, people will be able to enjoy the beaches around Paracas for years to come.

WHY IT MATTERS

You have seen how important natural resources are to people in Paracas. You have also seen one way that people in communities all over the world are alike. They are all concerned about protecting these resources.

By working together, people will be able to protect Earth's natural resources for many years to come.

✓ Reviewing Facts and Ideas

MAIN IDEAS

- Paracas is an ocean community in the country of Peru.
- There are many natural resources in Paracas.
- Pollution is dangerous to people and wildlife in Paracas.
- People are working together to help fight pollution in Paracas and other places.

THINK ABOUT IT

1. What do people like about living in Paracas?

2. **FOCUS** How are natural resources important to people in Paracas, Peru?

3. **THINKING SKILL** How are the resources in your community *like* the wildlife in Paracas?

4. **GEOGRAPHY** Paracas is a peninsula. How is this important to life in the community of Paracas?

MAKING A DIFFERENCE

Keep Eustace Lake Clean!

ZUNI, NEW MEXICO—If you visit Eustace Lake in Zuni, New Mexico, you might see a sign that says, "Keep Eustace Lake Clean." It was made by sixth graders who took action to protect their environment.

It all started in the classroom of Jim Bizell, a teacher at Zuni Middle School. One of his students' favorite spots was Eustace Lake. The lake was once a great place to swim, boat, and fish. But it became unsafe to use. Kelton Kallestewa, one of Mr. Bizell's students, described the lake this way: "It was filled with tires, garbage, and bottles. The picnic tables were broken, and the bathroom walls were knocked down."

Mr. Bizell decided that the students could make a difference by cleaning the lake. Here's Kelton's description of what they did: "We began hauling weeds and removing glass. Four kids went out on a boat and took trash out of the lake. Other kids repaired the bathrooms and picnic tables."

Soon other members of the community were helping too. Some gave pipes to make swing sets. Others helped make pathways and put fish back in the lake.

Making a difference is "up to the kids," said Kelton. "We have the ability to do it. It makes me feel proud to have other people proud of me. When I see the lake now, I'm happy. I'll be able to fish!"

"It makes me feel proud . . ."

Kelton Kallestewa

57

Geography Skills

Understanding Hemispheres

VOCABULARY
hemisphere
equator

WHY THE SKILL MATTERS

You have read about the community of Paracas in Peru. To describe where Peru is, you can say it is on the continent of South America. By learning about hemispheres, you will also know another way to locate Peru. Use the Helping Yourself box on the next page as you study hemispheres.

USING THE SKILL

Earth is a sphere. A sphere is round like a ball or a globe. Look at Maps A and B. They show Earth divided into hemispheres. *Hemi* means "half," so a hemisphere is half of a sphere.

The Western and Eastern hemispheres are opposite halves of Earth. Peru is in South America, in the Western Hemisphere. Is Asia in the Eastern or Western Hemisphere?

Maps C and D on the next page show the Northern and Southern hemispheres. The equator, an imaginary line around the middle of Earth, divides these two hemispheres.

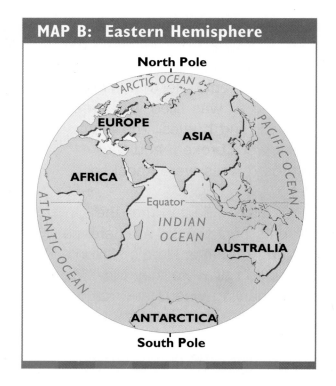

MAP A: Western Hemisphere

MAP B: Eastern Hemisphere

As you can see on Maps C and D, North America is in the Northern Hemisphere. What other hemisphere includes North America?

TRYING THE SKILL

Now try locating Europe and Africa on the hemisphere maps. Europe is in the Northern Hemisphere and what other hemisphere? Are Europe and North America in the same hemispheres? In which three hemispheres are parts of Africa?

Helping yourself

- **The equator divides Earth into Northern and Southern hemispheres.**
- **Earth can also be divided into Eastern and Western hemispheres.**

REVIEWING THE SKILL

1. Name the four hemispheres into which we divide Earth.
2. Which three hemispheres contain parts of South America? Which one contains all of South America? How did you find out?
3. Name all the continents found in the Northern Hemisphere.
4. What could you do to help a friend understand hemispheres?

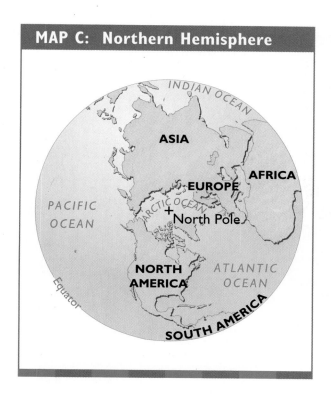

MAP C: Northern Hemisphere

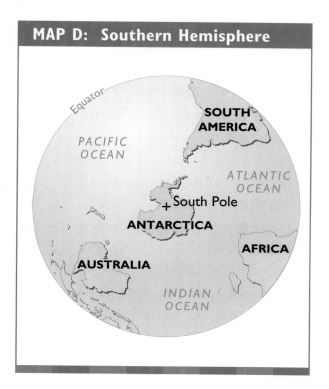

MAP D: Southern Hemisphere

CHAPTER 2 REVIEW

THINKING ABOUT VOCABULARY

Number a sheet of paper from 1 to 5. Beside each number write the word or term from the list below that best completes each sentence.

coast   recycling
minerals   wildlife
natural resources

1. Every Saturday my father and I bring bottles and newspapers to our community _____ center.
2. When I visit the _____, I love to walk along the sandy beach.
3. Today people are finding new ways to protect endangered _____ around the world.
4. Trees, water, and soil are three examples of our country's _____ .
5. Things found in the earth that are not plants or animals are known as _____ .

THINKING ABOUT FACTS

1. What covers most of Earth's surface?
2. How does a plain differ from a plateau? How are the two landforms similar?
3. Describe two ways in which your class can help save our country's natural resources.
4. Why are some people in Paracas protecting its natural resources?
5. How does climate influence the things that people do for fun in communities?

THINK AND WRITE

WRITING A JOURNAL ENTRY
Suppose that you are backpacking around the United States. Write an entry in your journal describing three kinds of natural resources that you observed on your trip.

WRITING A SPEECH
Write a speech explaining the importance of protecting endangered species around the world.

WRITING A LETTER
Suppose you were invited to spend a week in Paracas, Peru. Write a letter to your family describing everything you saw there. Remember to include a description of the kinds of natural resources found in Paracas as well as the kinds of things people do there for work and for play.

APPLYING GEOGRAPHY SKILLS

USING INTERMEDIATE DIRECTIONS

Answer the following questions about the map at the right to practice your skill at using intermediate directions.

1. What are the four intermediate directions?

2. Which city is southwest of Louisville?

3. Which community is southeast of Scotland?

4. In which direction is Cincinnati from Indianapolis?

5. Why is it important to understand intermediate directions?

Summing Up the Chapter

Look at the word map below. Then review the chapter to find at least three items to list under the four headings. When you have filled in a copy of the map, use it to discuss how we depend on Earth and its natural resources.

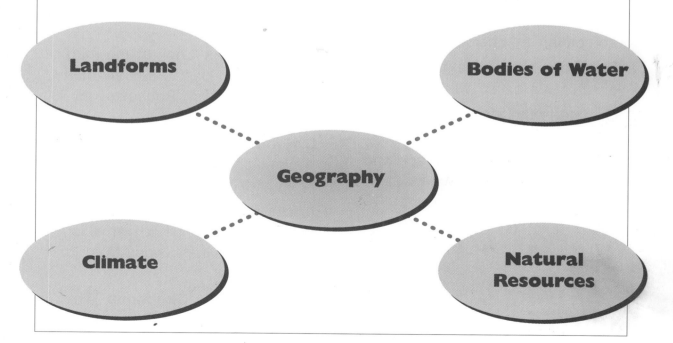

UNIT 1 REVIEW

THINKING ABOUT VOCABULARY

Number a sheet of paper from 1 to 10. Read the definition of each underlined word. Beside each number write **T** if the definition is true and **F** if it is false.

1. A <u>plain</u> is land that is raised above surrounding land.

2. A <u>rural</u> community is a place of farms or open country.

3. <u>Geography</u> is the study of the various plants and animals that live on Earth.

4. A <u>landform</u> is a kind of land, such as a plain, hill, or mountain.

5. A member of a community or a country is known as a <u>citizen</u>.

6. Land that stretches out flat is called a <u>plateau</u>.

7. A <u>volunteer</u> is someone who does something by choice, without pay.

8. The animals that live naturally in an area are called <u>wildlife</u>.

9. <u>Climate</u> is the way it is outdoors each day.

10. The study of Earth's surface and the bodies of water that cover it is called <u>environment</u>.

THINK AND WRITE

WRITING ABOUT COMMUNITIES

Write a paragraph to convince someone to move to your community. In your writing include those qualities that make your hometown special.

WRITING A POEM

The United States has many different landforms. Read the poem on page 42. Then write a poem describing our country's landforms.

WRITING ABOUT PERSPECTIVES

What if you had just moved to Cuajimalpa, Mexico? Write a letter to a friend in the United States describing how life in Mexico might be different from life back home.

BUILDING SKILLS

1. **Map Scales** Why are map scales included on most maps in this book?

2. **Map Scales** Look at the map of Indiana on page 23. How many miles is it from Rochester to Uniontown?

3. **Hemispheres** Which two hemispheres are divided by the equator?

4. **Intermediate Directions** Look at the map on page 51. In which direction is Las Vegas from Los Angeles?

5. **Intermediate Directions** Why are intermediate directions useful?

LOCAL *connection*

What are the names of places and streets in your community? How can you find out how these places got their names? Make your own posters to share this knowledge with others.

READING ON YOUR OWN

Here are some books you might find at the library to help you learn more.

KATE ON THE COAST
by Pat Brisson
A girl writes letters to her best friend describing life in the Northwest.

FAMILY PICTURES
by Carmen Lomas Garza
Learn what life is like for a Hispanic family living in Texas.

TOWN AND COUNTRY
by Alice and Martin Provensen
Here's a look at life in the United States, on a farm and in a city.

UNIT REVIEW PROJECT

Creating a Community Brochure

1. Suppose you could create a community brochure. What would you include in it?
2. Draw a map of the community.
3. List some facts about the history of the community.
4. Draw pictures of this community on separate pieces of paper. Include museums, parks, schools, and the post office.
5. Glue each picture onto colored construction paper.
6. Punch a hole in the left-hand corner of each page.
7. Tie the pages of your brochure together with a piece of yarn or string.

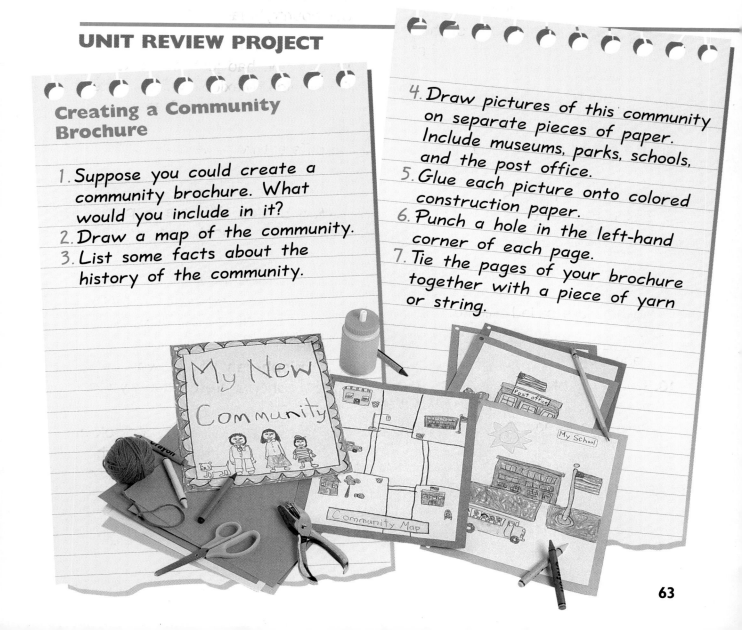

Looking Back to the Past

Why Does it Matter?

Who first lived in your community? Why do you think they decided to live there?

In this unit you will learn about three very different communities where people lived long ago. These communities were built in different places by different groups of people. Learning about them helps us to discover our country's past and to understand the story of our earliest communities.

As you explore these communities, think about how the past is still part of our lives today.

FIND OUT MORE!
Visit our website:
www.mhschool.com

*inter*NET
CONNECTION

Adventures
with
NATIONAL GEOGRAPHIC

LIVING HISTORY

It's morning at Plimoth Plantation, in Massachusetts. Time to gather firewood and feed the chickens. Later, the floor needs to be swept. It's hard work—especially when you're wearing Pilgrim-style clothes. Young people sometimes work at Plimoth Plantation. This village was built to look just like the one the Pilgrims built after they sailed across the Atlantic Ocean from England. These kids find out for themselves what daily life was like in the 1620s.

GEO JOURNAL

Write a letter to a friend telling about a job you'd like to have at Plimoth Plantation.

A Native American Community at Mesa Verde

THINKING ABOUT GEOGRAPHY AND HISTORY

The first American communities were started by Native Americans. They lived all across the land we now call the United States. People in these communities made their clothing, homes, and food from the natural resources they found where they lived.

In Chapter 3 you will learn about the Native Americans. You will also visit Mesa Verde, a Native American community built long ago high on the side of a cliff. The map shows you where Mesa Verde is located. The time line shows you when important events occurred.

1100s–1300s

The Anasazi build communities in cliffs

1300s–1450s

The Anasazi leave Mesa Verde

1100   1200   1300

Mesa Verde,
Colorado

TODAY

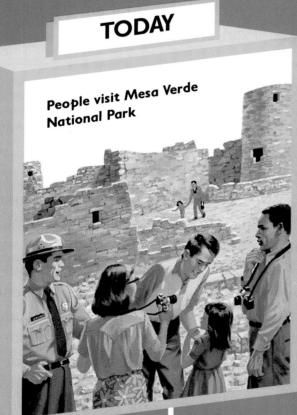

People visit Mesa Verde
National Park

Native American Communities

Focus Activity

READ TO LEARN

Who lived in the first American communities?

VOCABULARY

• history

Read Aloud

"All the time I learn things about my Cherokee culture. Sometimes when I'm doing chores for my mom like pulling up weeds in the backyard, I make little woven baskets out of grass like our people used to make long ago. I am happy to be Cherokee. I am proud of it."

The First Communities

These are the words of Stormi Welch. She is a nine-year-old Cherokee who lives in the state of North Carolina. She is very proud of her Cherokee culture and her past. The Cherokee are just one of many Native American groups who live in the United States today.

"Native American" or "Indian" are names for the first people to live in the land that became the United States of America. It is important to understand how Native Americans lived long ago. Native Americans are part of our country's history. History is the story of the past. In this lesson we'll look back at our country's first communities.

Native American Storytelling

Many different groups of Native Americans lived in this land long ago. Each group had its own culture. But one thing most Native Americans shared is a love of storytelling. They still do today. The following story was written by Tina Naiche (NAH chee), a young Apache. The Apache are a group of Native Americans who live in the southwest part of our country.

MANY VOICES
LITERATURE

Story by Tina Naiche, written in 1976.

Coyote Gets Turkey Up a Tree

Coyote is a great figure for the Apaches. He is good at tricking other animals but he is always getting fooled himself. Coyote stories show our pleasure in outwitting our enemies— and they also show how easy it is to be fooled.

Here's one way Coyote was fooled.

Coyote found Turkey up in a tree.

He knew it would be easy to catch him. All he had to do was chop down the tree.

Coyote chopped and chopped. Just as the tree was about to fall, Turkey flew to another tree.

Coyote knew what to do. He got busy chopping that tree down too. He chopped and chopped. Then just as the tree was falling, Turkey flew again.

That went on all day. By evening Coyote was lying on the ground panting. Turkey just flew away home.

Many Cultures

What does the story tell you about the Apache? Like most Native American groups, they believed people could learn from animals.

Long ago, Native Americans shared some beliefs, such as learning from animals. But they also had many differences. Some groups were as unlike each other as people from different countries are today. Each group of people had its own special culture. Each had its own language and its own religion.

Native American cultures were partly shaped by the natural resources around them. Look at the map on the next page. You can see that buffalo roamed the Great Plains in the middle of what is now the United States. The Plains Indians skillfully used the buffalo for food, clothing, and shelter. Look at the map again. What can you tell about the cultures of other Native American groups?

National Museum of the American Indian

The Plains Indians decorated buffalo hide and used it to make robes and moccasins.

Joslyn Art Museum

National Museum of the American Indian

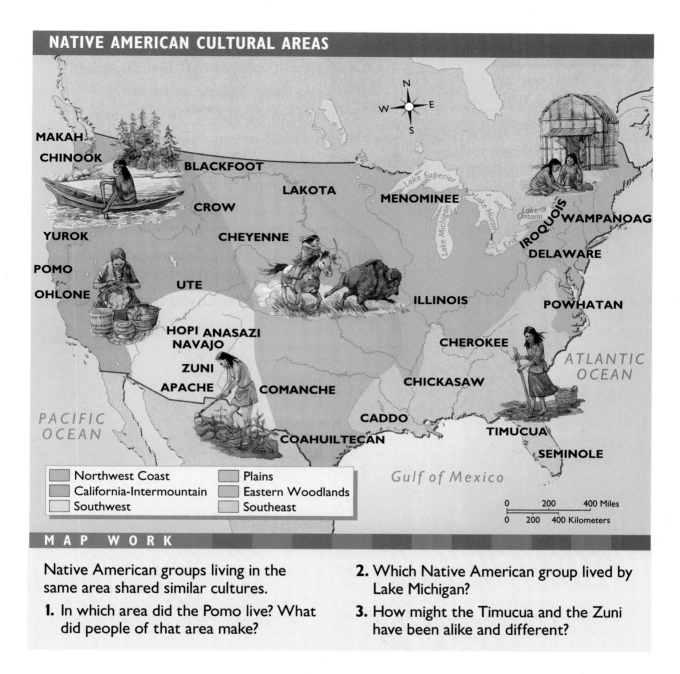

NATIVE AMERICAN CULTURAL AREAS

MAKAH
CHINOOK
BLACKFOOT
LAKOTA
CROW
MENOMINEE
CHEYENNE
YUROK
POMO
UTE
OHLONE
HOPI ANASAZI
NAVAJO
ZUNI
APACHE
COMANCHE
ILLINOIS
CADDO
COAHUILTECAN
TIMUCUA
SEMINOLE
IROQUOIS
WAMPANOAG
DELAWARE
POWHATAN
CHEROKEE
CHICKASAW

Lake Superior
Lake Michigan
Lake Huron
Lake Ontario
L. Erie

PACIFIC OCEAN

ATLANTIC OCEAN

Gulf of Mexico

Northwest Coast
California-Intermountain
Southwest
Plains
Eastern Woodlands
Southeast

0 200 400 Miles
0 200 400 Kilometers

MAP WORK

Native American groups living in the same area shared similar cultures.

1. In which area did the Pomo live? What did people of that area make?

2. Which Native American group lived by Lake Michigan?

3. How might the Timucua and the Zuni have been alike and different?

From this map you can see where different groups of Native Americans lived long ago. Each color stands for a different cultural area. Groups in the same area shared a similar culture. Find the Native American group called the Anasazi (ah nuh SAH zee) on the map. How did they probably get food? How can you tell?

Living Off the Land

Natural resources helped shape the way Native Americans lived in communities. Look again at the map on page 73. In the Eastern Woodland culture group, find the Iroquois. The land they once lived on is now part of New York State. It was mostly forests. On the rich land they grew corn, beans, and squash. The Iroquois lived in shelters covered with bark called longhouses. These houses held many families. Water came from the lakes and rivers in the Northeast. Today many Iroquois still live in this area.

Dr. Oren Lyons is a leader of the Iroquois people today (left). Long ago Iroquois families shared a longhouse made of wood and bark (below).

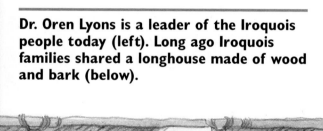

From the map on page 73, locate the Yurok (YUR ahk). How do you think their environment influenced the way they lived? They lived along the West Coast. The Pacific Ocean and the rivers were valuable resources. The Yurok were skilled fishers. Today about 3,700 Yurok still live in this area. Some of these Yurok are fishers.

WHY IT MATTERS

The Native Americans are an important part of our country today. The Cherokee people live in North Carolina and Oklahoma. As with many Native American groups, their culture continues to be an important part of Cherokee life today.

In learning about the history of the United States, it is important to study how Native Americans lived long ago. In the next lesson we will read about the Anasazi. We will learn about their land, resources, and culture. We will also see how part of their culture lives on today.

This otter fur arrow case is about 75 years old and is used in Yurok ceremonies today. The arrows are made of wood and flint stone.

✓/// Reviewing Facts and Ideas

MAIN IDEAS

- History is the story of the past.
- Native Americans were the first people to live in the land that is now the United States.
- There are many different Native American groups in our country today. Each has its own special culture.

THINK ABOUT IT

1. What is history?
2. **FOCUS** Who lived in the first American communities?
3. **THINKING SKILL** How was the Iroquois community *like* your community? How was it *different*? How can you tell?
4. **GEOGRAPHY** Look at the map on page 73. How do you think geography influenced the Seminole?

COMING TOGETHER AT A
POWWOW

Native Americans of yesterday and today have many different cultures. Yet one thing most share is a legacy of music and dance.

Today the powwow is one way Native Americans celebrate their culture and their past. Long ago, powwows were used to give good luck to hunters and farmers.

If you were part of a powwow today, you would watch and perform dances and songs from long ago. You might also make new friends. Let's see what it's like to join in at a powwow.

The players and singers around the drum are part of a group called "The Drum" (above). It provides the "heartbeat" for singing and dancing. Young people often make their own costumes (right).

Native Americans in the past also enjoyed visiting with each other. The woman and girls are doing beadwork.

Powwows bring together old and young, boys and girls, and men and women. Some people dress in everyday clothing. Others wear traditional Native American clothing.

77

The Geography of Mesa Verde

Focus Activity

READ TO LEARN

What is the geography of Mesa Verde like?

VOCABULARY

- desert
- canyon
- cliff
- mesa
- technology

PLACES

- Four Corners
- Mesa Verde

Read Aloud

Here the land is dotted with table-flat landforms that rise to the hot sun.

Here dramatic cliffs drop suddenly into deep canyons.

Life in the Desert

Have you ever seen a place like the one just described? It is an area in the southwestern part of our country called a desert. A desert is a very dry environment where little rain falls. On a summer's day, the temperature in the desert can get extremely hot. But at night, the temperature drops and it's much cooler.

Look at the map on the next page. It shows part of the states of Colorado, New Mexico, Utah, and Arizona. This desert area is often called the Four Corners. Can you see why? The four states all meet in one place. Long ago no states were there. But there were communities. And the people who lived in these communities were called the Anasazi.

A Difficult Environment

As you learned in the last lesson, Native Americans made good use of natural resources. The Iroquois lived in the northeastern part of our country. They used trees to make houses. The Plains Indians of the West hunted buffalo to use the skins for clothing and shelter. You read that the Yurok lived in the northwestern part of the United States. They skillfully used trees to build their homes and canoes.

The Anasazi also made the best of their very dry environment. The Anasazi were mostly farmers. They grew corn, beans, and squash. They also raised turkeys, which need little water.

The Anasazi used the resources of the desert to meet their other needs too. They used plants to make shoes and clothes. They also made pottery from the clay of the dry ground.

The Anasazi made sandals from the yucca (YOO kah) plant of the desert.

THE FOUR CORNERS	MAP WORK
UTAH · Colorado River · COLORADO · Rio Grande · Mesa Verde · ARIZONA · NEW MEXICO · 0 50 100 Miles · 0 50 100 Kilometers	The Four Corners area is in the southwestern part of our country. 1. What four states meet at the Four Corners? 2. In what state is Mesa Verde located? 3. In what direction is Mesa Verde from New Mexico? 4. Do any other four states meet in one place?

Mesas, Cliffs, and Canyons

The land of the Southwest is not all flat. As you can see in these pictures, there are many different landforms. To the Anasazi these shapes were not just beautiful. They were also great natural resources.

Deep canyons were carved into the land by mighty rivers. A canyon is a deep river valley with steep sides. Many communities were built along the walls of these canyons. Some Anasazi even made buildings and homes in the cliffs! A cliff is the steep face of a rock.

From the pictures here, find the landform that looks like a high, flat table. The name for that landform is mesa (MAY sah). In fact, *mesa* is the Spanish word for "table." Sometimes the Anasazi built their homes in the steep sides of mesas. Like canyons and cliffs, mesas protected them from enemies and the environment.

One Anasazi community in this area was Mesa Verde (VER deh). The Spanish word for "green" is *verde*. You already know what *mesa* means. Can you guess why this area is called Mesa Verde?

Mesas **and cliffs are two southwestern landforms. Desert wildlife includes lizards.**

Using Technology

The Anasazi made use of technology (tek NAHL uh jee) to help them in different ways. Technology is the use of tools and materials to serve people's needs. Pointed sticks were made to dig ditches for collecting the little rain that fell at Mesa Verde. The water was then used to grow crops.

The Anasazi made stone axes to clear fields for farming.

WHY IT MATTERS

Suppose it is a time long ago, before your community was built. There were no highways or telephones. The Native Americans have already built many communities. Like people today, they used the land around them for all of their resources.

In the next lesson you will learn how the Anasazi worked with the land around them. You will see how they lived in a special community in the land of mesas and canyons.

✓✓ Reviewing Facts and Ideas

MAIN IDEAS

- The environment of a desert is very dry.
- The landforms of the area now called the Four Corners include canyons, cliffs, and mesas.
- The Anasazi were one group who lived in this desert area. They worked as farmers to meet their needs.
- Technology improved the life of the Anasazi.

THINK ABOUT IT

1. What is the climate of Mesa Verde?

2. **FOCUS** What is the geography of Mesa Verde like?

3. **THINKING SKILL** What do you _predict_ would happen to the plants at Mesa Verde if it did not rain there for a long time? Explain your answer.

4. **WRITE** Look again at the pictures in this lesson. In your own words, describe the landforms you see.

Mesa Verde Long Ago

Read Aloud

A chickadee chirps in the distance. It is early morning, and an eight-year-old boy stirs in his bed. He has a busy day ahead of him.

Focus Activity

READ TO LEARN

How did the Anasazi live?

VOCABULARY

- kiva
- artifact

Morning at Mesa Verde

The description you have just read does not sound very unusual, does it? But let's take a closer look. The boy's bed is actually a mat made from the leaves of the yucca plant. His blanket is made from turkey feathers. His "pajamas" are woven from plants.

He lives with his family in a house with many rooms. It is built into the side of a mesa. It is called a cliff house. As he starts his day, the people in his community are already busy. Some men and women are making pots out of clay. Others are sharpening stones to use as knives. The young boy is eager to join them.

The boy's name is Little Rabbit. He is an eight-year-old Anasazi who lives at Mesa Verde. The time is 1,000 years ago. Let's see what Little Rabbit's day is like.

Community Life

To start the day, Little Rabbit finds his father, Strong Deer. He is outside sharpening an arrow. The Anasazi men sometimes hunt with spears and bows and arrows. They also farm and weave blankets. Little Rabbit is eager for the day he will be old enough to hunt and weave. "Not today," says his father. "Today you will help your mother."

Little Rabbit's mother is Swift Raven. Like many women, she takes care of the children and the home. She also cooks, makes pottery, and weaves baskets. Little Rabbit's new little sister, Bright Owl, is strapped to a board on her mother's back. "Good morning, Little Rabbit," his mother says. "Will you get me some water for the turkeys?" Little Rabbit takes a basket to the well. The baskets are woven so tightly that no water can spill. That is a good thing. Little Rabbit knows that water can be hard to find.

Soon all the women and children will go to the nearby field to gather beans and corn. All of the families work together and share their food. From the Infographic on the next pages, you can see different ways the Anasazi worked together.

DID YOU KNOW?

How were sandals made?

Anasazi children were helpful in making sandals. They were taught this skill not only by their parents but also by the older people in their community. Sandals were made from yucca. Children who made the best ones could trade them for blankets, arrowheads, and other things.

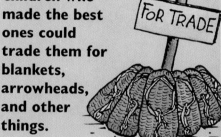

FOR TRADE

A Day with the Anasazi

Pretend you are standing across from the cliff house where Little Rabbit and his family lived long ago. What might you see?

Older women help care for the young children.

Older men are sitting in the sun, telling stories.

The hole in the ground is the entrance to a special room used for religious purposes called a kiva.

Little Rabbit is carrying a basket filled with water.

Many storage rooms are used to hold crops and grain.

Women and children are grinding corn.

Swift Raven is making clay pots for cooking and storage.

Strong Deer is sharpening an arrow for hunting.

The Anasazi Culture

Religion was an important part of Anasazi culture. In the Infographic you learned that the kiva was used for religious purposes. Sometimes it was also used as a workplace.

The drawing below gives you a close-up view of a kiva in Little Rabbit's community. It was used mostly by men. At times women used the kivas as well. The Anasazi believed that people came to Earth from special holes in the ground. A kiva had a hole for this reason.

The walls of the kiva have colorful paintings. Stone benches are built into the walls. A fire in the center of the floor provides warmth.

Not all religious ceremonies take place in the kiva. For Little Rabbit tomorrow will be an exciting day. There will be a dance held in a field. Dancers will give thanks for the ripe food from the fields. They will wear colorful outfits and masks. One day Little Rabbit will take part in the dance. It too is a part of Anasazi culture.

The Anasazi used a ladder to enter a kiva.

WHY IT MATTERS

How do we know what Little Rabbit's day might have been like 1,000 years ago? We do not know for sure. People did not write or take photographs back then. Scientists have tried to piece together the clues by looking at artifacts. Artifacts are objects left behind by a group of people. Pottery, tools, pieces of clothing, and buildings are all artifacts.

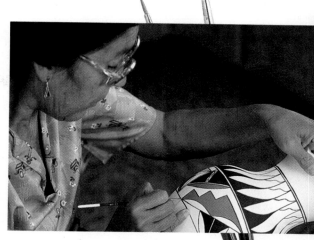

Today, Native Americans like this Pueblo woman still make pottery similar to the Anasazi pottery of long ago.

The Anasazi left Mesa Verde and other communities about 700 years ago. Scientists are not sure why. Some say that perhaps there was no rain for a long time. Or perhaps they were forced out by another Native American group.

Although the Anasazi have disappeared, parts of their culture remain. Today Pueblo (PWEB loh) villages have kivas. The kivas are just like the ones the Anasazi had long ago. In the next lesson you will learn another way the culture of the Anasazi continues today.

✓ Reviewing Facts and Ideas

MAIN IDEAS

- The Anasazi lived in communities built into the sides of mesas.

- Children helped with many tasks.

- Men hunted, farmed, and weaved.

- Women worked in the fields, made pottery, and took care of the younger children.

- Religion was an important part of Anasazi culture.

THINK ABOUT IT

1. How was the kiva important to people in the Anasazi community?

2. **FOCUS** How did the Anasazi live?

3. **THINKING SKILL** _Sort_ activities people did at Mesa Verde into fun activities and work activities.

4. **GEOGRAPHY** What landforms are in Little Rabbit's community?

Mesa Verde Today

Read Aloud

"Welcome to Mesa Verde National Park. My name is Maxwell Rudolph. Only people who work for the park can live here. My father is a Park Ranger."

Focus Activity

READ TO LEARN

What can be learned by visiting Mesa Verde National Park today?

VOCABULARY

- museum

PLACES

- Mesa Verde National Park

Mesa Verde National Park

You have just been welcomed to Mesa Verde National Park by Maxwell Rudolph. Maxwell is a nine-year-old boy who lives in the park with his family. Only a few people live in the park today. But long ago many Anasazi lived here in a big community.

As you have read, the Anasazi mysteriously left Mesa Verde long ago. No group of people has lived in the cliff houses since. Today visitors can see the place much as it used to be.

Over many years much of the land in our country has changed. Paved highways have been laid down. Skyscrapers and shopping malls have been built. But as a national park, Mesa Verde has been protected from change. Let's join Maxwell and his father for a tour to see how the Anasazi lived over 700 years ago.

Welcome to Mesa Verde!

From the entrance to the park, it takes a half-hour drive just to reach the Far View Visitor Center. That gives you an idea of how big the park is! At the Visitor Center, Maxwell's father greets thousands of visitors every year. Look at the map of Mesa Verde National Park below. It shows you where places to visit are located.

"The best place to start our tour is at the museum," says Mr. Rudolph. A museum is a place where people can look at objects of art, science, or history.

"From here, there are many places to go," says Mr. Rudolph. "Of these places, you can walk by homes from about 1,000 years ago."

By visiting Mesa Verde or looking at jewelry and other objects, people can learn about the Anasazi culture.

MESA VERDE NATIONAL PARK

- Cortez

COLORADO

- ■ Place of Interest
- ▭ Road
- — Park Boundary
- ⫻ Park Entrance

N
W E
S

Far View Visitor Center

Mancos River

Spruce Tree House

Long House

Museum

Cliff Palace

Balcony House

0   2   4 Miles
0   2   4 Kilometers

M A P   W O R K

Mesa Verde National Park was created in 1906.

1. What are some places of interest in the park?

2. How far is the museum from the Visitor Center?

3. What happens to the road before it reaches the Visitor Center?

Respecting the Past

Mr. Rudolph takes visitors to sites where the Anasazi lived long ago. On the paths, they hike past yucca plants like the ones used every day by the Anasazi. Visitors climb ladders to reach the old rooms. They also climb down ladders to see the kivas. There are many different things Mr. Rudolph hopes the visitors will learn.

"Of course, I want people to learn what life might have been like long ago," he says. "But that is not the most important thing. I want them to respect the past. I tell them to act as if they are walking through someone's home—because they are!"

Mr. Rudolph also tells visitors to Mesa Verde not to touch or remove any artifacts. He then reminds them that the kivas are still very important to some Native Americans today. Pueblo, Zuni, and Hopi people still live in nearby areas. Many of their beliefs and customs are similar to those of the Anasazi long ago.

Visitors climb a ladder to reach rooms at Long House (left) and see Anasazi homes at Cliff Palace (right).

As the tour ends Mr. Rudolph leaves visitors with an important reminder: "We study the past to learn something we can use today. One of the most important things we can learn from the Anasazi is to work well together in our communities. Another important lesson is to respect nature and think about the long-term effects of our actions."

WHY IT MATTERS

By studying the past we learn how people lived in communities. One way to study and learn about the past is to visit a museum or a place like Mesa Verde National Park.

Look around your own community. Ancient artifacts may not be in your backyard. But your community does have a history that goes back a long time. And chances are, if you study that history, you'll learn something about your community today.

Mr. Rudolph teaches children about the Anasazi at Mesa Verde.

✓ Reviewing Facts and Ideas

MAIN IDEAS

- Visitors to Mesa Verde National Park can learn about the past by seeing artifacts.
- Visitors can see what life was like long ago.
- Visitors must be respectful of the sites they see.
- By learning about the past, we can learn about our communities today.

THINK ABOUT IT

1. Why is the museum a good place to start the park tour?

2. **FOCUS** What can be learned by visiting Mesa Verde National Park today?

3. **THINKING SKILL** What do you _predict_ might happen to Mesa Verde if it were not a national park?

4. **GEOGRAPHY** Look at the map on page 89. Use the scale to find the distance from the Balcony House to the museum.

Thinking Skills

Making Decisions

VOCABULARY
decision

WHY THE SKILL MATTERS

Every day in your life you make **decisions**. A decision is a choice that is made. When you choose what clothes to wear in the morning, you are making a decision.

Sometimes making a decision is very easy. You might know that one choice would be a big mistake and the other would be exactly right. But sometimes, making decisions can be hard. Use the Helping Yourself box on the next page to guide you in making decisions.

USING THE SKILL

Suppose that you and your family are visiting Mesa Verde National Park. You have only one day to spend there. After you have visited the museum, your mother says it's up to you to decide where to go next. How would you decide what sites to see?

In making a decision, it is important to set a goal. Your goal could be to see and learn as much as possible at Mesa Verde in only one day.

You could then gather information to learn what your choices are. Pictured above is a visitor's guide to Mesa Verde National Park. It provides important facts about different sites.

Each choice from the guide has advantages and disadvantages. Cliff Palace is the biggest place. Spruce Tree House is not quite as large. Both are near each other.

Long House is the second largest place. It has a beautiful view. But it is far from both Spruce Tree House and Cliff Palace.

You decide that too much time would be spent traveling to Long House. Your decision could be to visit Cliff Palace. Then, if there were time, you could also visit Spruce Tree House. After all, you have only one day to spend at the park!

92

TRYING THE SKILL

Now suppose you are at the gift shop near the museum. Your mother has given you $5 to spend. From the picture below, you can see what things you can buy for $5. What will you decide to buy? What should you do first to make your decision? If your goal is to learn what Mesa Verde is like today, what would you choose to buy?

REVIEWING THE SKILL

1. What does it mean to make a decision?
2. What is one decision you made today?
3. How did you make your decision?
4. Why is it important to learn how to make good decisions?

PRICE LIST

History Book	$5.00	Photo Book	$5.00
Hat	$5.00	Patch and Pin	$5.00
Tour Guide	$5.00	Key Chains	2 for $5.00
Coloring Book	$5.00		

CHAPTER 3 REVIEW

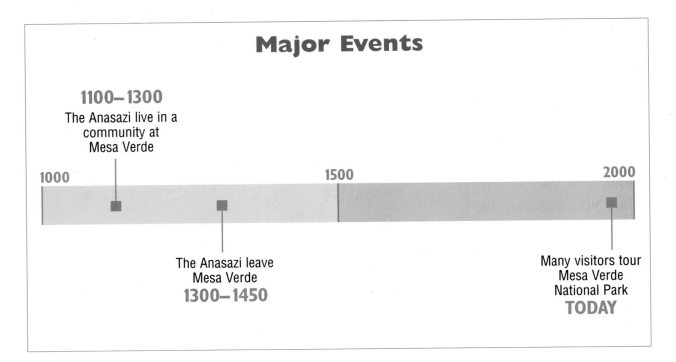

Major Events

1100–1300
The Anasazi live in a community at Mesa Verde

1000

1500

2000

The Anasazi leave Mesa Verde
1300–1450

Many visitors tour Mesa Verde National Park
TODAY

THINKING ABOUT VOCABULARY

Number a piece of paper from 1 to 10. Read the definition of each underlined word. Write **T** if the definition is true and **F** if it is false. If it is false, write a sentence correctly defining the word.

1. A <u>desert</u> is a very dry environment with little rainfall.

2. <u>Technology</u> is the study of how animals live on a farm.

3. <u>Artifacts</u> are tools used to dig up objects left by a group of people.

4. The landform that looks like a high, flat table is a <u>cliff</u>.

5. A <u>canyon</u> is a deep river valley with steep sides.

6. The story of our past is our <u>history</u>.

7. A <u>museum</u> is a place where people can look at objects of art, science, or history.

8. A <u>mesa</u> is a steep face of a rock.

9. A <u>kiva</u> is a large farming tool.

10. A <u>decision</u> is making a choice.

THINKING ABOUT FACTS

1. How did the natural resources in an area matter to the people living there? Give an example.

2. In what area of our country did the Anasazi live long ago?

3. Why did the Anasazi build their homes in cliffs and in the sides of mesas?

4. How do we know what life was probably like for Native Americans long ago?

5. Why do we study the past?

THINK AND WRITE

WRITING A JOURNAL ENTRY

Suppose you lived at Mesa Verde long ago. Write a journal entry about a day in your life. Describe what you eat, what you wear, and what you do during the day.

WRITING A COMPARISON

Write a paragraph comparing the life of the Anasazi and the Yurok. You may want to compare the area they lived in and what they ate.

WRITING A POSTER

Write a poster encouraging people to visit Mesa Verde National Park. What would you describe about the park? What places would you want to tell people about?

APPLYING THINKING SKILLS

MAKING DECISIONS

Answer the following questions to practice the skill of decision making.

1. What are the steps to follow in making a decision?

2. How do you decide what homework to do first? What do you think about before deciding?

3. Suppose you are invited to play by two different friends. One you play with often. The other you have wanted to play with for a long time. Identify the steps you would take in deciding. What are the possible results of each choice?

4. How do you decide what to do for fun on a rainy day?

5. Why is it important to consider all choices when making a decision?

Summing Up the Chapter

Review the chapter and complete a copy of the main idea table below. In the table legs, list how the Anasazi met the basic needs shown in the table feet. Then write an answer to the question: In what ways did the natural resources of the area help shape the way the Anasazi lived?

Main Idea The culture of the Anasazi is partly shaped by the natural resources around them.

FOOD   **CLOTHING**   **SHELTER**

An English Colony at Jamestown

THINKING ABOUT GEOGRAPHY AND HISTORY

About four hundred years ago, a group of people set sail from England to North America. They built a village called Jamestown.

The land where the English settled was home to a group of Native Americans called the Powhatan. It was a place rich in forests and rivers. As you read Chapter 4, see how both groups of people used the land's resources. Start by studying the map and time line here.

1607

Colonists arrive at Jamestown

1614

Marriage of Pocahontas and John Rolfe

1500   1600   1700

Jamestown,
Virginia

TODAY

People visit Jamestown Settlement
Museum

The Geography of Jamestown

Read Aloud

"There are fair meadows and goodly tall trees . . . beautiful strawberries and excellent good timber."

Focus Activity

READ TO LEARN

What is the geography of Jamestown like?

VOCABULARY

- bay
- coastal plain

PLACES

- Jamestown
- Virginia
- Chesapeake Bay

Land of Many Resources

These words were written a long time ago by George Percy. He was a passenger on a small ship that sailed from England to North America in 1607. Percy and other Englishmen on the ship dreamed of gold and other riches in the land that is now the United States.

Look at the map on the next page. The area where the Englishmen started their community is called Jamestown. It was named for the King of England, James I. Today it is in the state of Virginia.

As you can tell from George Percy's words, the environment of Jamestown seemed good. There were trees for building houses and food to eat. It looked like a fine place to build a community. In this lesson let's take a closer look at the geography of Jamestown.

Using Natural Resources

The English were not the first people to build communities in Virginia. Native Americans had lived in the area for thousands of years. They had learned over time how to make good use of natural resources. Tall pine trees were used for building houses and for making bows and arrows. They also carved out trees and used them as canoes.

Look at the map shown below. In 1607 a Native American people called the Powhatan (pow uh TAN) lived in what is now eastern Virginia. They fished in the James River and Chesapeake Bay. A bay is a body of water partly surrounded by land. Can you find where Chesapeake Bay meets the James River?

Native Americans used resources like trees to build canoes and other important items.

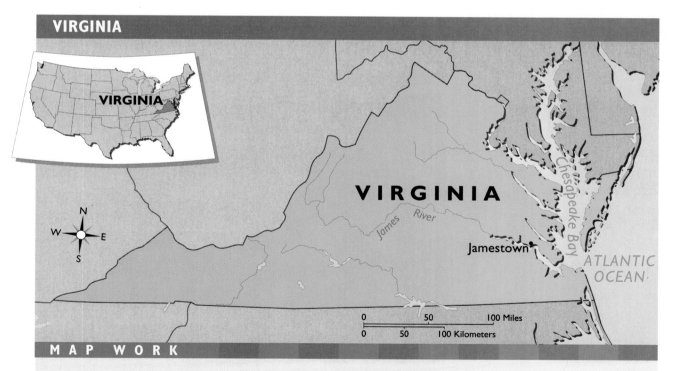

MAP WORK

English colonists built a community at Jamestown in 1607.

1. How far is Jamestown from the Atlantic Ocean?
2. What body of water is between the Atlantic Ocean and the James River?
3. Why do you think canoes were important to the Powhatan people?

99

Living with the Environment

In the last chapter you read about how the Anasazi used natural resources to survive in the dry environment of Mesa Verde. But the Powhatan's environment around Jamestown was different. There was plenty of rain for plants and trees. The area around Jamestown is a coastal plain. A coastal plain is flat land along the coast. It was good for farming. The Powhatan grew corn, beans, and squash. They also hunted deer and other animals.

The English also liked Jamestown's environment. They saw the location as a good place to build a community. Their boats had a good port in the deep waters of Chesapeake Bay. The waters, which surrounded the English on three sides, helped to protect the English against attack. The Native Americans and the Spanish often used land routes for attack.

Links to
CURRENT EVENTS

Catch of the Day!

What are new ways people use natural resources?

Virginia's waters have long provided people with food. Today fish and shellfish are not only found in the water, but also on land! They are now raised in tanks on fish farms in Virginia.

Where do the foods you eat come from? Keep a list. Then compare your list with others from your class.

This artwork from the 1800s shows the English using resources of the forest to build Jamestown.

The Granger Collection

WHY IT MATTERS

Environment makes a difference to communities. People need resources from the environment to live. This fact was true in our country's past too.

For the Powhatan long ago, the environment provided resources for farming and fishing. For the English, Jamestown provided a good port for ships. The port was also useful in protecting against attacks by their enemies. The land around Jamestown also provided wood for building houses.

For both the Powhatan and the English, survival meant living with the environment around them.

Squash and beans were among the foods that the Powhatan grew.

Reviewing Facts and Ideas

MAIN IDEAS

- Hundreds of years ago, people sailed from England to build a community in the area they named Jamestown.

- Native Americans were already living in communities in the area around Jamestown.

- Jamestown's environment was good for farming.

- The land around Jamestown was called a coastal plain.

- Chesapeake Bay provided a good port for the English ships. It also provided food for the Powhatan.

THINK ABOUT IT

1. How did the English and the Powhatan use the natural resources at Jamestown?

2. **FOCUS** What is the geography of Jamestown like?

3. **THINKING SKILL** Suppose you wanted to build a community. How would you _decide_ on a place? State your goals.

4. **GEOGRAPHY** Name two bodies of water near Jamestown. You can use the map on page 99.

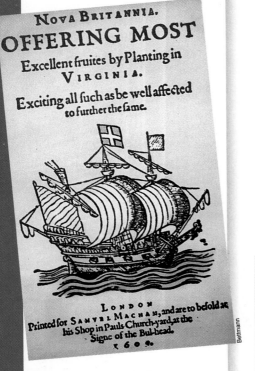

NOVA BRITANNIA.

OFFERING MOST
Excellent fruites by Planting in
VIRGINIA.

Exciting all such as be well affected
to further the same.

LONDON
Printed for SAMVEL MACHAM, and are to be sold at
his Shop in Pauls Church-yard, at the
Signe of the Bul-head.
1 6 0 9.

Bettmann

Focus Activity

READ TO LEARN

What was life like for the colonists?

VOCABULARY

- colony
- colonist
- slavery

PEOPLE

- Powhatan
- John Smith
- John Rolfe
- Pocahontas

Jamestown Long Ago

Read Aloud

"I insist that the guns and swords, the cause of all our jealousy and uneasiness, be removed and sent away."

Powhatan and the English Meet

These words were said by Powhatan, the leader of the Powhatan people in 1609. He was speaking to John Smith, the leader of the English at Jamestown. Powhatan was hoping for peace between his people and the English.

The Powhatan and the English met in 1607. That was the year the English first arrived at Jamestown. It was a very long time ago—almost 400 years!

The meeting between the Powhatan and the English is one of the early stories in the history of our country. It is a story of good times. It is also the story of hard times. The English struggled to build a community at Jamestown. The Powhatan struggled to find a way to live peacefully with the English. In this lesson you will meet some of the important people who helped the new community survive.

The English at Jamestown

Men like John Smith were sent by England to start a colony at Jamestown. A colony is a place that is ruled by another country. The English hoped that the colony would provide resources and riches like gold for people back in England.

The people sent to Jamestown were called colonists. A colonist is someone who lives in a colony. Colonists did not only want to build a new community. They also hoped that they, too, would get rich from Jamestown's resources.

Powhatan (below left) and his people were already living around Jamestown when John Smith (in frame) and other English colonists arrived.

Difficult Times

Soon after arriving at Jamestown, the colonists found life hard. They had problems growing food. Many of them were not farmers. They did not realize how hard they needed to work. Some colonists even refused to work.

A strong leader was needed to help the English. They found one in John Smith. He made a new rule. He said, "He that will not work, shall not eat."

Smith made another important decision. He asked the Powhatan for help. The colonists learned how to grow corn and other food from the Powhatan.

Even with the help of Powhatan and his people, the colonists struggled. The winter of 1609 was called a "starving time." There was little food. Colonists were dying from diseases. Read once again the words of colonist George Percy. What does he say about life in Jamestown?

Colonists had to learn how to farm for food in order to survive.

MANY VOICES
PRIMARY SOURCE

Written by George Percy, about 1609.

Our men were destroyed with cruel diseases and swellings and burning fevers and by wars. Some **departed** suddenly, but for the most part they died of **famine**. There were never Englishmen left in such misery as we were. The settlers began to feel the sharp hunger which no man can truly describe.

departed: died
famine: starving, hunger

The Granger Collection

The Colony Survives

Life continued to be hard for the colonists. Their dreams of finding gold never came true. But in 1612 some changes turned the colony around. A colonist named John Rolfe began growing a new kind of tobacco and sending it back to England. The tobacco was sold for a lot of money. It helped make the colony and England richer.

Until this time the English sometimes fought with the Powhatan. But in 1614 John Rolfe married Pocahontas. She was the daughter of Powhatan. Their marriage led to a long time of peace between the Powhatan and the English. The colony began to grow.

By 1624 other English colonies were also growing along the coast of the Atlantic Ocean. To learn more about the early years of these colonies turn the page.

The marriage of Pocahontas and John Rolfe brought peace to Jamestown. A statue of Pocahontas stands in Jamestown today.

The Granger Collection

105

The Thirteen Colonies

Virginia was not the only English colony in North America. Soon there were 13 English colonies along the Atlantic coast. These colonies later became the first thirteen states of our country.

PLYMOUTH, MASSACHUSETTS

The Pilgrims started Plymouth, Massachusetts, in 1620 to practice their own religion. The Wampanoag (wahm puh NOH ahg) people helped the Pilgrims fish and farm. To thank God for their harvest the Pilgrims had a Thanksgiving meal with the Wampanoag.

Maine (part of Massachusetts)

New York

New Hampshire
Massachusetts
Rhode Island
Connecticut

Pennsylvania

New Jersey

Delaware

Virginia

Maryland

North Carolina

South Carolina

Georgia

PHILADELPHIA, PENNSYLVANIA

William Penn followed the Quaker religion. In 1682 in Pennsylvania he started a community called Philadelphia. Penn became friends with the Delaware people. They signed a peace agreement that lasted many years.

SAVANNAH, GEORGIA

Savannah became the first colonial community in Georgia in 1733. Some of the colonists here were people who owed money in England. They repaid the money they owed by farming land.

Africans Arrive

Many different people came to the colonies. Some came to build new lives. Some came to seek riches. Others were looking for religious freedom. Some who came had been forced into slavery. Slavery is the practice of one person owning another.

People forced into slavery in the colonies came from Africa. They were captured and taken across the Atlantic Ocean in slave ships. They were then sold into slavery.

WHY IT MATTERS

Starting a community was hard for the colonists. But after years of struggle, the little community of Jamestown grew larger. It was joined by other colonies. Later, these colonies— 13 in all—came together as a new country, the United States of America.

Bettmann

African people were sold into slavery in the colonies.

✓✓ Reviewing Facts and Ideas

MAIN IDEAS

- The English colonists began Jamestown in 1607.
- The winter of 1609 was called a "starving time." Many colonists died.
- In 1612 John Rolfe introduced a new kind of tobacco. It made the colony richer.
- There were 13 English colonies, which later became the United States of America.

THINK ABOUT IT

1. Why did the English set sail for Jamestown?
2. **FOCUS** What was life like for the colonists?
3. **THINKING SKILL** Look at the Infographic on page 106. Put Plymouth, Philadelphia, and Savannah in *order* by the dates they were started.
4. **WRITE** Pretend you are a colonist living in Jamestown. Write a letter describing your new life to your family back in England.

Jamestown Today

Read Aloud

"We do many of the things that the Powhatan and the English did long ago. We have cooking fires burning. We tan deer hides. We even show kids making rope."

Focus Activity

READ TO LEARN

What do visitors see at Jamestown Settlement?

VOCABULARY

- living history museum

PLACES

- Jamestown Settlement

A Step Back in Time

These are the words of Erik Holland. He is a guide at Jamestown Settlement. The settlement is a living history museum. A living history museum takes you back in time. It is a place where people dress, talk, and do things as they did long ago. Erik's job is to show people how English colonists and the Powhatan lived here in the 1600s.

Let's visit Jamestown Settlement. The first thing you notice is people's clothing. Guides like Erik are dressed in clothes like those worn by Native Americans or colonists hundreds of years ago. While they may look different at first, Erik tells visitors: "My moccasins are almost like the tennis shoes kids wear today. Tennis shoes are made from animal skins. So are my moccasins."

English Village

Like Erik's moccasins, most of the things you see at Jamestown Settlement are not the actual artifacts from long ago. Instead, they are copies. People have studied Jamestown's history very carefully to create copies that look real.

Look at the pictures on this page. The English houses are built from plaster and grass. The clothes people are wearing are made from wool and cotton. The ship instruments they are using are made from iron and wood.

Near the houses are three ships docked in the James River. They are named *Susan Constant, Godspeed,* and *Discovery.* They are copies of the original boats colonists like Captain John Smith sailed on many years ago. Climb aboard! You will see how small the spaces are. You can imagine how crowded it must have been. After all, the colonists also had to bring pigs, chickens, goats, and lots of supplies.

Jamestown/Yorktown Foundation

Fun at Jamestown Settlement includes visiting ships and seeing how people lived in the 1600s.

Jamestown Virginia

Powhatan Village

In talking about visiting Jamestown Settlement today, Erik tells visitors, "It's fun to see different cultures from the past. You have seen how the English lived. Now let's see how the Powhatan lived."

In the Powhatan village you can see Native Americans grinding corn. You can see how they cooked their meals. You can even smell fish and meat cooking. But stand back. The fire is hot!

You can actually make rope like the Powhatan did long ago. You will even get to play games that children played long ago. The Powhatan houses were made from wood frames covered with grass. How are they different from the ones the colonists lived in?

At the Powhatan village visitors learn to make rope the way people did long ago.

Learning History

When you visit Jamestown Settlement, something may occur to you. In some ways the lives of these two groups were so different. But in other ways their lives were similar. They both needed to make homes, clothes, and food. They both took care of their communities. During his tour, Erik tells visitors, "By visiting us here you see and do things that people in the past did every day. It's a great way to learn history."

WHY IT MATTERS

Visiting a place like Jamestown Settlement is a fun and interesting way to learn about the history of people and their communities. Reading books, watching movies, and talking to people can also teach you about history.

In our country today, we live with our history all around us. In the next chapter you will learn about another community with a history that is important to its people today.

Jamestown Virginia

The Powhatan made needles from bone and used them to sew clothing made from animal skins.

✓// Reviewing Facts and Ideas

MAIN IDEAS

- Jamestown Settlement was created to show people what life was like long ago.

- Visitors can see and do many things. They can climb aboard ships, smell food cooking, and visit a Powhatan village and an English village. They can even make things like people did long ago!

THINK ABOUT IT

1. What is a living history museum?

2. **FOCUS** What do visitors see at Jamestown Settlement?

3. **THINKING SKILL** How was life in the Powhatan village _like_ life for the colonists? How was it _different_?

4. **WRITE** Write a brief travel guide for Jamestown Settlement. Describe what people can visit.

Reading Time Lines

VOCABULARY

time line

WHY THE SKILL MATTERS

The events you have read about in Jamestown happened hundreds of years ago. Sometimes reading about the past can be confusing. What happened first? What happened next? A time line can tell you the order in which events happened. Reading time lines will help you to understand history.

USING THE SKILL

You have read about how Jamestown grew as a community. How do you think a new community would grow today? Suppose that a group of people call their community "Newtown." Look at the time line below to see how this community might grow.

Read the time line from left to right. The dates tell you that the earliest event is the building of roads and houses. The last event is the opening of the shopping center. What happened the year before the Fire Department started?

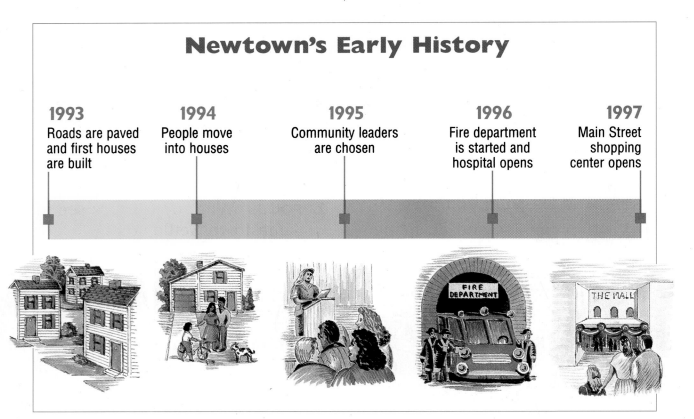

Newtown's Early History

1993	1994	1995	1996	1997
Roads are paved and first houses are built	People move into houses	Community leaders are chosen	Fire department is started and hospital opens	Main Street shopping center opens

TRYING THE SKILL

When you read about Jamestown, you saw words such as "long ago" and "starving time." These words told you something about time and let you know when things happened at Jamestown.

There were many important events in Jamestown's early history. The time line below will help you understand the order in which some of these events happened.

This time line shows events between 1600–1615. How many events does it show? Read the time line. What is first on the time line? In what year did the next event happen? What was it?

Helping yourself

- **Time lines** show the order in which things happen.
- Read time lines from left to right.
- Note the date of each event.

REVIEWING THE SKILL

1. What do time lines show?

2. Which did the people of Newtown build first—a shopping center or a hospital? How do you know?

3. In what year did John Rolfe and Pocahontas get married?

4. How do time lines help you to understand history?

Jamestown's Early History

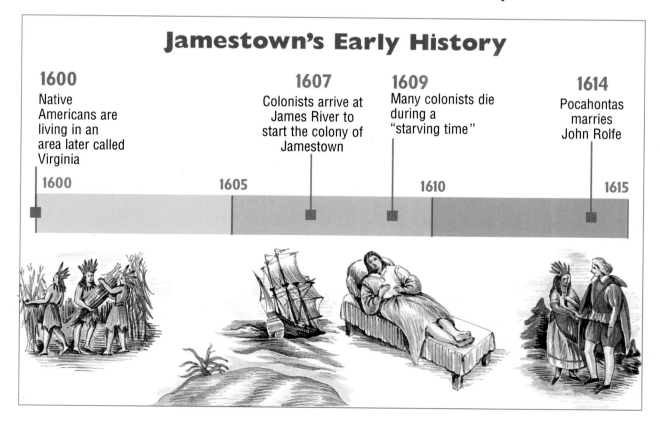

1600
Native Americans are living in an area later called Virginia

1607
Colonists arrive at James River to start the colony of Jamestown

1609
Many colonists die during a "starving time"

1614
Pocahontas marries John Rolfe

1600　　　　　1605　　　　　1610　　　　　1615

CHAPTER 4 REVIEW

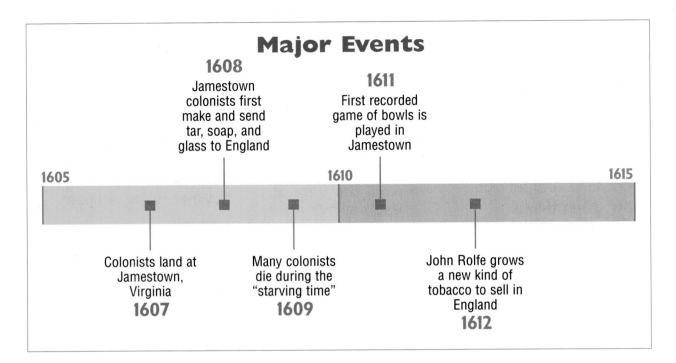

Major Events

1605 **1610** **1615**

1608
Jamestown colonists first make and send tar, soap, and glass to England

1611
First recorded game of bowls is played in Jamestown

Colonists land at Jamestown, Virginia
1607

Many colonists die during the "starving time"
1609

John Rolfe grows a new kind of tobacco to sell in England
1612

THINKING ABOUT VOCABULARY

Number a piece of paper from 1 to 5. Beside each number write the word or term from the list below that matches the statement.

bay
coastal plain
living history museum

colony
slavery

1. A place that is ruled by another country

2. A body of water that is partly surrounded by land

3. The practice of one person owning another

4. A place where people dress, talk, and do things as they did long ago

5. An area of flat land along the coast

THINKING ABOUT FACTS

1. Why was Jamestown a good spot to start a colony?

2. Why did England begin colonies in North America? Why did people come to the colonies?

3. What problems did the first colonists of Jamestown have?

4. Why do people visit Jamestown Settlement today?

5. In what ways were the Powhatan houses similar to the English ones? How were they different?

THINK AND WRITE

WRITING A COMPARISON
Write a paragraph comparing the geography of Mesa Verde with that of Jamestown.

WRITING A LETTER
Suppose you are a colonist at Jamestown in 1607. Write a letter to somebody in England about your life in North America. Include experiences such as meeting a Native American, building a home, and surviving a hard winter.

WRITING A CONVERSATION
Write a made-up dialogue between a Native American and a colonist at Jamestown.

APPLYING STUDY SKILLS

READING TIME LINES
Answer the following questions to practice the skill of reading time lines. Use the Major Events time line shown on the previous page.

1. What is a time line?
2. What happened in 1609?
3. Which event happened first, the first shipment of goods to England or the development of a new kind of tobacco? In what year did each take place?
4. What is one thing colonists did for fun at Jamestown?
5. When are time lines useful?

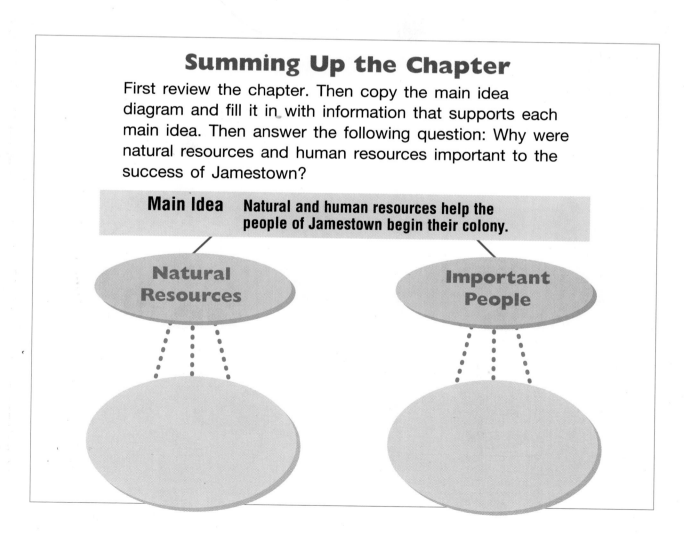

Summing Up the Chapter

First review the chapter. Then copy the main idea diagram and fill it in with information that supports each main idea. Then answer the following question: Why were natural resources and human resources important to the success of Jamestown?

Main Idea — Natural and human resources help the people of Jamestown begin their colony.

Natural Resources

Important People

A Spanish Mission in San Francisco

THINKING ABOUT GEOGRAPHY AND HISTORY

Today San Francisco is a busy city on San Francisco Bay. Long ago Native Americans lived along the bay. Their lives changed when Spanish people came and started a new kind of community.

In Chapter 5 you will learn about these new communities and the growth of San Francisco. You will also see how Spanish culture, and other cultures, are still a celebrated part of life in San Francisco today.

1600s

Native Americans live around San Francisco Bay

1836

Mission Delores is built

1600   1800   1850

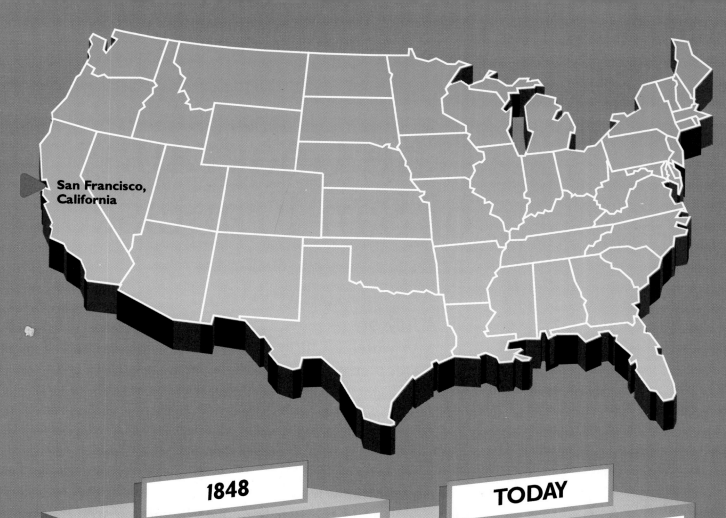

San Francisco,
California

1848

Gold is discovered near San Francisco

TODAY

Many people live and work in San Francisco

1900

2000

The Geography of San Francisco

Focus Activity

READ TO LEARN

How is the San Francisco Bay important?

VOCABULARY

- dam

PLACES

- San Francisco, California
- San Francisco Bay
- Golden Gate National Recreation Area

Read Aloud

A hilly city
with water on three sides,
a steep street
with eight curves,
cool, foggy summers
and warm winters, . . .
What City is this? . . .

Do you know what city the poet Tricia Brown is describing in the words above? If you guessed San Francisco, you are right!

The Golden Gate Bridge

Suppose that it is a typical day in the city of San Francisco. It is located in California. The air is cool, and fog rolls in off the San Francisco Bay. Then slowly the fog lifts. Up ahead you can begin to see the tall, bright orange towers of the Golden Gate Bridge.

The Golden Gate Bridge is almost two miles long. It was built in 1937 to join communities across the bay to communities in the city. Bridges are important to San Francisco because it is located on a peninsula.

Down by the Bay

San Francisco is often called "The City by the Bay." Can you guess why? Look at the map below. San Francisco Bay curls around the city from the north to the east. As you can see, the Pacific Ocean is to the west of the city. Connecting these two bodies of water is a narrow body of water known as the "Golden Gate."

If you walk south of the bridge, you'll be in the Golden Gate National Recreation Area. Along the bay here you can see people fishing and surfing. Look closely, and you might even see a sea lion!

At Golden Gate National Recreation Area, visitors often watch sea lions at play at Seal Rocks.

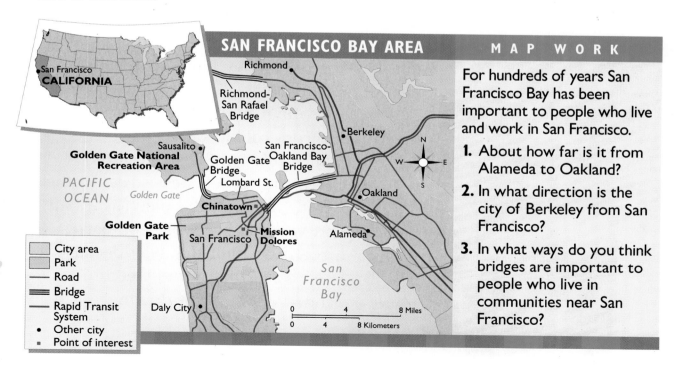

SAN FRANCISCO BAY AREA

San Francisco
CALIFORNIA

Richmond
Richmond-San Rafael Bridge
Berkeley
Golden Gate National Recreation Area
Sausalito
San Francisco-Oakland Bay Bridge
Golden Gate Bridge
PACIFIC OCEAN
Golden Gate
Lombard St.
Oakland
Golden Gate Park
Chinatown
San Francisco
Mission Dolores
Alameda
Daly City
San Francisco Bay

City area
Park
Road
Bridge
Rapid Transit System
Other city
Point of interest

0   4   8 Miles
0   4   8 Kilometers

MAP WORK

For hundreds of years San Francisco Bay has been important to people who live and work in San Francisco.

1. About how far is it from Alameda to Oakland?

2. In what direction is the city of Berkeley from San Francisco?

3. In what ways do you think bridges are important to people who live in communities near San Francisco?

Fog, Fog, and Hills

Fog often covers San Francisco (top). Long ago and today, cars have always gone slowly down Lombard Street (bottom).

If you ever visit San Francisco Bay, you might hear the sound of loud foghorns blowing over the bay. These horns help ship captains safely move their ships through the fog. San Francisco is famous for its thick, white fog. Warm winds blow in from the east. Cool ocean winds blow in from the west. When these winds meet, fog is made.

Fog is not the only unusual thing about San Francisco. The city also has 43 hills! The people who live in the city have had to adjust to the hills. They have built houses that slope along hills. They have even made special laws about how to park cars to keep them from rolling down hills.

San Francisco's Lombard Street is called the "crookedest street in the world." Look at the pictures at left and you will see why. Lombard Street was built this way because it is on a hill that is too steep to drive a car straight down.

120

Living With Natural Resources

For hundreds of years, Native Americans have caught crabs and clams in San Francisco Bay. Later, the bay was also used by settlers for shipping and fishing.

In the 1800s San Francisco grew quickly as people moved to the city for work. The need for natural resources such as water also grew. Fresh water from streams was shipped on rafts down the bay to the city. It sold for about $1 per bucket! In the early 1900s, dams were built east of San Francisco to give fresh water to the city. A dam is a wall built across a river to control the flow of water. Today, dams help to make electricity for the city's buildings.

In 1906 a terrible earthquake hit San Francisco. Many people died and buildings were destroyed. New water pipes were laid in the city during rebuilding.

WHY IT MATTERS

San Francisco Bay has been important for the growth of San Francisco. In the next lesson you will learn other ways in which "The City by the Bay" has grown.

✓// Reviewing Facts and Ideas

MAIN IDEAS

- The climate of San Francisco is cool and foggy.
- San Francisco has many hills.
- Bridges like the Golden Gate Bridge are important because San Francisco is located on a peninsula.
- San Francisco Bay has provided food and access to water to people in the area for hundreds of years.

THINK ABOUT IT

1. What is the climate of San Francisco?

2. **FOCUS** How is the San Francisco Bay important?

3. **THINKING SKILL** What would you _decide_ to do if you visited San Francisco?

4. **GEOGRAPHY** Look at the map on page 119. About how many miles is it from the Golden Gate Bridge to the San Francisco-Oakland Bay Bridge?

San Francisco Long Ago

Focus Activity

READ TO LEARN

What was life like in San Francisco long ago?

VOCABULARY

- mission
- missionary
- independence
- gold rush

PLACES

- **Mission Dolores**

Read Aloud

cheeyish (chay AY ish)
troot (TRO oat)
partaay (pawrt AW ay)

Do you know what these words mean? If you had been an Ohlone (uh LONE ee) living long ago near San Francisco Bay, these words might have been a part of your everyday language. A cheeyish is a jackrabbit. A troot is a deer and a partaay is a frog.

Early People in California

Long ago, the Ohlone and other Native Americans lived in the area that is now called the San Francisco Bay area. Each village often had a different language. In all, there were about eight Ohlone languages.

Like the Anasazi, the Ohlone used the land to meet their needs. They gathered acorns and ground them into flour to make bread and cereal. They gathered seaweed from the ocean and dug for clams in the sand. They made clothing from the skins of jackrabbits and deer. They also built rounded shelters covered with grasses and other plants.

The Spanish Begin Missions

For many years the Ohlone and other Native Americans lived in communities around San Francisco Bay. These were communities with rich traditions. But in the 1700s, they were changed forever. Catholic priests from Spain traveled north from Mexico to set up missions. Missions were communities led by Roman Catholic priests to teach their religion and way of life to Native Americans. These priests were called missionaries.

The missionaries believed they were helping the Native Americans. They thought their lives would be better if they became Catholic. But most Native Americans did not want to live and work in the missions. They wanted to live in their own communities.

In all, the Spanish missionaries forced Native Americans to build and work in 21 missions in what is now California. In 1776 one of the missions they set up was called San Francisco de Asís (ah SIS). It was in the area that is now San Francisco. Later it was called Mission Dolores. By 1830 about 230 Native Americans lived at Mission Dolores. To learn about life in a mission, turn the page.

The lives of the Ohlone (top) and other Native Americans were forever changed by Spanish missionaries like Junípero Serra (bottom).

FATHER JVNIPERO SERRA
ONE HVNDRED AND FIFTIETH ANNIVERSARY SAN GABRIEL MISSION 1771–1921

interNET
CONNECTION   Visit our website:
www.mhschool.com

Living at a Mission

This Infographic shows what life long ago may have been like at a mission in California. What were some of the things women did at the mission?

Men made wood and stone tools and other things needed at the mission.

The church was important to the community. Some missionaries lived in rooms behind the church.

Women spun cotton, weaved, and made pottery and baskets. They also fished, cared for the children, and prepared food. Corn was an important crop.

Some Native Americans lived in rooms built in the mission walls.

Missionaries taught Native American children to read and write in Spanish.

Every day started with a prayer. At noon and in the evening, the whole community gathered to pray again.

Gold and More Gold!

DID YOU KNOW?

How big is that nugget?

While most pieces of gold found during the great Gold Rush were quite small, some were very large. The heaviest gold nugget found weighed 195 pounds. That's about as heavy as 4 third graders!

Mission life continued for about 60 years. Over that time some Native American groups and their way of life survived. But many groups like the Ohlone were almost completely destroyed. Many died from diseases. Many of the lands they used to live and hunt on now belonged to the missions.

In 1821 Mexico won its independence from Spain. Independence is being free from others. Mexico then took much of the land owned by the missions. This made it hard for the missions to continue.

By the 1830s the missions were struggling. Then something important happened that changed California forever. On January 24, 1848, gold was found near San Francisco!

More than 50,000 men, and some women, rushed to California. As a result of the "Gold Rush," San Francisco grew very quickly. A gold rush is a quick movement of people to a place where gold has been discovered. In 1848 about 800 people lived in San Francisco. Two years later, about 25,000 people lived in the city.

During the Gold Rush people hoped to get rich by finding large gold nuggets, but few people did get rich.

126

California Becomes a State

In 1846 the United States of America declared war on Mexico. By 1848 the United States had won the war. After the war, Mexico was forced to give up the land area of California to the United States.

In 1849 many people wanted California to become a state. In 1850 Congress named California our thirty-first state.

WHY IT MATTERS

You read that Spanish missionaries brought their culture to California long ago. As a result, the lives of Native Americans were changed. Today, parts of Spanish and many other cultures are still an important part of life in San Francisco and other communities in our country.

People in California are proud of our country's flag and their state's flag.

Reviewing Facts and Ideas

MAIN IDEAS

- The Ohlone lived around what is now San Francisco Bay.
- Spanish missionaries forced many Native Americans to live and work in missions.
- Many Native Americans lost their culture as a result of mission life.
- Gold was discovered near San Francisco in 1848.
- In 1850 California became our nation's thirty-first state.

THINK ABOUT IT

1. How did the Ohlone use their natural resources?
2. Why did San Francisco grow rapidly during the Gold Rush?
3. **FOCUS** What was life like in San Francisco long ago?
4. **THINKING SKILL** How was life for Native American men in the mission _different_ from life for women? How was it _alike_?
5. **WRITE** Write a poem about mission life long ago. Use the Infographic on pages 124–125 to help you.

San Francisco Today

Focus Activity

READ TO LEARN

How do people live and work in San Francisco today?

VOCABULARY

- cable car

PLACES

- Chinatown

Read Aloud

"This is the most beautiful city in the world. Come and visit us. You will see many different people speaking many different languages. The kids who live here are lucky. They see so many different cultures and people and food!"

These words were spoken by Peter Pavlukevich (pahv lew KAY vitch). In this lesson you will also see why people like Mr. Pavlukevich are proud to call San Francisco their home.

A Growing City

In the last lesson you read about life in San Francisco long ago. Today San Francisco is very different. It has grown from the days of the missions and the Gold Rush. More than 700,000 people live and work in the city. San Francisco is the thirteenth-largest city in the United States of America.

Mr. Pavlukevich has seen a lot of changes in San Francisco. "When I was 8 years old in 1946, San Francisco was like a small town," he says. "Strangers would say hello to each other. My friends and I could even play baseball in the street because there were very few cars!"

The Past Lives On

San Francisco is a city that combines its history with its life today. Every year thousands of people visit the missions. Mission Dolores is still used as a church. It is one of the city's oldest buildings. Its original bells can still be heard. It also has a museum where people learn about how the Native Americans and Spanish missionaries lived long ago.

Take a look at the photo below. What kind of community do you think this is? It is a Chinese American community in San Francisco. This community is called Chinatown. Chinese people first came here over 100 years ago during the Gold Rush. Today there are about 85,000 Chinese people living in the city.

The past continues today in other ways as well. San Francisco is well known for its cable cars. A cable car is a small car that runs on a track and is pulled by a cable. They were first used in the 1870s. Today they still carry people up and down the hills. People in San Francisco really care about their cable cars. They even passed a law to use them in the city forever!

Mission Dolores is still an active church in San Francisco today (top). The past also lives on in Chinatown where traditional foods are eaten (bottom).

Living and Working in San Francisco

Whether designing sites for the Internet or cooking foods in a restaurant, people work at many different jobs in San Francisco.

People who live in San Francisco have many different kinds of jobs. Mr. Pavlukevich has a very special job. He works as a "gripman" on a cable car. His job is to stop and start the cable car. "It's a lot of fun," he says. "All types of people ride with me including teachers, lawyers, and police officers," he says. "There's even a chef on my cable car!"

Mr. Pavlukevich also meets lots of kids on his cable car. "Kids love to go to school by cable car," says Mr. Pavlukevich. "They like to hear the bell ring. They also love to see the different people who live and work in San Francisco."

In San Francisco people work in many different types of jobs. Some people make clothes in factories. Others work for computer companies. Still other people may work in businesses that take care of the many people who visit San Francisco every year.

A San Francisco Memory

Exciting things happen to people who live and work in communities like San Francisco. Mr. Pavlukevich has many memories about working on a cable car. You can read about his favorite memory below. What special memories do you have of your community?

MANY VOICES
PRIMARY SOURCE

Story told by Peter Pavlukevich in 1997.

One day a woman from Australia got onto my cable car. She told me that she was going to have dinner with her sister that night. They had not seen each other in 45 years!

A few blocks later I picked up some more people. One of these people told me that she was going to a very special dinner that night. Something clicked in my mind. I thought, "I wonder if I am right?" I said to her, "I bet you are going to meet your sister. You have not seen her in 45 years."

She asked me, "How did you know?" I said, "Because she is right over there!"

These two sisters found each other right in front of me! That was one of the most heartwarming feelings that I have had. And it happened right on my cable car!

Many People, Many Cultures

San Francisco is an urban community with people from many cultures.

For many years, San Francisco has been a city where many different people live and work together. "This is a city where people live with many different cultures and languages," says Mr. Pavlukevich. "That's what makes San Francisco so great. Kids who live here learn to accept and understand each other. That's the most important thing. Now, that's beautiful!"

WHY IT MATTERS

You have learned about San Francisco's rich past. You have also seen how people in San Francisco live and work together today.

Every community has its own special past. People enjoy remembering their past. People can also learn from the past and work together to make the present even better. These are some of the reasons why people enjoy communities.

✔/ Reviewing Facts and Ideas

MAIN IDEAS

- San Francisco has grown into a large, busy city of over 700,000 people.
- San Francisco is a city that combines its history with its present.
- People who live in San Francisco have different types of jobs.
- People of many different cultures live in San Francisco.
- Many people in San Francisco enjoy living and working in the city.

THINK ABOUT IT

1. What signs of San Francisco's past can still be seen today?
2. What does Mr. Pavlukevich like about living in San Francisco?
3. **FOCUS** How do people live and work in San Francisco today?
4. **THINKING SKILL** How is San Francisco _like_ your community today? How is it _different_?
5. **WRITE** Think of a memory you have of your community. Write a story about that memory.

MAKING A DIFFERENCE

Saving Animals in Danger

SAN FRANCISCO, CALIFORNIA—Amy Crisp is very proud of her mother. "My Mom saves animals," she says. Amy's mother is Terri Crisp. She is the director of the Emergency Animal Rescue Service, or "EARS." In San Francisco EARS has trained 236 volunteers. Whenever a major flood, fire, earthquake, or hurricane occurs, EARS members save animals that have been forced from their homes or natural environments. Volunteers from San Francisco and around the country have been to hurricanes in Florida, oil spills in Alaska, fires in Wyoming, and tornadoes in Arkansas.

Because of the dangerous work they sometimes do, EARS volunteers have to be at least 16 years old. But Amy Crisp, age 8, became a special EARS volunteer after a flood near her home in January 1997. During this flood, EARS workers rescued 878 animals. Besides dogs, cats, horses, and rabbits, they found pigs, hamsters, and an emu. EARS volunteers like Amy fed them and looked after them for 22 days. The animals stayed until their owners came to get them or EARS found new homes for them.

On this rescue, Mrs. Crisp put Amy in charge of 20 puppies. "My job," said Amy, "was to play with the puppies, walk them, and make sure they stayed warm. It was January and very cold. They wore little sweaters and we had to make sure they kept their sweaters on. It made me feel good to help out."

Mrs. Crisp agrees. "Animals that are pets are so helpless in an emergency. We owe it to our animals to help them."

"It made me feel good to help out."

a my crisp

Reading Bar and Line Graphs

VOCABULARY

bar graph   line graph

WHY THE SKILL MATTERS

You just learned about San Francisco today. In studying San Francisco it is helpful to compare its population with those of other cities in California. It is also useful to see how San Francisco's population has changed over time. One way to view this information is to use graphs.

READING A BAR GRAPH

Suppose you want to compare the populations of San Francisco and other California cities. Look at the bar graph at right. A bar graph uses bars of different heights to show amounts. This bar graph shows the populations of four of the largest cities today in California.

Look again at this bar graph. Which cities does it name? Look at the numbers on the left side of the graph. The numbers stand for populations.

Now "read" the graph. First find the bar for San Francisco. Slide your finger to the top of the bar. Now slide your finger across to the number

at the left. The number is below one million. The population of San Francisco is about 780,000 people.

Now find the bar for San Jose. About how many people live in San Jose?

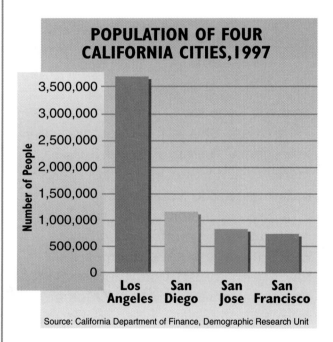

POPULATION OF FOUR CALIFORNIA CITIES, 1997

Source: California Department of Finance, Demographic Research Unit

READING A LINE GRAPH

Another kind of graph is a line graph. A line graph shows how something changes over time. Look at the line graph on the next page. It shows how the population of San Francisco has changed over time.

The dots for each year are connected by a line. The line shows you a picture of what happened to San Francisco's population.

Run your finger along the line. Note the dates at the bottom and the numbers at the left. How has the city's population changed between 1850 and 1997?

TRYING THE SKILL

You may find it useful to refer to the Helping Yourself box as you continue to study the graphs. Which graph would you use to find the population of San Diego in 1997? Which would you use to compare San Francisco's population in 1900 with its population in 1997? What happened during this time?

REVIEWING THE SKILL

1. Which city on the bar graph has the largest population? Tell how you know.

2. What is the earliest year shown on the line graph? How can you tell?

3. About how many people lived in San Francisco in 1950?

4. What would you tell someone to do to make it easier to read a graph?

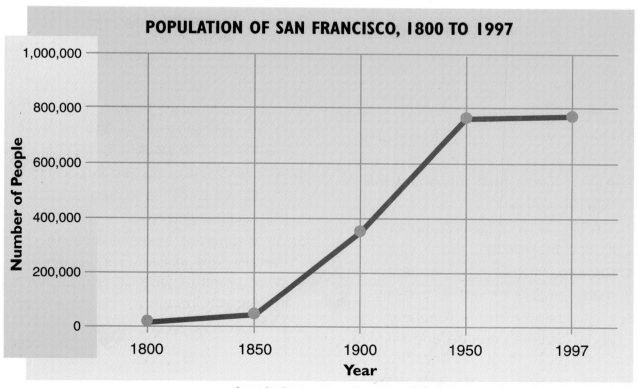

POPULATION OF SAN FRANCISCO, 1800 TO 1997

Source: San Francisco Almanac; World Almanac; California Department of Finance, Demographic Research Unit

135

CHAPTER 5 REVIEW

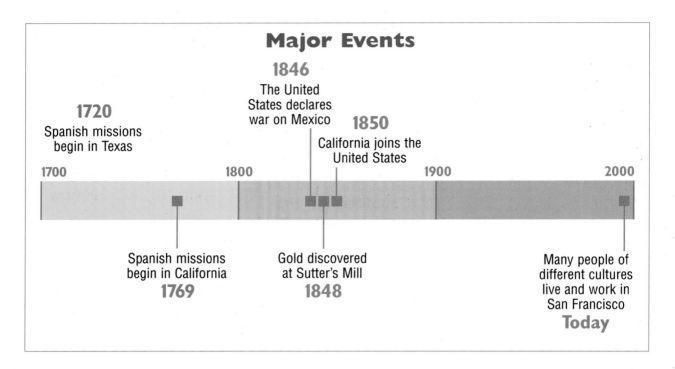

Major Events

1720
Spanish missions begin in Texas

1846
The United States declares war on Mexico

1850
California joins the United States

1700   1800   1900   2000

Spanish missions begin in California
1769

Gold discovered at Sutter's Mill
1848

Many people of different cultures live and work in San Francisco
Today

THINKING ABOUT VOCABULARY

Number a piece of paper from 1 to 5. Beside each number write the word that best completes each sentence.

dam   missionaries
Gold Rush   cable car
independence

1. Mexico won its _____ from Spain in 1821.

2. A _____ was built to control the flow of water.

3. The _____ took people up the hill in San Francisco.

4. Because of the _____ in 1849, many people moved to the city.

5. _____ taught Native Americans about Spanish culture and religion.

THINKING ABOUT FACTS

1. How did the missionaries change the lives of the Ohlone people?

2. In what year did California join the United States? What events took place before this happened?

3. In what ways was San Francisco Bay important to people who lived in San Francisco long ago? How is it important to people today?

4. Why is Chinese culture important to people who live in San Francisco today?

5. What different types of jobs do people have in San Francisco? What types of jobs do people have in your community?

THINK AND WRITE

WRITING A STORY

Write a brief story about a typical day of a child living at a mission long ago.

WRITING A SONG

Write a song about cable cars. In it describe San Francisco today.

WRITING AN ADVERTISEMENT

Suppose you work for an advertising company and have been asked to create a magazine advertisement about San Francisco. Write an advertisement to tell people what is special about San Francisco.

APPLYING STUDY SKILLS

READING BAR AND LINE GRAPHS

Answer the following questions to practice the skill of reading bar and line graphs. Use the graphs on pages 134–135.

1. What is the difference between a bar graph and a line graph?
2. Which city has the larger population, Los Angeles or San Diego? Which graph tells you this?
3. Did more people live in San Francisco in 1850 or in 1950?
4. Which graph tells you about changes over time?
5. What information about yourself could you show on a line graph?

Summing Up the Chapter

Fill in a copy of the Venn Diagram below. In the circle on the left, write the words that describe San Francisco in the 1700s. In the circle on the right, write the words that describe San Francisco today. Where the circles meet, write the words that describe both time periods. How has San Francisco changed since the 1700s? How is it still the same?

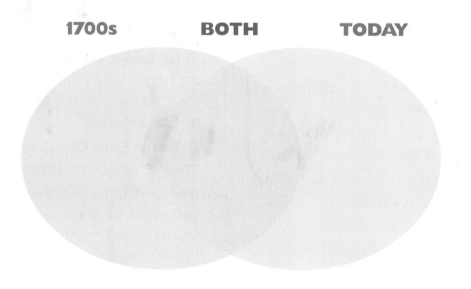

1700s   BOTH   TODAY

UNIT 2 REVIEW

THINKING ABOUT VOCABULARY

Number a sheet of paper from 1 to 10. Beside each number write the word from the list that best completes each sentence.

artifacts   kiva   technology
Bay   mesa   colony
decision   mission
missionaries   museum

1. _____ is the use of tools and materials to serve people's needs.

2. Ships heading into Jamestown sailed on the Chesapeake _____ .

3. A _____ was a community where Native Americans lived and practiced the Catholic religion.

4. Scientists often use _____ to learn about how a group of people lived long ago.

5. The tour book listed many places to visit. We had to make a _____ about where to go first.

6. A _____ was a room used by the Anasazi for religious purposes.

7. _____ set up Mission Dolores in San Francisco.

8. John Smith was sent to start a _____ at Jamestown.

9. A _____ is a landform that looks like a high, flat table.

10. At a _____ people can look at objects of art, science, or history.

THINK AND WRITE

WRITING A REVIEW

Suppose you have just visited Mesa Verde National Park and Jamestown Settlement. Write a paragraph reviewing why such places are important.

WRITING AN ESSAY

Write one paragraph explaining a special event in your community that is important to you. It could be a parade or a holiday celebration.

WRITING A NEWSPAPER ARTICLE

Suppose you went with the Spanish missionaries to California. Write an article that reports on the land, the people, and the problems you faced.

BUILDING SKILLS

1. **Making Decisions** What is the first step to take in making a decision?

2. **Making Decisions** Identify a decision you made today and how you made it.

3. **Time Lines** Look at the time line on page 113. Which happened first, the "starving time" or the marriage of Pocahontas?

4. **Bar and Line Graphs** What does the line graph on page 135 show?

5. **Bar and Line Graphs** Suppose you want to show how many students like various kinds of fruit. Would you use a line graph or a bar graph? Why?

LOCAL *connection*

How was the land around your community changed by people who once lived there? How was the land used? What does this tell you about how these people lived? Make a diorama showing how different groups of people left their mark on the land around your community.

READING ON YOUR OWN

Here are some books you might find at the library to help you learn more.

THE CITY BY THE BAY: A MAGICAL JOURNEY AROUND SAN FRANCISCO
by Tricia Brown
Take a fun tour around San Francisco, accompanied by colorful illustrations.

ON THE MAYFLOWER: VOYAGE OF THE SHIP'S APPRENTICE AND A PASSENGER GIRL
by Kate Waters
Read what it was like to be a young boy and girl on the Mayflower.

THE MUD FAMILY
by Betsy James
Read of a time when an Anasazi girl made mud dolls that gave rain to her community.

UNIT REVIEW PROJECT

Creating an Infographic

1. Create an Infographic showing how people lived in Jamestown long ago.
2. In a group, discuss facts to include in your Infographic.
3. Decide how you will present these facts. Use the Infographic on pages 84-85 as a guide.
4. Have each group member choose one part of the Infographic to complete.
5. Include colorful drawings to show what life in Jamestown was really like.

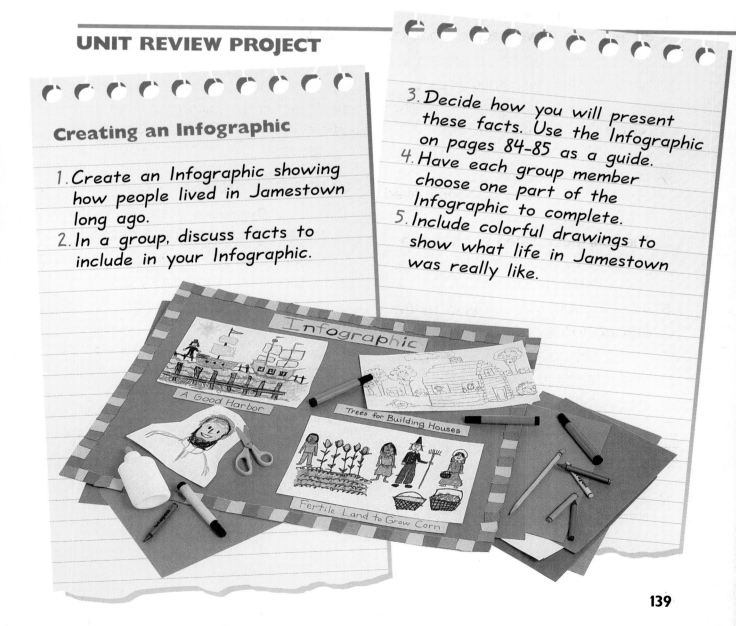

Building a Government

Why Does it Matter?

People in our country work together to make laws that help us live safely and fairly. Some were made a long time ago. Some of the laws were made much more recently. In this unit you will learn about how people and government work to make lives better for people in communities.

As a citizen of the United States of America, you have important rights and responsibilities. By learning about government and citizenship, you will be better able to make a difference to your country and your community.

FIND OUT MORE!
Visit our website:
www.mhschool.com

interNET
CONNECTION

Adventures
with
NATIONAL
GEOGRAPHIC

WHEN THE WHITE HOUSE IS HOME

The White House belongs to all Americans. But some kids have a special connection to the President's house. It's their home! Young Tad Lincoln liked to read there with his father, Abraham Lincoln. Quentin Roosevelt, Teddy Roosevelt's son, rode his pony in the driveway. "John John" Kennedy enjoyed hiding under the desk of his dad, John Kennedy. And Amy Carter, Jimmy Carter's daughter, played with her nephew in a tree house on the lawn. Kids who live in the White House give up a lot of privacy for the privilege of living there. But White House kids get to make history.

GEO JOURNAL

It's your first night in the White House. Describe your thoughts about being there.

A New Country Is Born

THINKING ABOUT
GEOGRAPHY AND HISTORY

As you have read, English colonies grew along the Atlantic coast of North America long ago. Some colonial communities, among them Philadelphia and New York, grew into busy cities.

From the time line and map, you can see that some major events happened in Philadelphia and New York. Match the triangles on the map to the picture that has the same color. In Chapter 6 you will meet some of the people who made Philadelphia and New York important and see how their ideas helped form our country, the United States of America.

1776

The Declaration of Independence is signed

1787

The Constitution is written

1776   1787   1788

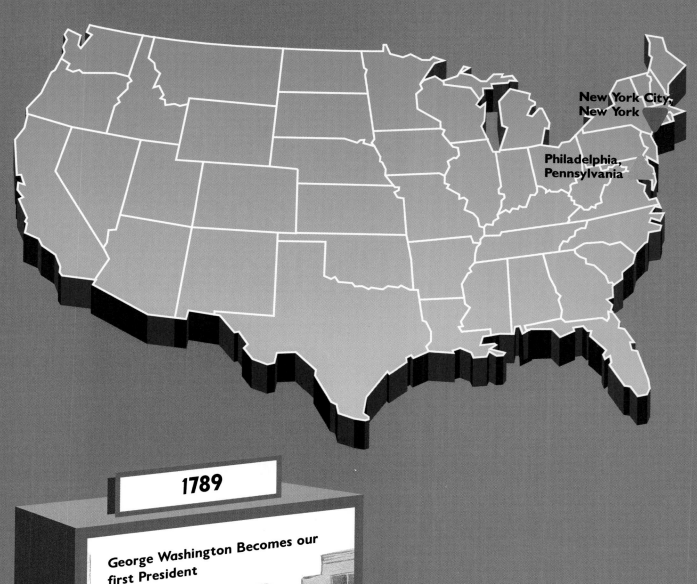

New York City, New York

Philadelphia, Pennsylvania

1789

George Washington Becomes our first President

The Bettman Archive

Focus Activity

READ TO LEARN

How did Ben Franklin make a difference in Philadelphia?

VOCABULARY

- almanac
- tax
- American Revolution
- Declaration of Independence

PEOPLE

- Benjamin Franklin
- Thomas Jefferson

PLACES

- Philadelphia, Pennsylvania

Ben Franklin and Philadelphia

Read Aloud

"Most of the shop fronts were painted red, blue, green, or yellow, and the big swinging signs in front of them were brilliant with paint. . . . The people of Philadelphia wore bright colors and had a taste for fine clothes."

Welcome to Philadelphia!

These are the words of a writer named Margaret Cousins. She describes what life was like in the city of Philadelphia, Pennsylvania in the early 1700s. At that time there were 13 English colonies in America. The colonies had many cities. The biggest, busiest city of all was Philadelphia. About 38,000 people lived there, more people than in Boston and New York City put together.

Philadelphia became one of the most important communities in our country's history. Many things happened there that led the colonies to become the United States of America. Let's take a look at what Philadelphia was like back in colonial days.

Meet Ben Franklin

Everyone in Philadelphia was talking about one person—Benjamin Franklin. He seemed to be everywhere, doing just about everything.

Ben Franklin grew up in Boston, Massachusetts, in a family of 17 children. When he was 12, his father sent him to live and work with his older brother James, a printer. Ben quickly learned a lot about printing. But he did not get along with his brother. When he was 17, he left for Philadelphia.

When he arrived in Philadelphia in 1723, Ben found an exciting city. He talked to everyone and soon made many friends. He loved his new city, and he set out to make it even better.

As a young man, Ben Franklin learned to use the printing press.

PENNSYLVANIA

Philadelphia

Poor Richard's Almanac

Ben quickly found work in Philadelphia as a printer. A few years later, in 1732, he wrote and printed *Poor Richard's Almanac*. An **almanac** is a book that comes out every year with lots of information in it. His almanac had a calendar, weather predictions, and information about the moon and sun. It was most popular for the helpful advice it gave readers. Read the following sayings from his almanac. Which sayings have you heard of?

From *Poor Richard's Almanac*, written by Benjamin Franklin, 1732-1757.

- Early to bed and early to rise, makes a man healthy, wealthy and wise.

- Lost time is never found again.

- Don't throw stones at your neighbors', if your own windows are glass.

- A penny saved is a penny earned.

- Little strokes fell great oaks.

- Well done is twice done.

- When the well's dry, we know the worth of water.

- The honey is sweet, but the bee has a sting.

Helping His Community

The almanac sold so many copies that soon Ben Franklin was a rich man. He didn't have to work as much as he used to. Franklin decided to spend his time doing things he loved, including helping Philadelphia and the colonies. Look at the chart on this page to learn about some of his many great ideas.

The Inventions of BEN FRANKLIN

The first lending library in the colonies was started by Franklin.

Franklin did many experiments with electricity. To save buildings from fires, he invented lightning rods, which conduct lightning straight into the ground.

The Franklin stove used much less wood and gave off more heat than fireplaces.

Franklin helped organize Philadelphia's first volunteer fire department. Volunteers carried leather pails to help fight fires.

Franklin created bifocal glasses to help people see close-up, for reading, as well as at a distance.

Fighting for Freedom

In Franklin's time the colonies grew and began to have problems with their English rulers. The colonists felt that they should make their own laws. They did not want to pay taxes to the English government. A tax is money that people pay to support the government. By the 1770s many colonists wanted to have their own government.

In 1775 the American Revolution broke out. Fighting began between the colonists and the English. The colonies wanted independence, or to be a free country.

It was the summer of 1776. The leaders of the colonies met in Philadelphia to work together to win the war. Ben Franklin was there. His wise advice and experience were highly valued. Thomas Jefferson from Virginia was also there. Jefferson wrote a statement about why the colonies should be free. It was called the Declaration of Independence. On July 4, 1776, the leaders all agreed to adopt it.

The artist John Trumbull painted *The Declaration of Independence, 4 July 1776* (bottom).

The United States of America

Most Americans were happy about the Declaration of Independence. But the real celebration could not take place yet. Freedom had not yet been won. People from every colony marched off to war against the English. Many battles were fought. Many lives were lost. Finally, in 1781, America won its independence. The 13 colonies were now the states of a new country, the United States of America.

WHY IT MATTERS

Philadelphia was an important city during the American Revolution. Ben Franklin worked to help his city and all the colonies. On July 4, 1776, Ben Franklin was one of 56 leaders to adopt the Declaration of Independence. This date is still important to us today. It is the birthday of our country.

In 1776, the Liberty Bell rang to celebrate the adoption of the Declaration of Independence.

✓// Reviewing Facts and Ideas

MAIN IDEAS

- Ben Franklin arrived in Philadelphia in 1723. He did many things to help the city.
- Starting in 1775 the American Revolution was fought to free the colonies from England. The colonies wanted to make their own laws and to stop paying taxes to England.
- On July 4, 1776, the Declaration of Independence was adopted.
- In 1781 the American Revolution ended.

THINK ABOUT IT

1. Why did the colonies fight against England?

2. **FOCUS** How did Ben Franklin make a difference in Philadelphia?

3. **THINKING SKILL** _Predict_ what might have happened if the American colonies had lost the American Revolution.

4. **WRITE** Suppose that you are writing your own almanac. Write two sayings that would be helpful to people today.

Our Country's Flag

What is red, white, and blue and has been waving in our country since the American Revolution? It is "Old Glory," our country's flag.

Before 1777 each colony had its own flag. But the colonies came under one flag when they became the United States of America.

The legacy of our "Stars and Stripes" celebrates the land, people, and history of the United States. It is a symbol of the past and future hopes of our country.

As you look at the legacy of our flag, see how it has stayed the same and changed.

In 1969 our "Stars and Stripes" waved far away on the moon.

The rattlesnake was a colonial symbol used in 1775.

Betsy Ross is said to have made our first flag. Today a copy of that flag, with 13 stars and 13 stripes, is flown outside the Betsy Ross House in Philadelphia.

Our First President

Read Aloud

The American Revolution was over. A new country called the United States was born. But who would lead this country? What kind of government would it have? There was one person many hoped could help the states reach an agreement. That man was George Washington.

Focus Activity

READ TO LEARN

How did George Washington help our country start a new government?

VOCABULARY

- **Constitution**
- **elect**
- **compromise**
- **Congress**
- **President**
- **Supreme Court**
- **Bill of Rights**

PEOPLE

- **George Washington**
- **James Madison**

Meet George Washington

People had good reason to pin their hopes on George Washington. During the American Revolution, he led the whole army. The army did not have a lot of money or supplies. But Washington's courage and leadership helped win the war. Afterward, he was praised by many people. One army leader described him as ". . . first in war, first in peace, and first in the hearts of his countrymen."

Some people even thought Washington should be crowned the king of the new country. Washington said the new country should not have a king. It should have a leader chosen by the people. Besides, he did not want to be king. He just wanted to go to his home in Virginia when the war ended. "I will rest under my own vine and my own fig tree," he said.

A Leader Is Needed

In 1787 the new country was facing new troubles. Many of the problems were about money. All the states were printing money to help pay the costs of the war. Each state had its own kind of money. The states started arguing with each other over these matters. They realized they needed a new government to make laws for printing money.

Leaders from the states decided to hold a meeting in Philadelphia. Their goal was to solve these problems. One of the leaders was George Washington. He was ill, but he knew he was needed once again to help his country.

George Washington and other leaders traveled to Philadelphia in 1787. At their meeting they discussed laws to help the country, including laws for making money.

Leaders came from each state to write the Constitution. James Madison (above) suggested a type of government with three different branches.

Writing the Constitution

The summer of 1787 was the hottest summer anyone in Philadelphia could remember. In spite of the heat, an important meeting was taking place to create a new government.

Imagine what it was like when the leaders met. The men wore wigs, long coats, ruffled shirts, and vests. Their pants came to their knees. Flies buzzed around and could bite right through their knee-high stockings.

Somehow none of that was important. The leaders were forming a new government. Their job was to write a Constitution. The Constitution states the laws and the plan for how the government of our country works.

One of the first things they did was to elect someone to lead the meeting. To elect is to choose by voting. George Washington was elected to be in charge.

A New Plan

Many leaders were at the meeting. Ben Franklin was there. So was **James Madison**. He spent the whole time taking careful notes. That's how we know what went on at the meeting.

Madison suggested a plan for three branches, or parts, of government. The leaders argued about the plan but worked out some **compromises**. A compromise is an agreement reached when each side gives up some demands.

When the Constitution was finally signed, Washington called it a miracle. Look at the chart below to see the three branches of our country's government.

Ben Franklin, over 80 years old, was carried to the meeting.

Our Country's National Government

Members of **Congress** are elected to the Senate or the House of Representatives. They make our laws. Congress meets in the Capitol building.

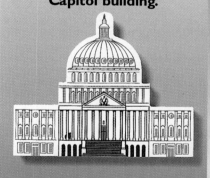

The **President**, our country's elected leader, sees that our country's laws are carried out. The President lives in the White House.

The nine appointed judges of the **Supreme Court** make sure our laws are fair. The judges meet in the Supreme Court building.

CHART WORK

The Constitution describes the job of each branch of government.

1. What are the two parts of Congress?

2. Who is the leader of our country?

3. In what building does Congress meet? In what building does the President work?

4. How do you think the three branches work together?

Our First President

As you can see on the chart on page 157, the Constitution made the President the leader of our country. The President would be different than a king. The President would be elected.

In February 1789, George Washington was elected the first President of the United States. A few months later, he rode to New York City for a special ceremony to become the President. In every town and city he passed through, people surrounded his carriage and cheered. There were parades and celebrations at just about every stop. When he reached New York City, the crowds were so thick that it was hard for carriages to move.

One of Washington's most important jobs was to choose good leaders to help him. Thomas Jefferson was one of the leaders chosen to help run the government. After four years Washington was elected President again.

Wherever George Washington traveled in the colonies, he was often greeted by large crowds of people.

158

WHY IT MATTERS

George Washington was an important leader in our country's history. He led the American Army during the American Revolution. He also helped write the Constitution. The Constitution is very important to all Americans. It has the most important laws of our country. But people found that it was not enough. It did not protect all people's freedom and rights.

In 1791 the Bill of Rights was added to the Constitution. It lists our most important rights. These include the right to free speech and the right to practice religion freely.

Throughout the history of our country, other changes have been made to the Constitution. But the ideas written in the summer of 1787 still guide us today.

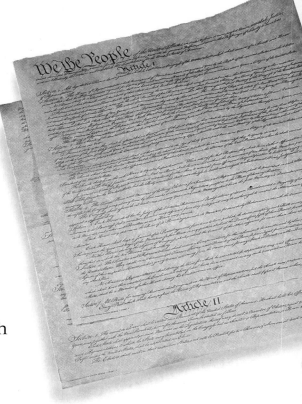

The Constitution and the Bill of Rights still guide our country.

Reviewing Facts and Ideas

MAIN IDEAS

- George Washington led the American Army in the American Revolution. He became our country's first President in 1789.

- Leaders gathered in 1787 in Philadelphia to write the Constitution. James Madison took notes at the meeting.

- Today, the Constitution is still the plan for how our government works.

- The Bill of Rights was added to the Constitution in 1791.

THINK ABOUT IT

1. What problems did the new country have?

2. **FOCUS** How did George Washington help our country start a new government?

3. **THINKING SKILL** Suppose you had to form a government. How would you _decide_ how to make laws? What would your new government be like?

4. **WRITE** Many people consider George Washington a hero. Write a paragraph about how he might be a hero to you.

Comparing and Contrasting

VOCABULARY
compare
contrast

WHY THE SKILL MATTERS

You have just learned about two very important documents in the history of our country, the Declaration of Independence and the Constitution. A document is a written statement that gives information about something. Suppose you wanted to better understand both documents. To do this you might want to compare and contrast them.

To compare things is to see how they are alike. To contrast things is to see how they are different. Comparing and contrasting can help you decide how the Declaration of Independence and the Constitution are important to the history of the United States.

USING THE SKILL

In comparing and contrasting these two documents, your first step might be to think about the Declaration of Independence. You know it was written in 1776. Then think about the Constitution. It was written in 1787, 11 years later. That is one difference. People gathered to write the Declaration of Independence in Philadelphia. They also gathered to write the Constitution in Philadelphia. That is one thing that makes the documents alike.

The Declaration was written during the American Revolution to tell why the colonies should be independent.

The Granger Collection

The Constitution was written after the Revolution was over, to set up the laws and plan for a new government. That is two ways they are different. Each document was written for a different purpose and at a different time in history.

TRYING THE SKILL

When our country was being formed, people did not have cameras. But we can get an idea of the way people looked from paintings and notes.

The Granger Collection

Look at the two paintings of Thomas Jefferson. Compare and contrast the paintings. You can use the Helping Yourself box for some tips as you try this skill.

What do you think you should do first? You could look at the clothes Jefferson is wearing in each painting. What about his clothes are alike? Different? How else do you think these two paintings of Jefferson are alike and different?

REVIEWING THE SKILL

1. What did you do to compare and contrast the two paintings?

2. What is the difference between comparing and contrasting?

3. Look at the chart of the three branches of government on page 157. How are the President and the Supreme Court alike? How are they different? How do you know?

4. When is it helpful to compare and contrast? Why?

161

CHAPTER 6 REVIEW

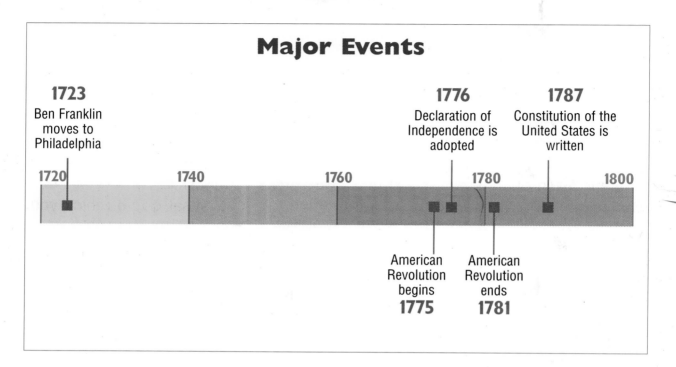

Major Events

1723
Ben Franklin moves to Philadelphia

1776
Declaration of Independence is adopted

1787
Constitution of the United States is written

1720   1740   1760   1780   1800

American Revolution begins
1775

American Revolution ends
1781

THINKING ABOUT VOCABULARY

Number a sheet of paper from 1 to 10. For each word listed below, write a sentence using the word correctly. The sentence should show that you know what the word means.

American Revolution   elect
Bill of Rights   President
compromise   Supreme Court
Congress   tax
Constitution
Declaration of Independence

THINKING ABOUT FACTS

1. What are some of the things for which Benjamin Franklin is remembered?

2. What is the Declaration of Independence? Who wrote it? When was it adopted?

3. In what year did the American Revolution begin? How long did it last?

4. What important things did George Washington do for our country? Which do you think was his greatest achievement?

5. Into what three different parts does the Constitution divide our government? Name another document important to our freedom. Tell what it does.

THINK AND WRITE

WRITING A NEWSPAPER STORY

Write a newspaper article about the creation of the Constitution. Discuss the meetings, the leaders involved, the disagreements that took place, and how Americans reacted to it.

WRITING AN INTERVIEW

Choose a person from this chapter to interview about the beginning of our country. Write the interview. Include your questions and the answers you think your subject may have given.

WRITING ABOUT A LEGACY

A legacy is something that we value in our lives today that is also a valued part of our past. Our flag is one example of a legacy. Write two paragraphs describing something that you consider to be a legacy.

APPLYING THINKING SKILLS

COMPARING AND CONTRASTING

Answer the following questions to practice the skill of comparing and contrasting.

1. What does it mean to compare and contrast two things?
2. How were Thomas Jefferson and George Washington alike? How were they different?
3. Compare and contrast the pictures of Benjamin Franklin on pages 147 and 157.
4. Compare and contrast the flags on pages 152 and 153. How has our flag changed?
5. What kinds of things might you want to compare and contrast?

Summing Up the Chapter

Review the chapter and then fill in a copy of the word map below. For each document, list the year it was written, its purpose, and any other important information. Then compare and contrast these documents.

Documents of the United States

- Declaration of Independence
- Constitution
- Bill of Rights

Countries Have Capitals

THINKING ABOUT
GEOGRAPHY AND HISTORY

Washington, D.C., is our country's capital. It is the center of our national government. In Chapter 7 you will learn about the beginnings of our capital city. Choosing its location and building it were among the first jobs of the United States government.

Today our capital has memorials and buildings that belong to everybody in the United States. As you will see, these structures honor important people and events in our country's history.

1791
Benjamin Banneker helps complete plans for the new capital city

1800
John and Abigail Adams move into the White House

1790   1795   1800

Washington, D.C.

TODAY

Many people visit the monuments and museums of Washington, D.C.

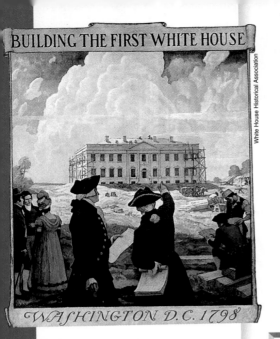

BUILDING THE FIRST WHITE HOUSE

White House Historical Association

WASHINGTON D.C. 1798

Focus Activity

READ TO LEARN

Who helped to build our country's capital?

PEOPLE

- John Adams
- Abigail Adams
- Pierre L'Enfant
- Benjamin Banneker

PLACES

- White House
- Washington, D.C.

A Capital for the U.S.A.

Read Aloud

"I pray heaven to bestow [give] the best of blessings on this house and on all that shall hereafter inhabit [live in] it. May none but honest and wise men ever rule under this roof."

A Capital Is Needed

The words above were written by President John Adams in 1800. They were written in a letter to his wife, Abigail, the day after he moved into the White House. John Adams was the second President of the United States and the first President to live in the White House.

Just a few years earlier, the leaders of the United States had trouble deciding where to build a capital city for the new country.

Thomas Jefferson, who was from the South, thought the capital should be in one of the southern states. Leaders from the North thought Boston or New York would be a good choice. Others thought Philadelphia should be the capital.

Planning a City

In 1790 members of Congress agreed that the capital should not be in any one state. Instead, it should be separate and belong to all the people of the country. Look at this map to see where the new capital was to be. As you can see, its location was a compromise. The new capital was really in the middle of the northern and southern states of our country.

Thirteen Original States

Washington, D.C.

President Washington hired a French builder named Pierre L'Enfant (pee AIR lah FAHN) to draw up plans for the new capital.

L'Enfant came to America in 1777. He was in the army and fought for the colonists during the American Revolution. L'Enfant designed a grand city, with wide streets and magnificent buildings. But he didn't get along with other planners. He left in the middle of the planning. And he took his plans with him!

Here is our capital city long ago. The new streets and buildings were built on land that once was a forest.

Life in the New Capital

Luckily, a man named Benjamin Banneker (BAN ih kur) had a good memory. Banneker had been one of L'Enfant's assistants. He had also worked hard on the plans for the new city. He sat down with other planners. Together they redrew L'Enfant's plans.

The new capital was named after George Washington. It was called Washington, D.C. The *D.C.* stands for District of Columbia.

The first building to be built in the new capital was the White House. In 1800 Abigail Adams was eager to start life in the new house. In her letters to her sister Mary, Abigail described life in the new capital. Read the letter below. What does it tell you about living in Washington, D.C., in 1800?

Benjamin Banneker was honored on a United States stamp.

MANY VOICES
PRIMARY SOURCE

Letter written by Abigail Adams in 1800.

MY DEAR SISTER:

I expected to find it a new country, with scattered houses over a space of ten miles, and trees and stumps in plenty with a castle of a house. I found the President's House is in a beautiful situation in front of which is the Potomac [River]. . . . The country around is romantic but wild, a wilderness at present.

168

WHY IT MATTERS

Abigail Adams's letters give us a look into the past. If she could have looked into the future, she might have been very surprised. There have been many changes to the White House since she lived there. Every year has also brought other changes to our country's capital. In the next lesson you will look at Washington, D.C., today.

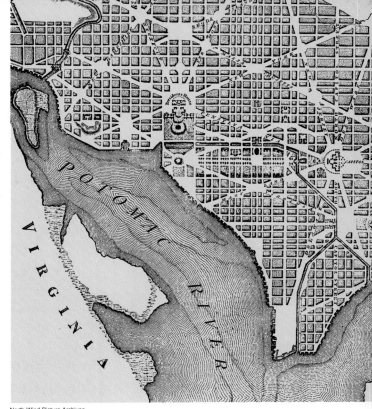

Early plans for Washington, D.C., included wide streets and open areas.

North Wind Picture Archives

Reviewing Facts and Ideas

MAIN IDEAS

- John Adams was the second President of the United States. In 1800 he and his wife Abigail became the first people to live in the newly built White House.

- The leaders of the country compromised and chose Washington, D.C., as the location for the capital. The new capital city would be in the middle of the country and would not be part of any one state.

- Pierre L'Enfant drew up the first plans for the capital. When he left in the middle of planning, Benjamin Banneker helped to redraw the plans.

THINK ABOUT IT

1. Why did people disagree about where the new capital should be? How did they compromise?

2. **FOCUS** Who helped to build our country's capital?

3. **THINKING SKILL** Suppose you had to choose a location for the United States capital today. Where should it be? How would you *decide*?

4. **GEOGRAPHY** Leaders chose to build the new city along the Potomac River. Most cities at that time were located on or near rivers. Why do you think that was so?

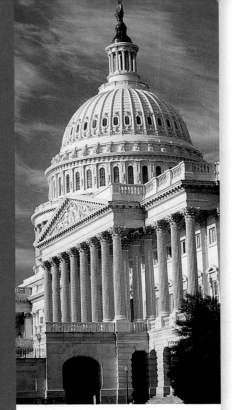

Our Nation's Capital Today

Read Aloud

"It's great to live in Washington. There are a lot of things to see and do. My favorite place to go to is the National Zoo."

Focus Activity

READ TO LEARN

What interesting things can you see and do in our capital today?

VOCABULARY

- memorial

PLACES

- Capitol
- Washington Monument
- Jefferson Memorial
- Lincoln Memorial
- Vietnam Veterans Memorial
- Lafayette Park

Come See the Capital

Gary Senn is a third grader who lives in Washington, D.C. Not far from his home, the President and other leaders of the United States are busy every day. They are making decisions that are important to the future of our country and the world. Washington, D.C. is home to many people. But it is the capital for all Americans.

Washington, D.C., has changed a lot since it was first built. Many more people live and work here. There are many shops and office buildings where forests once grew. Wide streets have replaced dirt paths and roads. Today cars and buses carry people through the city. There are no more horses and carriages. But you can still see some of the buildings that were built long ago.

Getting Around Town

Look at the map below. Find Anacostia. Here is where Gary Senn and his family live. Gary can walk to his school. To travel to other places in the city, Gary can take the Metro. The Metro is a train system that runs underground. People in Washington are proud of how fast and clean the Metro is.

Not very far from Gary's home is the Capitol. The Capitol is the building where Congress meets. *Capitol*, the word for the building, sounds like *capital*, the word for the city. But, as you can see, these words are spelled differently. Since 1800 Congress has met to make laws inside the Capitol.

Gary Senn is a third grader living in Washington, D.C.

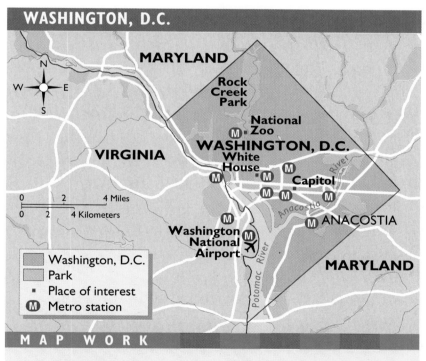

MAP WORK

Washington, D.C., is bordered by the states of Maryland and Virginia.

1. Which different rivers run through Washington, D.C.?

2. In which direction is the National Zoo from Rock Creek Park?

3. Why do you think many people travel by Metro?

interNET CONNECTION Visit our website: www.mhschool.com

A Capital

WASHINGTON D.C.

Washington Monument

Washington, D.C., has many memorials and monuments to help people remember the past. A memorial is something that is a reminder of a person or event. The Infographic on these pages shows some important monuments and memorials in Washington, D.C. Which memorials would you like to visit?

The Washington Monument, the tallest stone structure in the world, is 555 feet high. You can take an elevator to the top for a fantastic view.

The Jefferson Memorial was built in honor of the man who wrote the Declaration of Independence. Thomas Jefferson was also our third President. A large statue of Jefferson is part of this memorial.

to Remember

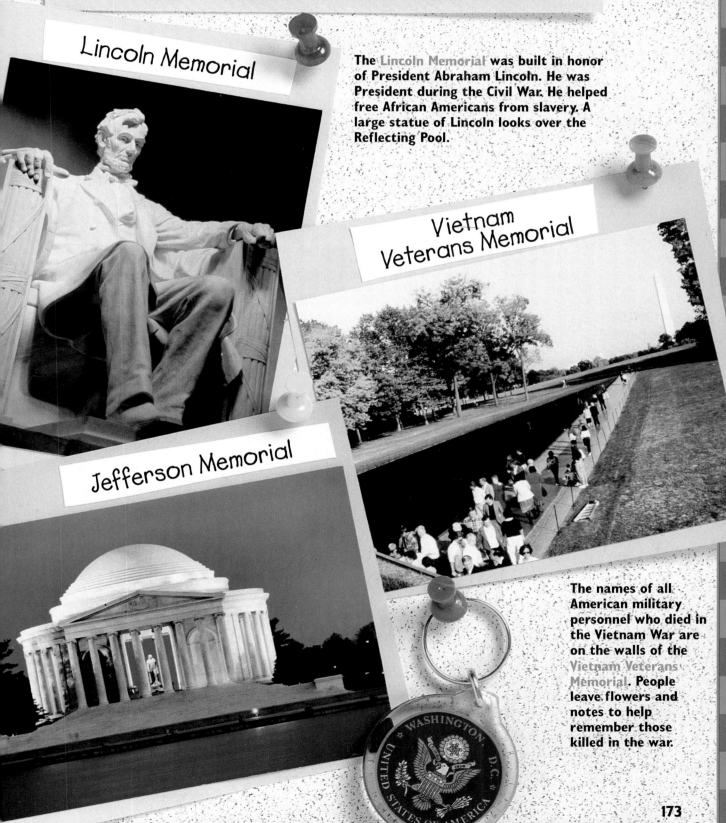

Lincoln Memorial

The Lincoln Memorial was built in honor of President Abraham Lincoln. He was President during the Civil War. He helped free African Americans from slavery. A large statue of Lincoln looks over the Reflecting Pool.

Vietnam Veterans Memorial

Jefferson Memorial

The names of all American military personnel who died in the Vietnam War are on the walls of the Vietnam Veterans Memorial. People leave flowers and notes to help remember those killed in the war.

Links to ART

In Memory Of...

The design for the Vietnam Veterans Memorial was the idea of a young woman named Maya Ying Lin. Her design reminds us of all the Americans who died in the Vietnam War.

As a class make a drawing for a memorial to honor someone who made a difference in your community in the past.

The Government at Work

Early in the morning Washington, D.C., is already bustling. Thousands of people are going to work. Many of them work for the government.

Right across from the White House lawn is another interesting place in Washington, D.C.— Lafayette Park. This park is public. *Public* means anyone can go there. On many days you can see people holding large signs. They are expressing their opinions. They want the President and other leaders to know how they feel about certain issues. Thanks to our Constitution, people in our country are free to share their opinions.

You might see some people who live in Lafayette Park. They live there because they have no homes. They are a reminder that our country still has problems to solve.

In Lafayette Park people often make signs that express their opinions (left). Many people work for our government in buildings in Washington, D.C. (above).

WHY IT MATTERS

The President of the United States and Gary Senn have at least two things in common. They both live in Washington, D.C. They are both Americans.

Many different people live and work in our country's capital. There are also interesting things to see and do there. Some places will show you how our government works today. There are also memorials and monuments to remind us of important people and events in our country's past.

In different countries around the world, capital cities are important to people. Capitals are not only centers of government. They are also places where people are proud to learn about their country. In the next lesson you will learn about a capital city in Africa.

The President is one of the elected people who work in Washington, D.C.

Reviewing Facts and Ideas

MAIN IDEAS

- Washington, D.C., is a busy city today. Many people live and work there.

- Memorials and monuments, such as the Washington Monument, remind us of our country's past.

- In Washington, D.C., people work hard trying to make our country a better place for all Americans.

THINK ABOUT IT

1. What is a memorial?

2. **FOCUS** What interesting things can you see and do in our capital today?

3. **THINKING SKILL** _Sort_ different places to visit in Washington, D.C., into two groups: memorials and buildings.

4. **GEOGRAPHY** Look at the map of Washington, D.C., on page 171. In what direction would you travel to go from Washington National Airport to the White House?

Geography Skills

Reading Grid Maps

VOCABULARY

grid map

index

WHY THE SKILL MATTERS

You have read about some places to visit in Washington, D.C. You have already seen a map of our capital city. But sometimes it is hard to find different places on a map. A **grid map** can help. A grid map has a grid, or a set of crisscrossing lines, to help you locate places on the map.

USING THE SKILL

Look at the grid map below. You can see two sets of lines. One set runs across, the other set runs up and down the map. The two sets crisscross to form boxes, or a grid. This grid map shows you the area in our capital called the National Mall. It is an area where many memorials, monuments, museums, and also government buildings are located.

Suppose you want to find the Library of Congress. It has many books. It is the biggest library in the world. First look at the **index**. An index is a list that tells you where to find information. Indexes are usually in alphabetical order.

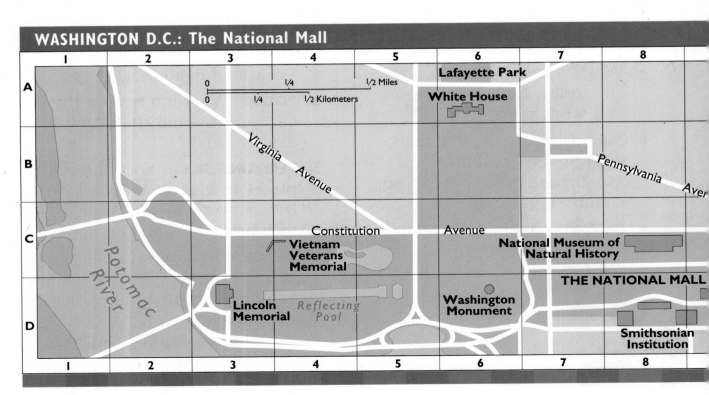

WASHINGTON D.C.: The National Mall

Look in the index for the Library of Congress. Find D13 next to its name. D13 is the letter and number of a box on the grid. Find the letter D along the side of the map. Then move your finger across until it is over number 13. Your finger is now in box D13. Can you find the library in this grid box?

TRYING THE SKILL

Use the Helping Yourself box as you find more places on the grid

Helping yourself

- **Grid maps** have crisscrossing lines that help you find places.
- The **index** lists the grid box in which places appear.
- To find a grid box, point to the grid letter on the side of the map. Slide your finger over to reach the right grid number.

map. To find the Capitol, look in the index. What grid boxes is it in? Find the Capitol on the map. Next look at box D6. What place of interest is located here?

REVIEWING THE SKILL

1. In what box is the Supreme Court located? How did you know?
2. Which buildings can be found in two boxes?
3. Why is it helpful to use a grid map?

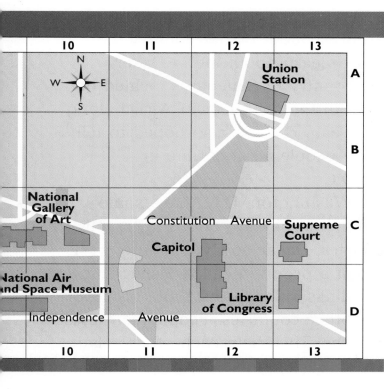

A Capital in Senegal

Focus Activity

READ TO LEARN

What is life like in Dakar, Senegal?

VOCABULARY

- mayor

PLACES

- Dakar, Senegal

Read Aloud

"Dakar is a great place. Everyone smiles and helps each other."

A Capital Connection

These words come from Damian Padilla (puh DEE yuh). He is a 19-year-old ambassador for his school in Washington, D.C. An ambassador is someone who is sent to another country to represent his or her country. Damian went to learn about life in Dakar, Senegal. The country of Senegal is located on the west coast of the continent of Africa along the Atlantic Ocean. Damian also hoped to tell the Senegalese people all about life in Washington, D.C.

Dakar and Washington, D.C., have some things in common. They are both the capitals of their countries. Dakar and Washington, D.C., are also part of a program called Sister Cities. This program links cities in the United States with cities in other countries. People from these cities share ideas. They help each other solve problems.

Governing Senegal

"I had a great time in Senegal," said Damian. "I even met the mayor of Dakar." A mayor is the head of a city government.

Damian learned that the governments of the United States and Senegal have things in common. Senegal's government has a parliament (PAHR luh munt), which is similar to our Congress. It has a supreme court, just as we do. Both countries are also led by a president elected by the people.

Look at the grid map below. In Dakar parliament meets in a building called the Palais (pa LAY) de l'Assemblée (de lah sum BLAY) Nationale (NAH see ah nahl). In which box is it located?

Damian Padilla (left) met the mayor of Dakar (right).

DAKAR, SENEGAL

INDEX

Cathedral...................B4
Chamber of
  Commerce.............B5
French Embassy.........B5
Great Mosque............A3
Independence
  Square....................B5
Palais de
  l'Assemblée
  Nationale.................C4
Palace of Justice.........D5
Presidential Palace.....B5

Great Mosque
Chamber of Commerce
Independence Square
French Embassy
Cathedral
Presidential Palace
ATLANTIC OCEAN
Madeleines Cove
Palais de l'Assemblée Nationale
Bernard Cove
SENEGAL
AFRICA
Palace of Justice

0   .25   .5 Miles
0   .25   .5 Kilometers

MAP WORK

Dakar is the capital of Senegal, a country in western Africa.

1. In which grid box is the Palace of Justice, or Supreme Court building?

2. How would you find Independence Square on the map?

3. How is Dakar similar to Washington, D.C.?

A Colorful Culture

For Damian one interesting thing about Senegal is its culture. "When I arrived, I first noticed that people wore really colorful clothes. Many children dressed as we do in the United States. Older people wore more traditional clothes. The colors of their clothes were so bright. They seemed to enjoy wearing such amazing colors."

There are many different groups of people in Senegal. The largest group is the Wolof (WUL uf). Their language is the most common one in Senegal. Senegal used to be a French colony, so many people also speak French.

Dakar is located on a peninsula that is nearly surrounded by the Atlantic Ocean. The city is one of Africa's main ports. Goods arrive by ship and are sold in markets. The ocean is also important in another way. People love to go to the beach and swim and play in the warm waters all year round.

A Senegalese woman carries goods from the market (left). People exercise on a beach in Dakar (below).

Living in Two Worlds

You have read about life in Dakar. What do you think someone from Senegal might say about living in the United States? Abdoulaye Diouf (ahb DOO lay DOOF) is a student from Senegal. He lives in Washington, D.C. "I was nervous when I first got here. It was my first time in the United States. But now I'm having fun," he said.

Abdoulaye sees some similarities and differences between the two cities. "In Dakar they are building houses more like American houses," he said. "And in Washington, D.C., the buses are faster."

WHY IT MATTERS

Like Washington, D.C., other cities in our country have sister cities around the world. People from these cities learn about and help each other. Both Damian and Abdoulaye learned that, like two sisters, Dakar and Washington, D.C., have a lot in common.

The Senegalese flag flies over the home of the president of Senegal. It is called the Presidential Palace.

Reviewing Facts and Ideas

MAIN IDEAS

- Dakar is the capital of Senegal.
- The Sister Cities program helps people in different cities around the world meet and work together to solve problems.
- The governments of Senegal and the United States have things in common.
- People speak Wolof and French in Senegal. Wolof is the main language.

THINK ABOUT IT

1. How are the governments of Senegal and the United States similar?

2. **FOCUS** What is life like in Dakar, Senegal?

3. **THINKING SKILL** *Compare* and *contrast* Dakar and Washington, D.C.

4. **GEOGRAPHY** Is Senegal in the Northern or Southern Hemisphere?

CHAPTER 7 REVIEW

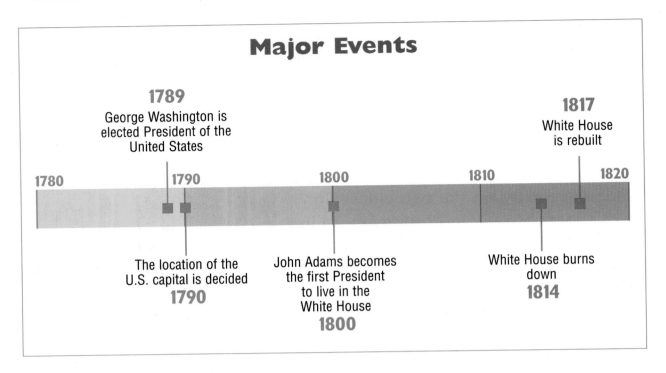

Major Events

1789
George Washington is elected President of the United States

1817
White House is rebuilt

1780   1790   1800   1810   1820

The location of the U.S. capital is decided
1790

John Adams becomes the first President to live in the White House
1800

White House burns down
1814

THINKING ABOUT VOCABULARY

Number a sheet of paper from 1 to 5. Write the word or words that best complete the sentences in the paragraphs below.

mayor   index
Capitol   memorials
grid map

In Senegal a visitor might meet the person in charge of city government. He is called the ___1___. On a visit to Washington, D.C., you can visit the ___2___ building where Congress works. You can also see the ___3___ that honor people and events.

When visiting cities it is useful to use a ___4___. It is made up of a set of crisscrossing lines to help you locate different places to visit. To find information on this map, you would look in the ___5___.

THINKING ABOUT FACTS

1. Why is our capital located where it is?

2. How was Benjamin Banneker important to the building of Washington, D.C.?

3. In what year did President Adams move into the White House?

4. What is the difference between the Capitol and the capital?

5. Why do we build memorials? What are some memorials in Washington, D.C.? What are some memorials in your community?

THINK AND WRITE

WRITING TO PERSUADE

Write a letter about a person from your school or community who you think should be honored. The letter is to persuade local leaders that this person should have a memorial. Include the things this person has done, and the type and location of the memorial you have in mind.

WRITING A JOURNAL ENTRY

Suppose the President has asked you to plan a new capital. Write a journal entry about a day at this new job.

WRITING A TRAVEL BROCHURE

Write a travel brochure about Washington, D.C. List places to visit and describe one.

APPLYING GEOGRAPHY SKILLS

READING GRID MAPS

Answer the following questions using the map on pages 176–177 to practice your skill of reading grid maps.

1. What is a grid map?

2. How is an index helpful in reading a grid map?

3. In which box is the White House located? What building is located in box C8? How did you find the answer to each question?

4. Through which boxes does Virginia Avenue run?

5. When might you use a grid map?

Summing Up the Chapter

Review the chapter before completing a copy of the main idea map below. Fill in at least one fact under every heading. Then write a paragraph explaining the development of Washington, D.C.

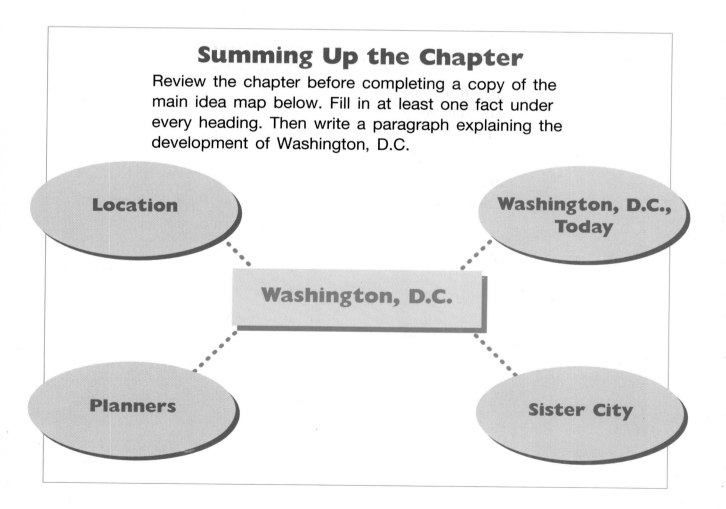

Location

Washington, D.C., Today

Washington, D.C.

Planners

Sister City

Citizens Make Communities Work

THINKING ABOUT GEOGRAPHY AND CITIZENSHIP

Citizens work together to make their communities better places. One way they do this is through government. Large or small, each community and state across our country has a government. In Chapter 8 you will learn what governments do. You will also see other ways people help each other and their communities.

Larchmont, New York

Frankfort, Kentucky

Los Angeles, California

Local government makes decisions about schools in communities like Larchmont, New York.

Government taxes pay for highways like this one in Los Angeles, California.

State government in Kentucky meets in the State Capitol.

185

Focus Activity

READ TO LEARN

Why do communities have governments?

VOCABULARY

- governor
- local government
- city council
- town meeting

PLACES

- Shapleigh, Maine
- New England

Community Government

Read Aloud

These are some signs you might see in your community. Have you ever thought about where they come from? Who decides where to put the signs? Who decides on the laws?

State and Local Governments

In the last chapter you read about our country's government. But the country's government does not make all of the laws.

Every state in our country has its own government. At the head of each state's government is the governor. A governor is elected by the people of the state. The governor and other state leaders make laws for the state. The state government is responsible for such things as fixing state highways and cleaning state parks.

A community can make its own laws too. Local government is the government in each city or community. Many local governments are led by a mayor. The mayor chooses people to help run the community. Many cities also have a city council. A city council is a group of elected people who make the laws for the city.

Welcome to Shapleigh

Potholes, parking, and parks. What do these three things have in common? They are all things a local government takes care of. Does the community want potholes in the local roads to be paved over? If so, how will they be paid for? Are streets too crowded? How can more parking spaces be built? Local governments are responsible for these things. And, as a group of students in Shapleigh (SHAP lee), Maine, found out, local government can also help to build a park.

Look at the map on this page. Shapleigh is a community in the northeast part of our country known as New England. Since colonial times, many communities in this area have held town meetings. Town meetings are a type of local government. They are usually held once a year. People come to a town meeting to decide on the laws and rules that are important to their community. Everyone in the community can come and have a say in what happens. At the end of the town meeting, people vote.

Every year there is a town meeting in Shapleigh, Maine. Community members meet in Town Hall to discuss important issues.

At the Town Meeting

All around New England, early March is an exciting time. The town meetings are about to be held. There will be many discussions and many compromises.

Mr. Jim Brown teaches sixth graders in Shapleigh. A few years ago his students decided that some land in Shapleigh was going to waste. When the yearly town meeting was about to happen, Mr. Brown's students decided to take action. They studied and planned. Then they convinced people at the town meeting that they could build a park on the land. And the result, a beautiful park, has improved their community!

With the help of students and others, a new park was built in Shapleigh.

Students Speak Up

Taking part in the town meeting was important for Mr. Brown's students. "I was surprised," said Adam Pierce. "We made a difference in how people thought about the park in Shapleigh. We changed their opinions."

"It felt good that Shapleigh was getting something out of our hard work," said Wendy Wehmeyer. "I knew it would be nice to have a park for people to enjoy the trees and flowers." A vote by citizens at the town meeting showed that they agreed with Mr. Brown's students.

WHY IT MATTERS

Your community and state have their own governments. They decide on many things that matter to you, like your schools, libraries, parks, streets, and your safety.

You are not old enough to vote yet. Still, you can take part in your government. The next lesson shows you how. You will also see how citizens can improve their communities.

Wendy Wehmeyer and Adam Pierce helped build the new park.

✓// Reviewing Facts and Ideas

MAIN IDEAS

- The state government makes state laws. A governor is the head of each state government.

- Many local governments have a city council to make laws. Mayors are the heads of many local governments.

- Some communities have town meetings where people vote on important issues.

- Everyone can get involved in community decisions.

THINK ABOUT IT

1. What is a town meeting?
2. **FOCUS** Why do communities have governments?
3. **THINKING SKILL** _Compare_ and _contrast_ local government with state government.
4. **WRITE** Suppose you are going to a town meeting. Write a speech with your classmates about something you would like to tell your community's leaders.

Using the Library

VOCABULARY

research   nonfiction
reference   fiction
encyclopedia   author
guide word

WHY THE SKILL MATTERS

The students of Shapleigh wanted to learn about gardening before they planted grass and trees in their park. To find the information they wanted, they did research. To research is to look for information. The library is often a good place to do research.

USING THE SKILL

At the library there are books of all kinds. Many libraries also have internet and CD-ROM technology. If you need help, a librarian can show you how to use these library resources.

The Shapleigh students wanted to find information about gardening. If you were going to help them, where would you look?

The first place you might go is the reference section. Reference books have many facts in them. You can look things up, but you usually cannot take reference books home.

One useful reference is the encyclopedia. Encyclopedias are books or sets of books with facts about people, places, things, and events. If you find encyclopedias on CD-ROM, you can view information on a computer screen.

The topics in an encyclopedia are listed in alphabetical order. If you wanted information on gardening, where would you look? You might use the encyclopedia with the letter G on the cover. Encyclopedias also have guide words on the top of each page. Guide words tell the first subject and the last subject that appear on a page.

After reading about gardening in an encyclopedia, you might decide to learn more about planting trees and flowers. Where could you go in the library to do more research?

Next you could go to the nonfiction section. Nonfiction books are about real people, places, and events. They are grouped by topics such as environment, history, and science. Suppose the librarian suggests a book called *My Garden Companion* by Jamie Jobb. It is a nonfiction book on growing different kinds of plants. To find it you would look at the environmental books in the nonfiction section of the library.

While you are at the library, you might go to the fiction section. Books of fiction are made-up stories of people, places, and events.

Fiction books are grouped on the shelves in alphabetical order by the last name of the author. The author is the person who wrote the book.

TRYING THE SKILL

Suppose you want to research your own community and its government. Where would you begin your research? Use the Helping Yourself box to guide you in using the library.

Which encyclopedia should you use to research your state? Where

would you look in the library for a book about your community?

REVIEWING THE SKILL

1. Where would you go in your community if you needed to do research? Why?

2. What are some of the resources that are in the library? Which ones have you used before?

3. How are guide words helpful in finding information on a page?

4. What is a fiction book? How are fiction books organized on shelves in the library?

Citizens in Action

Read Aloud

"I pledge allegiance to the flag of the United States of America and to the Republic for which it stands, one Nation under God, indivisible, with liberty and justice for all."

Focus Activity

READ TO LEARN

What can people do to be good citizens?

VOCABULARY

• Pledge of Allegiance

PLACES

• Tampa, Florida
• Portland, Oregon
• Oakland, California

Being a Good Citizen

What do these words mean? You have probably heard and said the Pledge of Allegiance many times. When you "pledge allegiance," you are promising to be loyal. The flag is one of the most important symbols of our country. When you promise to be loyal to the flag, you are really promising to be loyal to your country.

One of the most important things you can do for your country is to be a good citizen. Being a good citizen may mean taking part in your government. What else does being a good citizen mean to you? In this lesson we will see some of the many ways you can be a good citizen in your community and your country.

Citizens Get Involved

In this book you have read about many communities. All communities have one thing in common. They work best when people work together and help each other.

When you pick up litter, you are helping your community. When you help someone cross the street, you are helping your community. There are many ways to help people.

Alberta Reed lives in Tampa, Florida. She helps people by being a volunteer for a group called Meals on Wheels. Volunteers for Meals on Wheels deliver meals to people who cannot leave their homes.

Once a week Alberta Reed drives to the Meals on Wheels center. She picks up meals and delivers them to people in their homes. "These people cannot go out and shop or cook," she says. "Sometimes the meal I bring them is the only meal they get that day. They really just like seeing someone.
I always smile and talk with them."

One way you can help your community is by picking up litter (below). Alberta Reed (top) and other volunteers deliver meals to people in their communities.

Free Bicycles

Good citizens work together to improve their community. In Portland, Oregon, Joe Keating had a great idea on how to be a good citizen and improve community life.

Mr. Keating leads a group called the United Community Action Network. He decided to put free bicycles on the streets of Portland. A person could use a bicycle and then leave it at the end of the trip. Someone else who came along could use it next!

"We wanted to make Portland more livable and to protect the environment," he said. "The bikes worked perfectly for both goals."

Look at the special license plates Mr. Keating and others put on the backs of the bicycles. What do these license plates tell us about being a responsible citizen in the community of Portland?

Free community bicycles are available for use by people on main streets in Portland, Oregon.

FREE COMMUNITY BIKE

Please return to a main street for others to reuse.

USE AT YOUR OWN RISK.
Repair or pickup call
331-0526
U.C.A.N.

Becoming a Leader

Some good citizens also get involved in government. John Russo lives in Oakland, California. A few years ago he decided he wanted to be elected as a member of the City Council. He worked to tell people his ideas about improving community life in Oakland. He knocked on people's doors. He talked to anyone who would listen to his ideas about making Oakland a better place to live.

Since he was elected, Councilman Russo has been making laws to help find housing for people who don't have homes. He's also trying to get other citizens to do volunteer work.

Students can be active in government too. They can discuss issues with government leaders. "I talk to children all the time," said Councilman Russo. "Even though they can't vote, children are important citizens. They will be the leaders in the future!"

Links to
MATHEMATICS

And the Winner Is . . .

Many people do not vote. They do not think their vote makes a difference. But many elections have been decided by just a few votes.

Suppose you wanted to run for president of your class. One other person is running against you. How many votes would you need to win the election?

Councilman John Russo talks with children in Oakland, California.

195

WHY IT MATTERS

The next time you pledge allegiance or sing a song like "America," think about what it means to be a good citizen. One important thing makes our country and our communities strong: people working together to help each other.

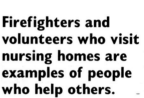

Firefighters and volunteers who visit nursing homes are examples of people who help others.

✓ Reviewing Facts and Ideas

MAIN IDEAS

- There are many ways to be a good citizen.
- Volunteering to help others is one important part of citizenship.
- Students can be good citizens by talking and writing to their leaders about things that are important to their community.
- Voting is an important part of citizenship.

THINK ABOUT IT

1. Why do communities need good citizens?

2. **FOCUS** What can people do to be good citizens?

3. **THINKING SKILL** Suppose there are two people running for mayor of your town. How would you _decide_ for whom to vote?

4. **WRITE** Think of a project you would like to start in your community. Make a sign asking others to help you with your project.

CITIZENSHIP
VIEWPOINTS

Citizens of the United States vote in booths like this one.

Should voting be required?

United States citizens 18 years or older have the right to vote. In most states voters must also register before their first election and any time they move. To register means giving proof of your citizenship and address.

Although United States citizens have the right to vote, many don't use this right. In our country only five out of ten people vote.

Some people suggest that citizens should be made to vote. Suzanne Hee's viewpoint on the next page expresses this idea. Others like Debbie Macon believe that it is best not to vote if you are not informed. Still others, like Joel Rosch, say that voting should be made easier. If Election Day was a national holiday, for example, people would find it easier to vote.

Consider the viewpoints at right, then answer the questions that follow.

Three DIFFERENT Viewpoints

1 SUZANNE HEE
Researcher, Santa Monica, California
Excerpt from Interview, 1997

I think voting should be required. Voting should be what each citizen gives back to society for all that he or she receives from society. I think it is very important for people to know about the issues that affect them and have a say on those issues. I don't think people realize that their votes count.

"...voting should be required."

2 DEBBIE MACON
Community Leader, West Bloomfield, Michigan
Excerpt from Interview, 1997

I believe that every citizen should be encouraged to vote, but not required. In our country freedom of choice is as important as the right to vote. Many times people don't vote because they feel they don't have enough information. If people have enough information, they will vote on their own without forcing them.

"...freedom of choice..."

3 JOEL ROSCH
Teacher, Raleigh, North Carolina
Excerpt from Interview, 1997

Forcing people to vote is a good idea, but there have to be certain conditions. People should not have to take time off from their jobs. Instead, voting should take place when people have time off. Democracy involves not only rights but responsibilities. If we are going to live in a democracy, going out to vote is a small price to pay.

"...not only rights but responsibilities."

BUILDING CITIZENSHIP

1. What is the viewpoint of each person?
2. How are they alike? In what ways are they different?
3. What other opinions might people have on this issue?

SHARING VIEWPOINTS

Discuss what you agree or disagree with in these and other viewpoints. Be sure to give reasons to support your opinions. Then as a class try to write one statement about which you can all agree.

CHAPTER 8 REVIEW

THINKING ABOUT VOCABULARY

On a sheet of paper write the word or term from the list below that matches the statement.

city council Pledge of Allegiance
governor   town meeting
local government

1. We say this when we salute the flag.
2. This type of local government is common in New England.
3. Town meetings are an example of this type of government.
4. This group works with the mayor to make community laws.
5. This person is the elected head of our state government.

THINKING ABOUT FACTS

1. What is the role of the state government?
2. What type of local government does your community have? Who heads your local government?
3. Who are some of the leaders in a local government?
4. Why is the Pledge of Allegiance important?
5. Why do you think people get involved in their local government?

THINK AND WRITE

WRITING A VOLUNTEER LISTING

Think of ways you and your classmates could help others. Write a list on posterboard to display in your classroom. Your list could include ways to help people in class, in school, or in the community. For example, you and your classmates could help improve the school grounds by picking up litter.

WRITING ABOUT A MEETING

When town meetings are held, someone writes a record of what happened. Suppose you are writing a record of a class meeting about classroom rules. Your record must note who was at the meeting, what was discussed, and any decisions that were made.

WRITING A JINGLE

Suppose you work for your state or local government. Your job is to create a jingle, or a saying set to music, that will get people to vote. Write a jingle about the importance of voting, or about voting and citizenship.

APPLYING STUDY SKILLS

USING THE LIBRARY

Answer the following questions to review your skill of using the library.

1. What type of research materials can you find in the library?

2. What is the difference between nonfiction and fiction books? Give an example of each.

3. Where would you look to find out about the history of voting in the United States?

4. How would you go about finding a fiction book by Mark Twain?

5. Why do you think it is important to divide the library into fiction, nonfiction, and reference sections?

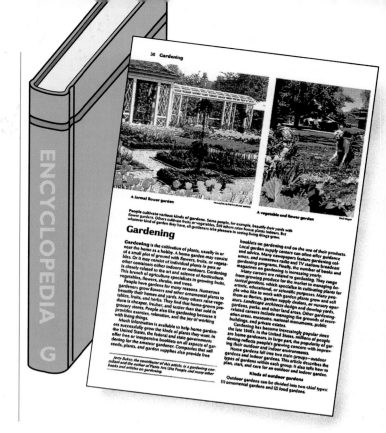

Summing Up the Chapter

Review the chapter before completing a copy of the main idea pyramid below. Read the chapter theme at the top and the main ideas in the middle of the pyramid. Fill in the bottom with details that support each main idea. Then answer the following question: Why are good citizens important to a community?

Good citizens take part in their government.

Communities and states have their own government.

Being a good citizen is important to your community and country.

UNIT 3 REVIEW

THINKING ABOUT VOCABULARY

Number a sheet of paper from 1 to 10. Read the definition of each underlined word or words. Write **T** if the definition is true and **F** if it is false. If the definition is false, write a sentence that correctly defines the underlined word or words.

1. <u>Town meetings</u> are a type of local government.

2. A <u>city council</u> is a group of people who are hired to give advice to local governments.

3. The <u>Constitution</u> is a statement about the laws and plans for how our government works.

4. The <u>author</u> is the head of city government.

5. The <u>Declaration of Independence</u> is a statement about why the colonies should be free.

6. A <u>memorial</u> honors an important person or event.

7. To <u>elect</u> is to choose by voting.

8. A <u>tax</u> is money you are paid by the government.

9. A <u>compromise</u> is the constitutional way we run the Supreme Court.

10. The <u>Bill of Rights</u> is a list of our country's most important rights.

THINK AND WRITE ◄ ▭

WRITING ABOUT ART

Describe the memorials and monuments in the Infographic on pages 172–173.

WRITING A PROFILE

Choose one important person from this unit. Write a paragraph describing this person.

WRITING A POEM

Write a short poem or song about our country and the importance of being loyal.

BUILDING SKILLS

1. **Compare and Contrast** What is the first step in comparing and contrasting two things?

2. **Compare and Contrast** Look at the pictures of George Washington on page 155 and Thomas Jefferson on page 160. How are they alike? How are they different?

3. **Grid Map** How does a grid map work?

4. **Grid Map** Look at the grid map on pages 176–177. Where is the Reflecting Pool?

5. **Using the Library** How could you research more information about the memorials in Washington, D.C.?

LOCAL *connection*

What monuments are located in your community to honor local and national heroes? How can you find out about the history of these monuments? Make your own monument or sculpture by honoring a hero or a legend in your community. Work with other students to display your work.

READING ON YOUR OWN

Here are some books you might find at the library to help you learn more.

DEAR BENJAMIN BANNEKER
by Andrea Davis Pinkney
A biography of the man who helped plan the city of Washington, D.C.

A MORE PERFECT UNION:
THE STORY OF OUR CONSTITUTION
by Betsy and Giulio Maestro
Read this colorful story of how the Constitution was drafted.

THE STORY OF THE WHITE HOUSE
by Kate Waters
Tour the White House and learn what it was like over two hundred years ago.

UNIT REVIEW PROJECT

Make a Citizenship Mobile

1. In a group, make a list of what it means to be a good citizen.
2. Have each group member draw and cut out a shape on a piece of colored paper.
3. On each shape, write one thing that a good citizen does.
4. Decorate your shapes with different colors and glitter.
5. Punch a hole in the top of each shape. Attach each shape to a piece of string.
6. Wrap colorful pipe cleaners around a wire hanger. Attach the strings to the hanger.

Communities on the Move

Why Does it Matter?

Our country has a history of movement and change. From colonists long ago to people today, the United States has always been a country on the move. Whether they have come from communities within our country or from far away, people on the move have helped make our country a special place. Another important part of our country's history is change. As you will see, the changing technology of transportation and communication has helped our country become what it is today: a land of many people and many exciting ideas.

FIND OUT MORE!
Visit our website:
www.mhschool.com

*inter*NET
CONNECTION

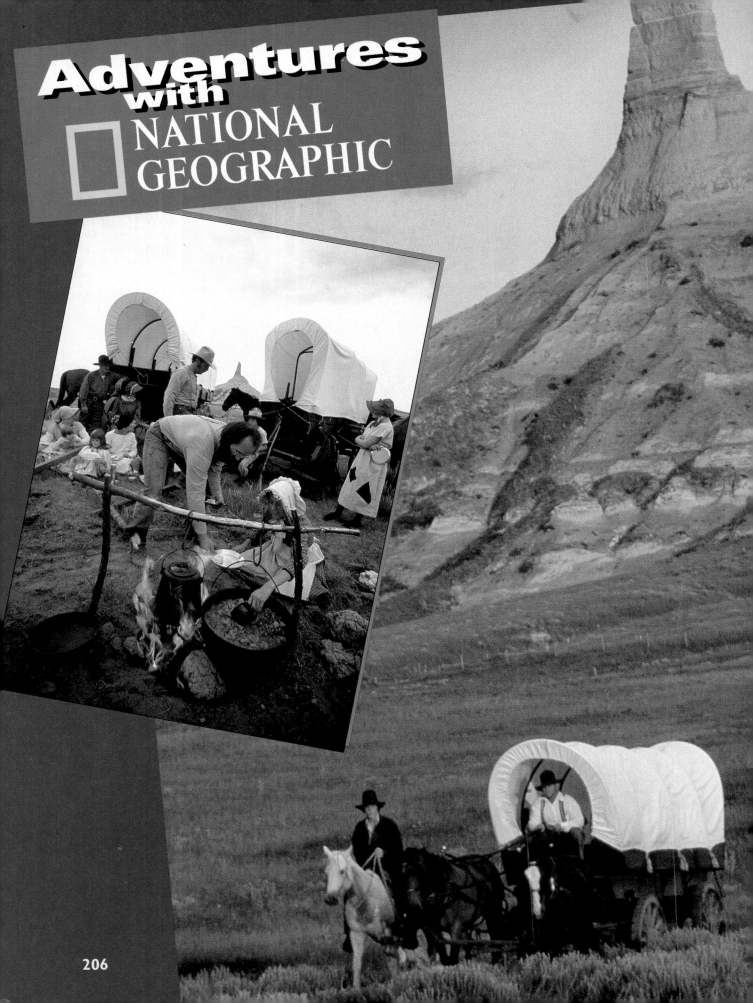

Adventures with
NATIONAL GEOGRAPHIC

ON THE OREGON TRAIL

Your wagon bumps along. So many other wagons have come this way, there are ruts carved into the ground! Sometimes you ride; sometimes you walk. When it gets dark, you help light a fire to cook supper. Is it 1841, or today? It's hard to tell. Modern kids who take part in re-creating the 2,000-mile wagon trip on the Oregon Trail share an experience that thousands of settlers had as they headed west over 100 years ago. They find out what it's like to travel through prairie and desert without a motel in sight.

GEO JOURNAL

Would you like to travel on the Oregon Trail today? Why or why not?

Building New Lives

THINKING ABOUT
GEOGRAPHY AND HISTORY

Long ago, people traveled over the oceans to start new communities in the United States. They also moved within our country to start new communities. This is still true today. This time line and map show how our history is filled with people on the move throughout our country.

In Chapter 9 you will learn how our country has grown and changed. You will also meet some of the many people who helped make the United States a special country.

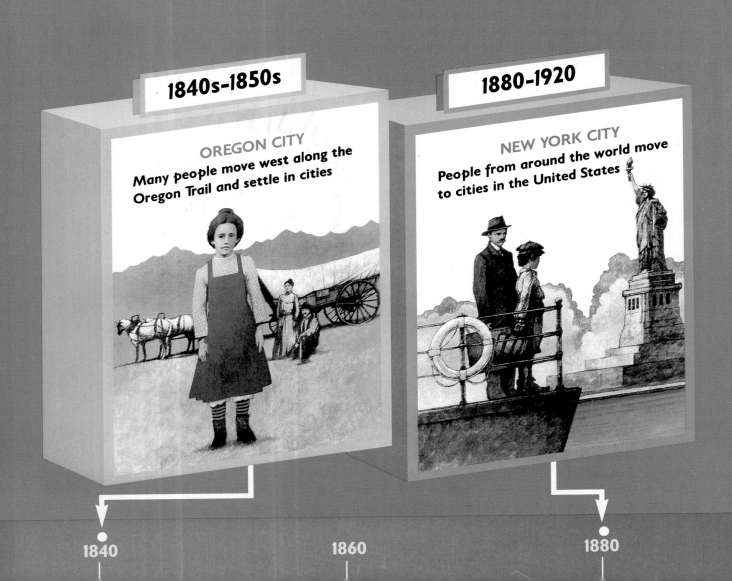

1840s–1850s

OREGON CITY

Many people move west along the Oregon Trail and settle in cities

1880–1920

NEW YORK CITY

People from around the world move to cities in the United States

1840   1860   1880

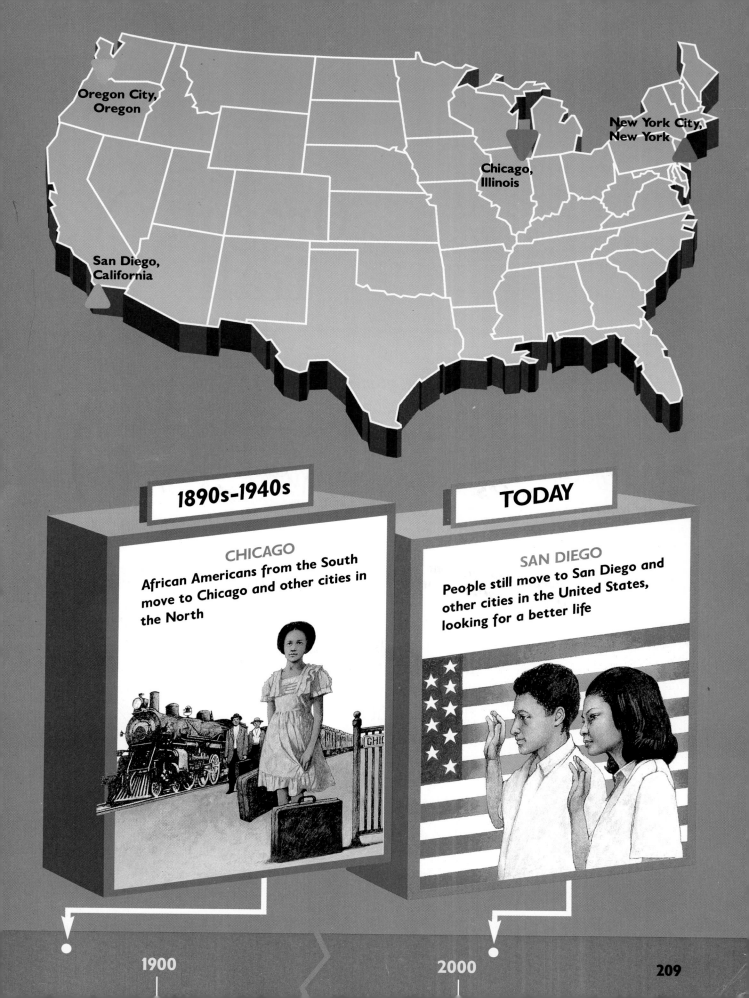

Oregon City,
Oregon

Chicago,
Illinois

New York City,
New York

San Diego,
California

1890s–1940s

CHICAGO
African Americans from the South move to Chicago and other cities in the North

TODAY

SAN DIEGO
People still move to San Diego and other cities in the United States, looking for a better life

1900

2000

The Oregon Trail

Focus Activity

Read Aloud

"The prairie, oh, the broad, the beautiful, the bounding [hilly], rolling prairie! Imagine the ocean, when the waves are rolling mountains high, becoming solid and covered with beautiful green grass and you have some faint idea of it."

Leaving Home

These words were written in 1853 by a young woman named Rebecca Ketchum. She was describing the prairie in the middle of the United States. A prairie is flat or rolling land covered with tall grasses. Many Native American groups lived west of the Mississippi River on these prairie lands.

People in the East heard that these areas had rich land for farming. In the 1840s and 1850s, many people left their homes to move west. They became pioneers. Pioneers are people who are among the first to explore and settle an area not known to them. Their adventures are part of our country's history.

Moving West

The map on this page shows some of the routes that thousands of pioneers used to move west. As you can see, the Oregon Trail was one of these routes. Pioneers traveled together in groups of wagons called wagon trains. Why do you think they traveled in groups?

Many wagon trains left from Independence, Missouri. This community had shops that sold supplies and animals for the long journey west.

Many pioneers began their trip west from Independence, Missouri.

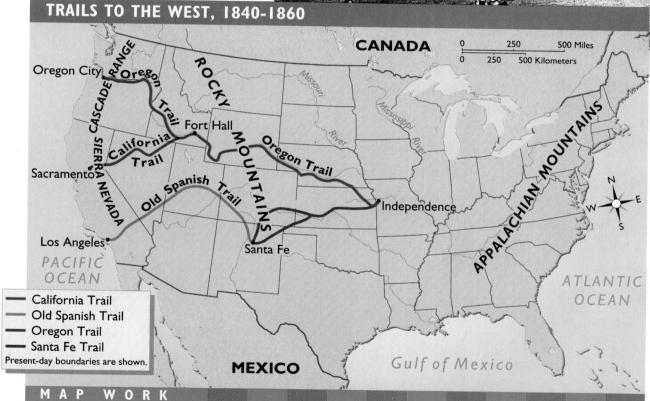

TRAILS TO THE WEST, 1840-1860

Legend:
- California Trail
- Old Spanish Trail
- Oregon Trail
- Santa Fe Trail

Present-day boundaries are shown.

Map labels: CANADA, 0 250 500 Miles, 0 250 500 Kilometers, Oregon City, CASCADE RANGE, Oregon Trail, ROCKY MOUNTAINS, Missouri, Mississippi River, River, APPALACHIAN MOUNTAINS, Fort Hall, California Trail, Oregon Trail, Sacramento, SIERRA NEVADA, Old Spanish Trail, Independence, Los Angeles, PACIFIC OCEAN, Santa Fe, ATLANTIC OCEAN, MEXICO, Gulf of Mexico, N E W S

MAP WORK

Pioneers could take several different trails to travel west.

1. Which is the longest trail? How long is the California Trail?

2. At what place do the Santa Fe Trail and Old Spanish Trail meet?

3. Where might a trip on the Oregon Trail be difficult? Why?

A World of Wagons

The wagon trains were a useful way to make the long, difficult journey. The 2,000-mile trip took over five months. The wagons were pulled by oxen, mules, and horses. They crossed rivers and mountains. They ran into snow, rain, and mud. Many pioneers got sick and died along the way.

At night the wagons were set up front-to-end in a big circle. Children would play together in the middle of the circle. People would meet to discuss their problems. Perhaps someone had a broken wagon wheel, another's mule was sick, another was out of flour. Everyone helped each other. Even children had responsibilities. They helped cook and wash dishes. They milked the cows and helped tie up the animals at night. Sometimes children had school lessons from parents or older brothers and sisters.

Settling in for the night often meant a hot meal and rest before the next day's difficult journey.

Corcoran Gallery of Art

Life on the Trail

Life on the trail was oftentimes uncertain. Native Americans lived in many of the areas along the way. In fact, the Oregon Trail was not made by the pioneers. It went along a path that had been used years before by Native Americans. Sometimes Native Americans gave settlers advice about traveling along the trail. But sometimes the two groups fought with each other over the land.

One way we know about the pioneers is from the diaries they kept. A diary is a written record of what someone has done or thought each day. Read the following words from a diary written by a 14-year-old girl named Sallie Hester. How was a day on the Oregon Trail different from one of your days?

Pioneers carved their names and dates of passage on big rocks to record their journey for others.

PRIMARY SOURCE

Diary written by Sallie Hester, May 21, 1849.

Camped on the beautiful Blue River with plenty of wood and water and good grazing for our cattle. Our family all in good health. We had two deaths in our train within the past week of **cholera** (KAHL ur uh). When we camp at night, we form a **corral** with our wagons. We sleep in our wagons on feather beds. We live on bacon, ham, rice, dried fruits, molasses, packed butter, bread, coffee. Occasionally some of the men kill an antelope and then we have a feast; and sometimes we have fish on Sunday.

cholera: disease of the intestines
corral: fenced-in area for animals

New Communities

After many months and thousands of miles, most of the pioneers reached Oregon. Some of them had lost family and friends along the way. One traveler wrote, "Our journey across the Plains was a long and hard one. We lost everything but our lives."

Most pioneers were planning to settle around Oregon City, Oregon. Many new cities were starting up. Oregon City was the largest. Some people were planning to farm the rich land. Others were planning to open up shops. Some were looking for gold in Oregon and California. Once there, though, life was not easy. Many people arrived with no money and few belongings. They were starting new lives.

Newly arrived pioneers built farms and houses (top). Communities like Oregon City grew quickly (bottom).

The Granger Collection

Our Country Grows

In 1869 a railroad was built across the country. Soon railroads replaced the Oregon Trail. Today people still move to different parts of the country looking to start new lives. But the ways people travel have certainly changed! How do people travel between communities in our country today?

WHY IT MATTERS

Earlier in this book you read that English settlers came to Jamestown hoping to build new communities in our country. In the same way, the pioneers who traveled west along the Oregon Trail dreamed of building better lives.

The history of our country is filled with stories of people moving to new communities. As you read the next lesson, think about what it would be like to come to a new community, in a new land, to build a better life.

Trails were filled with ruts and holes, which often damaged wagon wheels.

✓// Reviewing Facts and Ideas

MAIN IDEAS

- In the 1840s and 1850s many pioneers traveled west on the Oregon Trail.

- The route over the prairie and mountains was difficult.

- Stories of people moving to new communities are part of our country's history.

THINK ABOUT IT

1. What was the Oregon Trail?

2. **FOCUS** What was it like to travel west on the Oregon Trail?

3. **THINKING SKILL** Can you _predict_ what responsibilities you might have had on a wagon train? In what ways are they like yours today?

4. **WRITE** Write a diary entry describing a day you spent traveling with your family.

Classifying

VOCABULARY
classifying

WHY THE SKILL MATTERS

Heading west on the Oregon Trail required careful planning. Travel conditions were very difficult. Pioneers had to plan what to carry with them in their wagons. If a wagon was too heavy to pull, the oxen would get tired and sick. On the other hand, the pioneers were going on a long journey across the country. There were no repair shops or stores with supplies along the way. Pioneers had to bring the things they needed for the trip and for the new homes and farms they were going to build.

One skill that can help in making choices like these is **classifying**. Classifying is grouping similar things together. Classifying helps us to understand things better.

USING THE SKILL

Look at the pictures on the next page. They show some of the different things people wanted to bring with them on the Oregon Trail.

Suppose you were traveling west in the 1840s. Not everything shown in the picture can fit in your wagon. To plan what to take, you could classify the items into things that you will surely need and things that could be given up.

First select an item that you think is necessary. Supplies of food, such as flour and sugar, are necessary. Find other items that are also needed, such as the hammer and nails for repairs. What items are not needed? A favorite old piece of furniture is not absolutely necessary. Could the doll stay behind if there were no room? Continue to sort the items into two groups, those that would be needed and those that would not.

TRYING THE SKILL

There is more than one way to classify the items shown in the picture. Suppose your goal is to find items for mending and making clothes. Which items are those? Which items are useful for cooking? Which items would help a child enjoy a long trip?

Use the Helping Yourself box to guide you in classifying.

REVIEWING THE SKILL

1. What is classifying?
2. Look through the different items in your desk or schoolbag. What can you do to classify these items into groups?
3. Why do you think it is helpful to classify things?

Coming to America

Focus Activity

READ TO LEARN

Why did immigrants come to America?

VOCABULARY

- immigrant
- oral history

PLACES

- New York City
- Ellis Island

Read Aloud

"That was the first time I saw the Statue of Liberty, when I was standing on deck. And I had a hat on, and the wind came along and took my hat off. I said to my mother in Italian, 'Mama, there goes my hat!' And I said to her, 'Look at the lady, the lady over there!'"

Journey by Sea

These are the words of Joseph Allatin (a lah TEEN). The "lady" he saw was the Statue of Liberty. Joseph was six years old. His family had left Italy in 1894. The family sailed across the Atlantic Ocean to make new lives in the United States. The Statue of Liberty is in the harbor of New York City. It brought great joy to people like Joseph. It meant that they had arrived in the United States.

The Statue of Liberty is still a symbol that our country welcomes many immigrants. An immigrant is someone who comes to live in a new country. Like the pioneers who moved west in the 1840s and 1850s, immigrants were seeking a new life. During the early 1900s, they came to the United States looking for freedom. They also came because they could not find good jobs in their own country.

Arriving in New York

Once the ships carrying immigrants arrived in New York, they sailed past the Statue of Liberty to Ellis Island. Ellis Island was an immigration center. Officers there decided if people could stay in the United States. Immigrants who were sick might be forced to return to their country.

Many Americans today had a relative who came through Ellis Island. Lauren Buchter (BUHK ter) is 11 years old. Her great-grandfather came from Austria in 1902. He went through Ellis Island and then lived in New York City. Lauren's great-grandmother followed in 1916.

Lauren lives in New York City today. She never knew her great-grandparents. But she likes to learn about her past by talking to her grandfather, Jerry Selinfreund (SE lihn froynd). He was born a few years after his parents came to New York City.

When she asks her grandfather questions, Lauren is listening to oral history. Oral history is telling people what life was like in the past.

Children of all ages arrived with their families at Ellis Island (top). Lauren Buchter learns about the past from her grandfather (below). Here he is as a young boy long ago (left).

The Lower East Side

Like many other immigrants, Lauren's great-grandparents went to live on New York City's Lower East Side. It was very crowded. Most people lived in small, run-down apartment buildings called tenements.

"Even though living conditions were tough, my mother did not mind," said Mr. Selinfreund. "She lived in a tenement. She had to walk up to the fifth floor."

Immigrants came from many countries. They came for different reasons. Lauren's great-grandparents came for religious freedom.

Immigrants on the Lower East Side had different cultures. They also spoke many different languages. Having their children learn English was important. "My mother spoke many languages," Mr. Selinfreund said. "But none of them was English. That was one of the hardest parts. But she was so happy to be in the United States."

The Lower East Side was a community alive with very crowded apartments and busy streets.

Work and Play

Most immigrants worked very hard. Often they did several jobs to make a living. "My father was a glazier *(window-maker)* and a religious leader," said Mr. Selinfreund. "He also taught dancing. He even drove a taxi and became a button-maker."

Many women and children worked, too. Some worked in factories. Children sold pencils, candy, or newspapers on the streets. But life was not all work for children. The streets were also their playgrounds. They played tag and stickball. Instead of a baseball bat, they used a broomstick. Many neighbors came out to play or watch. But everything stopped when the soda man came by selling cold sodas!

Life was both difficult and fun. Children often worked to earn money to help their families (top). But there was also time to play street games like stickball (bottom).

A Country of Immigrants

The early 1900s was a time when many immigrants came to our country. They came from many different places around the world. The graph on this page shows you how many people came during this time period. Most came through New York. Others arrived in such cities as Boston and San Francisco.

Immigrants came from many different cultures. The one thing they had in common was hope—hope that life in the United States would be better.

Each group of immigrants has brought many important things to our country. They brought different languages, religions, and other parts of culture. They have made our country rich and strong.

Immigrants arrived with suitcases filled with personal items. Their few belongings were all they had to start new lives.

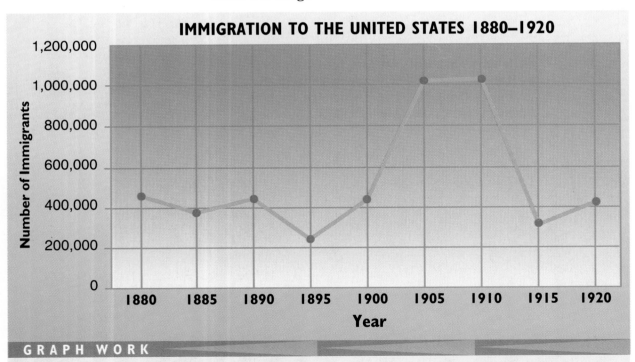

IMMIGRATION TO THE UNITED STATES 1880–1920

Number of Immigrants (y-axis): 0, 200,000, 400,000, 600,000, 800,000, 1,000,000, 1,200,000

Year (x-axis): 1880, 1885, 1890, 1895, 1900, 1905, 1910, 1915, 1920

GRAPH WORK

The United States grew as more and more immigrants came each year.

1. About how many immigrants came to the United States in 1905? About how many came in 1920?

2. What happened to the number of immigrants who came between 1900 and 1905?

3. What can you say about the pattern of immigration between 1880 and 1920?

Source: **U.S. Census Bureau**

Oral History

When Lauren is older, she may tell her children about how she lived in New York too. Then she will continue her family's oral history. "It's fun to hear my family stories," said Lauren. "It helps explain who I am today."

Do you have older people in your family or community? Ask them about their lives. Then you, too, will be learning from oral history.

WHY IT MATTERS

In the early 1900s, millions of new people came to the United States. They formed new communities. But immigration was not new for our country. Immigrants have been coming to our country for hundreds of years.

Today people still move here from other countries. People here also move from place to place. There is one thing you can say about our country—it is always changing!

Visitors to Ellis Island can learn about immigration and our country's history.

✓// Reviewing Facts and Ideas

MAIN IDEAS

- In the early 1900s, millions of immigrants came to the United States. Life was often difficult for the new immigrants.

- Immigrants came from many different countries.

- Many immigrants settled in New York's Lower East Side. Others settled in communities throughout the country.

- One way we learn about the past is through oral history.

THINK ABOUT IT

1. Why was the Statue of Liberty important for immigrants?

2. **FOCUS** Why did immigrants come to America?

3. **THINKING SKILL** *Classify* the years shown on the graph on page 222 into two groups. Group 1 is when over one million people immigrated. Group 2 is when under one million people immigrated. What have you learned?

4. **WRITE** Write a short poem about the Statue of Liberty.

Moving to Northern Cities

Focus Activity

Read Aloud

"The Great Migration is part of my life. I grew up knowing about people on the move. . . . There was always talk in my house of other families arriving from the South."

People on the Move

These are the words of an artist named Jacob Lawrence. He is describing a great journey. It was made by many African Americans in the early 1900s. During this time many African Americans left their homes in the southern part of the United States. They hoped to build new lives in northern cities.

In the last lesson you read about people moving from other countries to the United States. That type of movement, as you know, is called immigration. Another type of movement is called migration. Migration is the movement of people from one part of a country or area to another.

In this lesson you will learn more about Jacob Lawrence. You will also learn about the Great Migration, the movement north of many African Americans.

The Civil War

Since colonial times most African Americans had been living as slaves. They were forced to work for the people who owned them. They were not allowed to read and write. They were not free people.

Look at the map below. From 1861 to 1865 the Northern and Southern parts of the United States went to war against each other.

This war was called the Civil War. People in the South wanted to be separate from the North. People in the North wanted both sides to stay together as one country. During the war President Abraham Lincoln wanted to end slavery. Finally, in 1865, the war ended. Slavery was over. African Americans were free.

Abraham Lincoln said, "slavery must die that the nation might live."

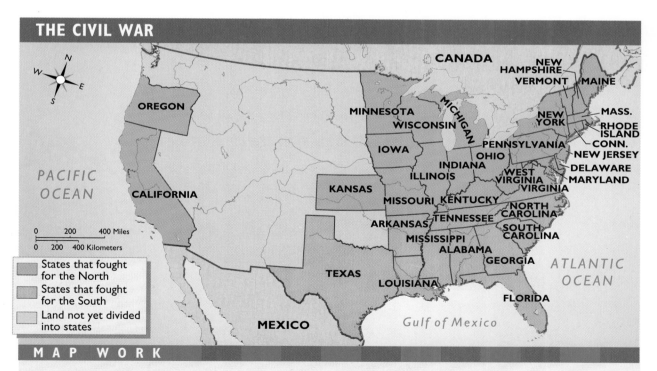

THE CIVIL WAR

States that fought for the North
States that fought for the South
Land not yet divided into states

MAP WORK

About 620,000 soldiers died during the Civil War.

1. Locate California on the map. For which side did people in California fight?

2. How many states fought for the South?

3. Can you name any states today that did not exist during the Civil War?

225

Difficult Lives

Although they were free, African Americans living in the South still had a difficult time after the Civil War. There were very few chances for good jobs or education. They still were not treated fairly.

In the early 1900s, African Americans heard there were good jobs and better opportunities in northern cities like Chicago, Detroit, New York, and Philadelphia. Thousands of people moved north hoping for a better life. The Great Migration began.

Many African Americans in the South lived in rural communities where they were not treated fairly.

Starting Over

Starting a new life in the North was exciting for many African Americans. One woman wrote of her life in Chicago, Illinois: "I am well and thankful to be in a city. . . . The people are rushing here by the thousands. The houses are so pretty, we [have] a nice place. Hurry up and come to Chicago. It is wonderful. . . ."

As communities grew in the North, there were more opportunities to find jobs. People worked in iron and steel mills. Some made buildings. Many worked in factories where they made products like bricks and glass. Others worked on railroads. Their lives were improving. As their community grew, some people started their own businesses. Many people were happy with their decision to migrate to the North.

These photos of life in the North were taken in the 1920s by the photographer James Van Der Zee.

Painting the Great Migration

You have read about the artist Jacob Lawrence. About 1917 his parents migrated north to Philadelphia. As a young boy Jacob Lawrence became interested in painting. He knew he wanted to be an artist. Later, in 1941, he made a series of paintings about the Great Migration. Look at the painting on this page. Describe what it tells about the Great Migration.

MANY VOICES
PRIMARY SOURCE

Painting by Jacob Lawrence, completed in 1941.

The Phillips Collection

Martin Luther King, Jr.

As African Americans soon found out, life was still difficult in the North. Although they did have a better chance for work and education, they still faced unfair treatment. They often received less pay than a white worker for the same job.

Unfair treatment continued in both the North and South. In the 1950s and 1960s thousands of people joined together to work for change. One African American leader was Martin Luther King, Jr. He spent his life working to make sure all people were treated fairly.

WHY IT MATTERS

You have read about immigration and migration. Our country's history includes many stories of people moving to new communities to build new lives. In the next lesson you will learn how people today still move to the United States with hopes of starting new lives.

Martin Luther King, Jr., wanted to make laws fair for all Americans.

✓✓ Reviewing Facts and Ideas

MAIN IDEAS

- The Civil War was fought between the North and South from 1861 to 1865.

- President Abraham Lincoln helped to end slavery.

- The Great Migration took place during the early 1900s.

- Martin Luther King, Jr., worked to end the unfair treatment of people.

THINK ABOUT IT

1. Why did African Americans migrate to the North?

2. **FOCUS** What was the Great Migration?

3. **THINKING SKILL** How is migration *like* immigration? How is it *different*?

4. **GEOGRAPHY** Look at the map on page 225. In what direction is Maine from Florida?

Legacy

A Family Reunion

During the Great Migration, some members of the Pressley family in South Carolina moved north to Philadelphia.

Today people in this family live in many different communities. Every year they return to South Carolina to have a family reunion. At the reunion they see people they care about. They also learn about their family history. It is a special time.

Today, as in the past, families sometimes move. They may move to new communities in the United States or even to another country.

At the airport Felicia Green welcomes cousins traveling to the reunion from faraway places.

Felicia's scrapbook includes a page on fun at the family reunion. Whether it's storytelling (top left), singing or playing baseball, there's lots to do!

It doesn't matter who wins in the tug of war, as long as it's fun for everyone.

Immigration Today

Focus Activity

READ TO LEARN

What is it like to immigrate to the United States today?

VOCABULARY

• oath
• port

PLACES

• San Diego, California
• Veracruz, Mexico

Read Aloud

"I like it in the United States. School is a little bit hard for me now. But it's getting better. I have new friends. But sometimes I miss my old friends."

Moving to a New Country

These are the words of a student named Delores Stivalet (stee vah let). She and her family moved to **San Diego, California**, from **Veracruz, Mexico**, just a few years ago. Delores was 11 years old. It was an exciting time for her and her family.

Maybe you and your family at one time moved to a new community. If so, you know how the move made you feel. Perhaps you were excited, nervous, or a little sad. On the first day of school, you may have been shy.

Perhaps you or someone you know has moved to the United States from another country. Moving to a new country can be very hard. There are many things to learn and many changes to make. In this lesson you will see how immigrants like Delores and her family build new lives in the United States.

Settling in San Diego

For Delores and her family, moving to a new country like the United States was challenging. Her family felt that there were better schools and more jobs for people in the United States. "If you really want to do something in the United States," her father said, "you can do it. That's why we moved here."

Delores's new community in San Diego is similar to Veracruz. They both have busy **ports**. A port is a place where ships load and unload goods. The climate is warm in both cities.

There are also many differences between the two cities. In San Diego, Delores and her family have to learn English. "I am learning to speak English," said Delores. "But we still speak Spanish at home."

Veracruz and San Diego are port cities. In Veracruz a woman sells goods (top). San Diego has many tall office buildings (bottom).

infographic

United States Immigration Today

Immigrants continue to come here from around the world. The United States offers people the chance for a better life. Let's see what some recent immigrants have to say about living in the United States.

❝I never saw snow where I lived in India. It's colder here. I like to go sledding and to make snowmen.❞

—**Aditya Nochur**
(AH deet yah noh CHAWR)

From India
Lives in Cambridge, Massachusetts

❝I missed foods like fried bananas. Someone offered me spaghetti. I said 'No, thank you!' But now I eat it.❞

—**Oyeyinka Oyelaran**
(oh YEAH yin kah oh YEAH la RIN)
From Nigeria
Lives in Winston Salem, North Carolina

❝I was surprised by how big the United States is. It has big airports, big roads and big shopping malls.❞

—Joanna Jawdosiuk
(joh AHN uh yahv DOH shook)
From Poland
Lives in Glendale, Wisconsin

Becoming a Citizen

From the Infographic you can see that people immigrate to the United States from different countries around the world. Many of these immigrants, like Delores and her family, hope to become citizens of the United States.

Study the chart below. It shows how some adult immigrants can become citizens of the United States today.

BECOMING A CITIZEN OF THE UNITED STATES OF AMERICA

STEP 5: Receive a certificate of citizenship.

STEP 1: Fill out form about you and your life.

STEP 4: Take an oath of loyalty to the United States. An oath is a statement or promise in which a person swears that what he or she said is true.

STEP 3: Meet with Judge, who can grant citizenship.

STEP 2: Answer questions in English about United States of America history and government.

WHY IT MATTERS

Immigration is even older than our country. From the early English settlers to the Ellis Island immigrants, people kept coming to this land to build new lives. The United States is still growing because of new immigrants and new citizens. The Statue of Liberty stands in New York harbor as a symbol of hope and friendship to all.

Taking the oath is an exciting event for immigrants who hope to build new lives in the United States.

Reviewing Facts and Ideas

MAIN IDEAS

- Many people immigrate to the United States from different countries around the world.

- Immigrants face a new language and a new way of life in their new country.

- Immigrants continue to help the United States grow.

THINK ABOUT IT

1. Name some countries where immigrants to the United States come from.

2. **FOCUS** What is it like to immigrate to the United States today?

3. **THINKING SKILL** What is the *sequence* of steps needed to become a citizen?

4. **WRITE** Write a paragraph describing your community to someone who just moved there.

MAKING A DIFFERENCE

Building a Folk Life Library

ABITA SPRINGS, LOUISIANA—"You never know what will be going on at Abita Springs Elementary School as we build our folk life library," said third grader Alonzo Behame (BAY ham).

The folk life library is an exciting way to learn about the people who came to live in the community long ago. To collect material, students in grades 1–3 first met with different people from the community. One day some students met with a Choctaw Native American. They learned how to make a necklace from the seeds of a tree. Another time students cooked foods with a Cajun (KAY juhn) chef. They prepared dishes made from alligator meat and shrimp. Cajuns were French-speaking people who came to live in Louisiana long ago. "I learned that many different groups of people helped make our community special," said Alonzo.

Students then use computers to write stories about what they learned. These stories are added to the folk life materials in the school library. There are always new stories and people to read about. Sometimes there are even new things to see—like a real Native American canoe that students made with the help of a Choctaw boat builder. It is in the school library.

As the folk library grows, students like Alonzo hope it will remain an important resource in Abita Springs. "It's something nice that will be here when I grow up," said Alonzo. "After all, it's easy to forget how things were made long ago. It's better to write things down to have for the future."

"... many different ... people helped make our community special."

Alonzo

237

CHAPTER 9 REVIEW

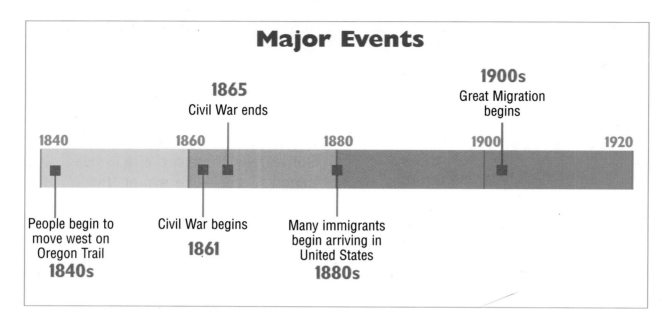

Major Events

1900s
Great Migration begins

1865
Civil War ends

1840   1860   1880   1900   1920

People begin to move west on Oregon Trail
1840s

Civil War begins
1861

Many immigrants begin arriving in United States
1880s

THINKING ABOUT VOCABULARY

Number a sheet of paper from 1 to 10. Beside each number write the word or words from the list that best fit each definition.

Civil War   immigrant   oral history
classify   migration   pioneer
diary   oath   prairie
Great Migration

1. People telling what life was like in the past

2. A statement in which a person swears to tell the truth

3. Flat or rolling land covered with tall grasses

4. To group similar things together

5. The movement of people from one part of a country to another

6. Someone who comes to live in a new country

7. A person who leads the way into a land not known to them

8. The movement north of African Americans in the early 1900s

9. The war between the northern and southern states from 1861–1865

10. A written record of what someone has done or thought each day

THINKING ABOUT FACTS

1. Why did pioneers travel west in groups known as wagon trains?

2. How do diaries help us learn about the past?

3. Why did immigrants come to the United States in the early 1900s?

4. What led to the Great Migration? Did the people who migrated north find what they hoped for?

5. What are some of the steps adult immigrants take to become citizens of the United States?

THINK AND WRITE

WRITING INTERVIEW QUESTIONS

Choose an older person to interview. To prepare, write some questions to ask about the person's childhood.

WRITING A WELCOME GUIDE

Create a guide to your community for new immigrants. Include helpful information such as where to buy groceries, how to get a library card, and how to get emergency help.

WRITING A COMPARISON

Write a paragraph comparing how people dressed long ago with how people dress today.

APPLYING THINKING SKILLS

CLASSIFYING

Review the classifying skill on pages 216–217 before answering the following questions.

1. How do you classify things?
2. How could you classify the things in your school?
3. List items you would take on an overnight camping trip. Classify the items into those needed for survival and those not needed.
4. Look at your list again. How else could you classify the items on it?
5. What are things you classify during a normal day?

Summing Up the Chapter

The movement of people into and within the United States is classified into four groups on the main idea map below. Review the chapter. Then complete a copy of the map by listing several reasons why each group migrated or immigrated. What goal did these groups have in common?

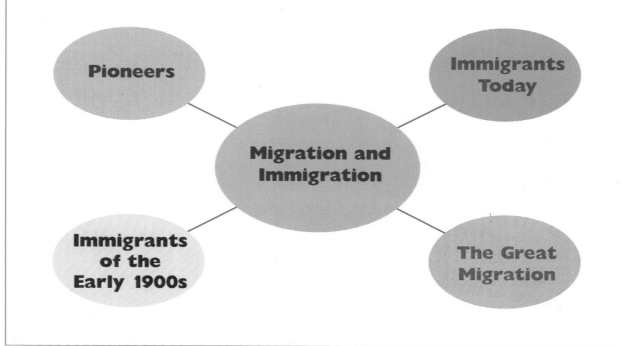

Changing the Way People Live

THINKING ABOUT GEOGRAPHY AND TECHNOLOGY

Two hundred years ago, moving to a new community may have meant a difficult trip and no news from old friends and neighbors. Since then, new methods of transportation and communication have made traveling and staying in touch much easier for people.

In Chapter 10, you will learn how technology has changed the ways we travel and get news. Technology is not only part of our history, it is part of our lives today and tomorrow.

1807

HUDSON RIVER, NEW YORK

The first steam-powered boat, the Clermont, travels upriver from New York City

1839

VANDALIA, ILLINOIS

The National Road, started in the East, reaches Vandalia, Illinois

1800　　　　1820　　　　1840

Hudson River,
New York

Washington, D.C.

Vandalia, Illinois

Kitty Hawk,
North Carolina

1844

WASHINGTON, D.C.
The first telegraph message is sent by Samuel Morse

1903

KITTY HAWK, NORTH CAROLINA
The Wright brothers make the first successful airplane flight

1860

1900

Focus Activity

READ TO LEARN

In what ways has transportation changed over time?

VOCABULARY

- fuel

PEOPLE

- **Robert Fulton**
- **Peter Cooper**
- **Henry Ford**
- **Wilbur Wright**
- **Orville Wright**
- **Elisha Otis**
- **Amelia Earhart**
- **Eduardo San Juan**
- **Mae Jemison**

PLACES

- **National Road**

On the Go

Read Aloud

In the last chapter you read about people moving to new communities. What were some of the ways they traveled? They bumped along in wagons over the Oregon Trail. They sailed long distances on ships across the Atlantic Ocean. They also chugged along in trains to cities in the North.

Transportation Before 1800

You probably travel somewhere almost every day. You may walk, ride a bike, or take a bus to get to school or to visit friends. Maybe you ride in a car or on a train. Can you imagine what your life would be like without these forms of transportation?

Before 1800, people walked to get most places. There were no cars or trains. If people had to go far, they rode on horses or mules, or used wagons pulled by animals. People also used canoes and boats if they had to travel over water.

Often travel over land was difficult because there were few roads in the United States. There were only paths and trails. They were nothing like the wide, smooth roads you often see in our country today.

Steam-Powered Engines

People had always traveled along waterways. But it was hard for boats to travel against the currents of the water. Robert Fulton thought there must be a way that technology could improve travel by water. He worked for years on the idea of using steam engines to power boats. Finally, in 1807, he got to test his idea. People lined the Hudson River in New York to watch Fulton's boat, the *Clermont*. Everyone was excited to see the boat move up the river.

The National Road

In the early 1800s people began to build new roads. Some of these new roads were covered with stone. Other roads were made from logs and planks of wood. Each new road made it easier to travel between places. One road became the busiest of all. It was called the National Road. It was built over many years, by many people. From the map below you can see that it helped people to move west.

This drawing shows Robert Fulton's steamboat, the *Clermont*, chugging up the Hudson River.

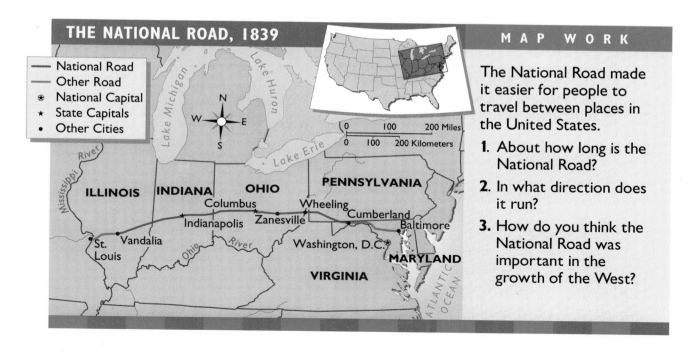

THE NATIONAL ROAD, 1839

— National Road
— Other Road
⊛ National Capital
★ State Capitals
• Other Cities

0 100 200 Miles
0 100 200 Kilometers

Lake Michigan
Lake Huron
Lake Erie

Mississippi River

ILLINOIS   INDIANA   OHIO   PENNSYLVANIA
Columbus   Wheeling
Indianapolis   Zanesville   Cumberland
St. Louis   Vandalia   Ohio River   Baltimore
Washington, D.C.⊛
MARYLAND
VIRGINIA
ATLANTIC OCEAN

MAP WORK

The National Road made it easier for people to travel between places in the United States.

1. About how long is the National Road?

2. In what direction does it run?

3. How do you think the National Road was important in the growth of the West?

Railroads from Coast to Coast

It was not long before steam engines were also used in other forms of transportation. Around 1825 steam engines in the United States were used for the first time to power railroad trains. Before then trains were pulled by horses.

One of the first railroad engines was called the *Tom Thumb*. Peter Cooper built the engine so it would be able to travel over hills and around curves. Cooper was proud of the *Tom Thumb*. He wanted people to know how fast his engine was. He set up a race. His engine would race against a "gallant gray" horse pulling a train car. When the day came for the big event, Cooper was disappointed! The mighty *Tom Thumb* broke down. The horse went on to cross the finish line.

But the age of the railroad was coming. Soon steam-powered railroads ran between most big cities. They made it easier for people to travel. Railroads also made it easier to move goods across the country.

The year is 1885. These construction workers are in front of railroad tracks built along the Cascade Mountains.

The Auto and the Airplane

With roads and steamboats and railroads, traveling long distances kept getting easier. Soon another invention changed the way people traveled between communities.

In 1908 a man named **Henry Ford** made a car he called the Model T. For the next several years Ford worked on making cars cheap enough so that many people could afford to buy them. People could now travel on their own to different places in less time than ever before. How do you think automobiles changed the way people live in your community?

Henry Ford's Model T (top) and the Wright Brothers' airplane (bottom) changed forever the way people travel.

Another invention that changed the way we live was the airplane. **Wilbur** and **Orville Wright** were brothers who owned a bicycle shop. Together they completed the world's first airplane flight in Kitty Hawk, North Carolina. Airplanes made people think that anything was possible.

Faster and Further

Transportation and technology are always changing. Today people travel in space. There are even machines that have landed on the moon and the planet Mars. Look at the chart below. It shows that the history of transportation has many exciting people and events. What did Eduardo San Juan (ed WAHR doh san HWAHN) do?

PEOPLE IN TRANSPORTATION

Elisha Otis invented an elevator with a safety clamp in 1852. This led to the first passenger elevator and encouraged the building of skyscrapers.

In 1932 Amelia Earhart was the first woman to make a cross-Atlantic flight alone. In 1937, she disappeared on a flight around the world.

Eduardo San Juan, a scientist and engineer, designed the lunar rover vehicle. Called the "moon buggy," it carried astronauts across the moon's surface in 1971 and 1972.

Mae Jemison became an astronaut in 1988. She was the first African American woman to prepare, launch, and travel in space shuttles.

CHART WORK

Many people have helped to shape the way we travel today.

1. Who was the first woman to fly alone in a plane across the Atlantic Ocean?

2. How do you think elevators changed the way people live in communities?

3. In what ways is the work of Eduardo San Juan and Mae Jemison similar?

Public Transportation

Sometimes new types of transportation bring new problems. Most forms of transportation today use **fuel**. Fuel is something that is burned to provide power. Gas and oil are examples of fuel. But burning fuel can cause pollution and use up our natural resources.

Today people are working to solve these problems. Public transportation is one solution that saves fuel. When people ride buses and trains instead of taking their own cars, there are fewer vehicles on roads. How do you think public transportation helps the environment?

Public transportation is helpful in fighting pollution by saving fuel.

WHY IT MATTERS

The United States has always been a country of people on the move. Today people move faster and further than ever before. Transportation is one way to bring people closer together. In the next lesson you will see some other ways that bring people in communities closer together.

✓// Reviewing Facts and Ideas

MAIN IDEAS

- In the 1800s Americans began to build many roads.
- Robert Fulton developed steam engines to power boats.
- Steam engines were also used for railroad trains.
- Henry Ford made cars that many people could afford.
- The Wright Brothers made the first successful airplane flight.
- New types of transportation change the way people live.

THINK ABOUT IT

1. How did the steam engine change transportation?

2. **FOCUS** In what ways has transportation changed over time?

3. **THINKING SKILL** *Classify* into groups different ways people travel. Make a chart. What headings could you use?

4. **GEOGRAPHY** Look at the map on page 243. What direction is Vandalia from Cumberland?

Reading Transportation Maps

VOCABULARY
transportation map

WHY THE SKILL MATTERS

By the middle of the 1800s there were several different ways for people to travel. You can see these different ways by reading a **transportation map**. A transportation map shows the routes people can use to travel from place to place. Transportation maps often show roads, railroads, and other kinds of transportation all on the same map.

Use the Helping Yourself box on the following page to guide you in reading transportation maps.

USING THE SKILL

Look at the map on the next page. It shows some other ways people traveled in the United States in 1860. Look at the map key. Find the symbols for roads, railroads, and canals. Canals are waterways dug across the land and used for boat travel.

Look at the painting of the Erie Canal below. Canals helped people move goods between bodies of water. A trip that had taken up to six weeks on rough trails and rivers took about a week on the Erie Canal. Find the Erie Canal on the map on the next page. It connects the Hudson River and Lake Erie.

Suppose that you wanted to travel from Cumberland, Maryland, to Vandalia, Illinois. The red line shows you that the National Road connected these two cities. With your finger follow the route from Cumberland to Vandalia on the map. You will pass through Maryland, Virginia, Pennsylvania, Ohio, Indiana, and Illinois. The brown line shows you that a railroad connected Cumberland and Vandalia.

The Granger Collection

TRYING THE SKILL

The map shows more than one way to get from one place to another. Suppose you wanted to travel north from Augusta, Georgia, to Boston, Massachusetts. What were two ways you could get there? If you wanted to take a train trip from the city of Philadelphia, where were two places you could go?

REVIEWING THE SKILL

1. What types of transportation are shown on the map below?

Helping yourself

- A **transportation map** shows various ways to travel.
- **The map key shows the symbols for different kinds of transportation on the map.**
- **Sometimes there is more than one way to travel between two places.**

2. In what ways can people travel now that were not possible in 1860?

3. What kinds of transportation could people use to travel from Augusta to Montgomery in 1860? How do you know?

4. Look at the cities on the map. In 1860 most cities were near railroads or along the water. Why do you think that was so?

5. When is it helpful to use a transportation map?

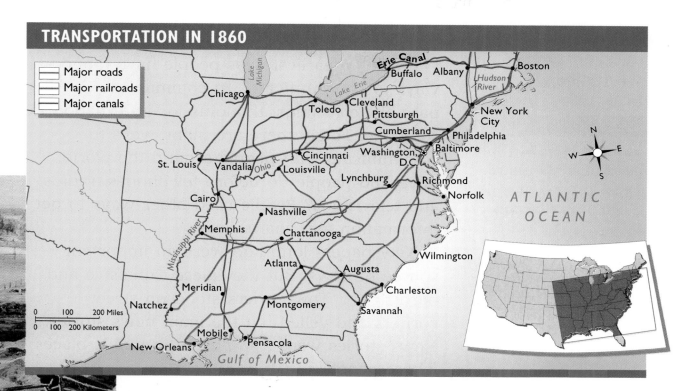

TRANSPORTATION IN 1860

Major roads
Major railroads
Major canals

Erie Canal
Buffalo   Albany   Boston
Lake Michigan   Lake Erie   Hudson River
Chicago   Cleveland
Toledo   Pittsburgh   New York City
Cumberland   Philadelphia
Cincinnati   Washington, D.C.   Baltimore
St. Louis   Vandalia   Ohio   Louisville
Lynchburg   Richmond
Norfolk
Cairo   ATLANTIC OCEAN
Nashville
Memphis   Chattanooga
Mississippi River
Wilmington
Atlanta   Augusta
Meridian   Charleston
Natchez   Montgomery   Savannah
Mobile   Pensacola
New Orleans   Gulf of Mexico

0   100   200 Miles
0   100   200 Kilometers

N W E S

Keeping in Touch

Read Aloud

The whole family gathered in the living room. Everyone was so excited as the switch was turned on. Slowly, like a miracle, a picture appeared on the screen and voices came out of the box.

Your grandparents probably remember a scene like this from the first time they watched television. In this lesson you will read about how television and other inventions have changed our lives.

Focus Activity

READ TO LEARN

In what ways has communication changed over time?

VOCABULARY

- communicate
- pony express
- telegraph
- satellite

PEOPLE

- Samuel Morse
- Alexander Graham Bell
- Guglielmo Marconi

Communicating Long Ago

From the earliest days people have found ways to communicate. To communicate is to pass along feelings, thoughts, or information to someone. Today there are many ways to communicate with people around the world. What did people do before telephones, radios, and televisions? People used other ways to get information and share ideas.

Newspapers long ago were an important source of news. But they were expensive and hard to get. Town criers stood on street corners and yelled out the main news stories. News stories were also posted in public places where people could read them.

Riding the Pony Express

Pioneers often left friends and family behind as they moved to new communities and built new lives. These people wanted news from their families and old communities.

In the 1800s mail service was not reliable. But in 1860 a group of men developed a mail service called the pony express. The pony express was a team of daring horseback riders. They rode across the western United States to deliver mail from one place to another. They would hand off the mail to another rider, who would continue the route. Look at the map below. Find the route of the pony express. People in Sacramento, California, could get mail from people in St. Joseph, Missouri, in just 10 days.

Pony express **riders traveled by horse both day and night, no matter what the weather.**

Buffalo Bill Historical Center

THE PONY EXPRESS, 1860–1861

CANADA

VERMONT
MAINE
NEW HAMPSHIRE
MASSACHUSETTS
RHODE ISLAND
CONNECTICUT
NEW JERSEY
DELAWARE
MARYLAND

OREGON
MINNESOTA
MICHIGAN
WISCONSIN
NEW YORK
PENNSYLVANIA
OHIO
IOWA
INDIANA
ILLINOIS
VIRGINIA

Sacramento
Carson City
Salt Lake City
St. Joseph
MISSOURI
KENTUCKY
CALIFORNIA
ARKANSAS
TENNESSEE
NORTH CAROLINA
ATLANTIC OCEAN

PACIFIC OCEAN

Snake River
Missouri River
Platte River
Colorado River
Ohio River
Rio Grande
Mississippi River

SOUTH CAROLINA
ALABAMA
GEORGIA

TEXAS
MISSISSIPPI
LOUISIANA
FLORIDA

MEXICO
Gulf of Mexico

0   250   500 Miles
0   250   500 Kilometers

— Pony Express Route
★ State Capital
• Other City
☐ Land not yet divided into states

MAP WORK

At each city riders used fresh horses to carry the mail to the next city.

1. About how many miles is the trip from St. Joseph to Sacramento?

2. Along what river does the pony express route travel?

3. Where might the trip be most difficult for riders?

Communication by Wire

The pony express was a new step for communication. But soon an invention was to change everything. Samuel Morse was one of the early inventors of the machine called the telegraph. The telegraph used special codes to send words long distances over wires. In 1844 Morse had workers run a wire from Washington, D.C., to Baltimore, Maryland. He then sat in the Capitol building and tapped out the first telegraph message: *"What hath [has] God wrought [made]!"* The telegraph worked! By 1861 telegraph wires ran across the country. People could now get news from faraway places in minutes. The pony express was no longer needed.

It was not too much longer before another invention changed how people communicated. In 1876 Alexander Graham Bell built a working telephone. People could now speak to each other directly from faraway places.

This telegraph register (left) was used by Samuel Morse (right) in 1844. It received and printed codes sent by wire.

On the Air

The telegraph and the telephone were exciting inventions. Messages could travel in seconds! But there was one problem. The messages had to run through wires. It was impossible to connect all places around the world with wires.

Guglielmo Marconi (goo LYEHL moh mahr KOH nee) was an Italian inventor. He wanted to find a way to send signals without using wires. He studied the ideas and inventions of other people who had been working on the same idea. Finally, in 1895 Marconi invented the wireless telegraph. Now, even ships at sea could send signals back and forth to each other. The wireless telegraph then led to the invention of the radio.

Later, scientists invented a way to send pictures through space. That led to the invention of the television. Today, televisions and radios are in many homes. We can instantly see clear pictures and hear voices from all over the world.

The radio (above) was a popular form of communication before television. Alexander Graham Bell (bottom) built this telephone in 1875.

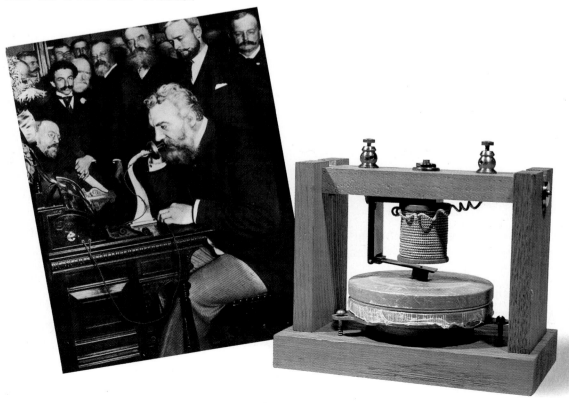

Latest Connections

Satellites **are used by scientists to help them learn about faraway places like the sun, Venus, and Mars.**

Look at the time line. You can see that people have continued to look for new ways to improve communication. In the 1960s the first communications satellites were used. A satellite is a spacecraft that is used to connect radio, telephone, and television communications. Satellites make it possible for people to communicate in seconds across oceans to other countries.

Can you think of other machines that people use to communicate with each other? Computers and faxes are used every day to send and receive information.

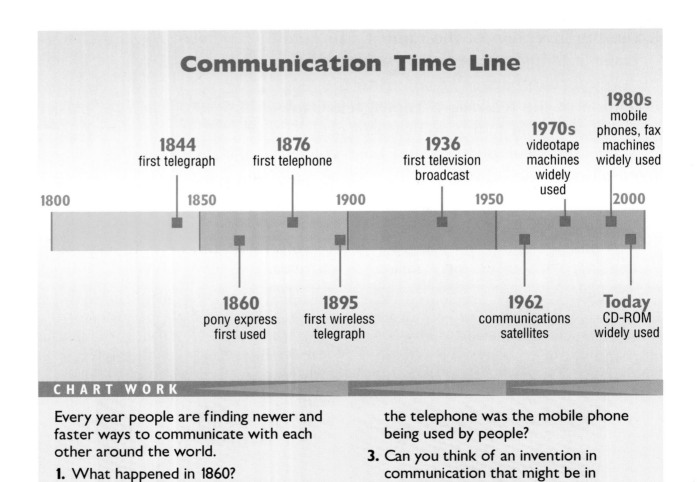

Communication Time Line

1800

1844 first telegraph

1850

1860 pony express first used

1876 first telephone

1900

1895 first wireless telegraph

1936 first television broadcast

1950

1962 communications satellites

1970s videotape machines widely used

2000

1980s mobile phones, fax machines widely used

Today CD-ROM widely used

CHART WORK

Every year people are finding newer and faster ways to communicate with each other around the world.

1. What happened in 1860?
2. How many years after the invention of the telephone was the mobile phone being used by people?
3. Can you think of an invention in communication that might be in people's homes in the future?

254

WHY IT MATTERS

It has always been important for people to communicate. It used to take days to get a message across the country by pony express. Now it can happen in less than a second.

Over the years people have found new and better ways to share ideas and information. As people communicate more quickly with each other, they learn more about communities and the world around them. By communicating more easily around the world every day, people learn about many cultures and new ideas. By working together to understand each other and by using new ways of communication, people can solve many problems in our world today.

Just fifteen years ago, few people used personal computers. Today they are used by many people at work and home.

Reviewing Facts and Ideas

MAIN IDEAS

- People have always found ways to communicate.

- The pony express used horses and daring riders to speed mail across the western part of the country.

- Samuel Morse invented a way to send messages across wires.

- Guglielmo Marconi invented a way to send messages without wires.

- Radios and televisions soon followed. Communication continues to improve today with satellites and computers.

THINK ABOUT IT

1. How did people receive news long ago?

2. **FOCUS** In what ways has communication changed over time?

3. **THINKING SKILL** Make your own time line about some of the changes in communication. Put the events in the correct _sequence_.

4. **WRITE** Write a newspaper headline about the invention of the personal computer.

A Tunnel in Europe

Read Aloud

"Fog in Channel. Continent Cut Off."

These words appeared in a newspaper headline in England long ago. It describes what happened when fog prevented ships from sailing across the English Channel.

But thanks to technology, things have changed. Today people do not have to rely on ships and planes to cross the English Channel.

Focus Activity

READ TO LEARN

What is the English Channel Tunnel?

VOCABULARY

- channel

PLACES

- France
- England
- English Channel

Two Countries and a Channel

In 1994 the first passengers boarded the Eurostar train. They were about to take a special trip. It was the first time France and England were connected by railroad. Look at the map on the next page. England is an island off the continent of Europe. It is separated from the rest of Europe by the English Channel. A channel is a narrow waterway between two larger bodies of water. The English Channel connects the Atlantic Ocean and the North Sea.

England and France are only about 21 miles apart at their closest points. But to travel between these two countries, people had to take a ship or fly. Now the English Channel Tunnel has connected them in a new way.

256

A Dream of Many Years

For over 200 years people have dreamed of linking England with France. In 1802 a French scientist came up with a plan for two long tunnels with a little island in between. The horse-drawn carriages could stop at the island to get fresh horses! The plan never came to life. Over the years many other plans were made. However, some people in England were afraid to connect their country with the rest of Europe. They thought they were safer as an island. But in 1986 the decision was made to build the tunnel. It took eight years to complete.

A ferry trip across the English Channel includes a view of these chalk cliffs at Dover, England.

THE ENGLISH CHANNEL TUNNEL

Thames River

North Sea

London

ENGLAND

Dover

Folkestone

Calais

BELGIUM

Brussels

Boulogne-sur-Mer

Lille

FRANCE

English Channel

EUROPE

England

France

Seine River

Paris

Legend	
━━	English Channel Tunnel
──	Railroad
•••	Ferry Route
▭	Highway
✈	Airport
✷	National Capital
○	Other City

N W E S

0   25   50 Miles
0   25   50 Kilometers

M A P   W O R K

Before the English Channel Tunnel was built, people traveled between England and France by ferry or plane.

1. About how far is it from Folkestone to Calais?

2. What are two ways to get from Calais to Paris?

3. What might be some differences in traveling by ferry instead of by tunnel?

Special machines dug a tunnel below the channel (left). When the digging was done, English and French workers had a big party (right).

Building the Tunnel

Finally we reach the breakthrough site. The two machines that dug this tunnel started from opposite sides of the Channel and worked toward the middle. [The] cutter-head—a huge wheel with . . . teeth—chews into the last trace of rock separating England from France.

These are the words of a writer named Cathy Newman. She was describing the moment when workers broke through the rock that separated the two halves of the tunnel. It was an important moment. The digging of the tunnel was completed. French and English workers hugged each other.

A special machine called the "tunnel-boring machine" was used to dig the tunnel. Many pounds of earth were dug up from the bottom of the English Channel to make the tunnel. That earth was then piled along the English and French coasts. These areas will be used to build parks.

All Aboard!

The English Channel Tunnel is more than one tunnel. It is really three tunnels. Trains from England to France run through one tunnel. Trains from France to England run through the second tunnel. The third tunnel is just for workers and service crews. The service crews help keep the tunnel safe.

Two different trains run through the tunnel. *Eurostar* is the train for passengers without cars. The other train is called *Le Shuttle* (le shuh TELL). It carries people with their cars. It also carries trucks filled with goods that will be sold in other countries.

The tunnels are actually dug in the ground below the bottom of the English Channel (right). Trains (below) travel through the tunnel faster than cars on the highway.

A Big Change

Because of the tunnel, people in England and France can do business with each other more easily. Goods can be trucked from one country to the other without having to be loaded and unloaded onto a boat or plane.

The French and English have different cultures, different histories, and different languages. But now they can visit each other more easily. The poem below was written by a ten-year-old English boy named Adam Westgarth. In what ways do you think he is excited about the tunnel?

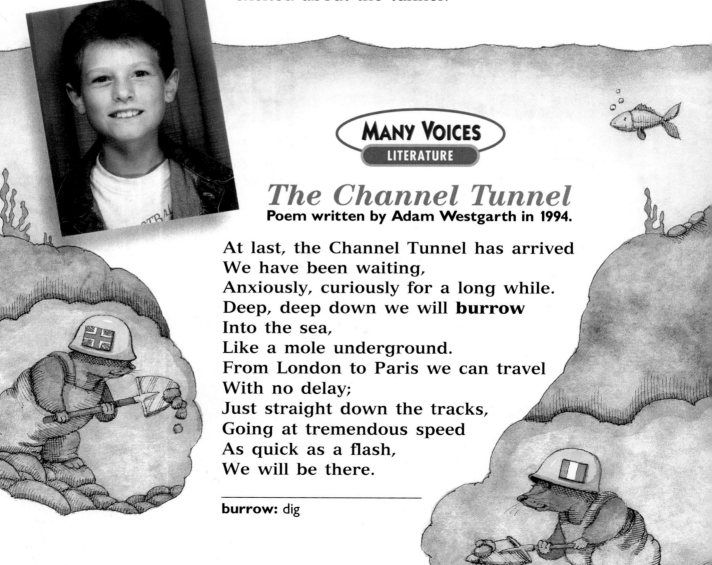

MANY VOICES
LITERATURE

The Channel Tunnel
Poem written by Adam Westgarth in 1994.

At last, the Channel Tunnel has arrived
We have been waiting,
Anxiously, curiously for a long while.
Deep, deep down we will **burrow**
Into the sea,
Like a mole underground.
From London to Paris we can travel
With no delay;
Just straight down the tracks,
Going at tremendous speed
As quick as a flash,
We will be there.

---

burrow: dig

260

WHY IT MATTERS

In this chapter you have read about changes in transportation and communication. Each of these changes has brought people closer together in different ways.

Trains, planes, and automobiles have allowed people to travel between places faster than ever. The telegraph allowed people to send messages quickly to each other over wires. Today the computer lets people around the world communicate quickly without wires. And in Europe the English Channel Tunnel makes it easier for people in England and France to share ideas and lives every day.

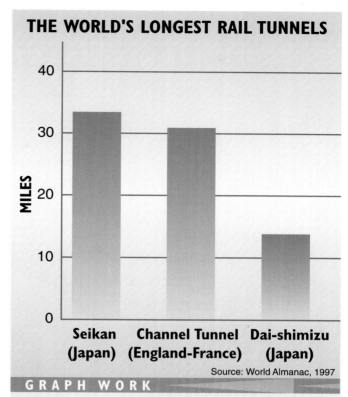

THE WORLD'S LONGEST RAIL TUNNELS

MILES

Seikan (Japan)   Channel Tunnel (England-France)   Dai-shimizu (Japan)

Source: World Almanac, 1997

GRAPH WORK

Japan has two of the three longest tunnels in the world.

1. About how long is the Seikan Tunnel?

2. Can you think of one way a tunnel might be better for travel than a bridge?

✓// Reviewing Facts and Ideas

MAIN IDEAS

- England is separated from the rest of Europe by the English Channel.

- For hundreds of years people dreamed of ways to connect England and France.

- The English Channel Tunnel has made it easier to travel between England and France.

THINK ABOUT IT

1. What are two ways to cross the English Channel today?

2. **FOCUS** What is the English Channel Tunnel?

3. **THINKING SKILL** List in *sequence* some of the new kinds of transportation that have been invented since 1800.

4. **GEOGRAPHY** Look at the world map in the Atlas on pages R10 and R11. What are some other places a tunnel might be built?

HERE WE GO

Modern ways of transportation help people travel between communities quickly. But for many people transportation is more than just traveling from one place to another. Transportation is also a legacy of fun and excitement. Look at the pictures here. See why being on the move has been fun for people of all ages, yesterday and today.

Look out pony express! In some communities today, people still use horses as a main form of transportation. Others ride horses just for fun.

Moving on! In the 1920s children rode carts they made from wooden boxes and baby carriage wheels (left). Today children keep rolling with in-line skates.

Whether paddling a canoe on a warm river or ice skating on a frozen lake, people enjoy having fun on the go in all kinds of weather.

CHAPTER 10 REVIEW

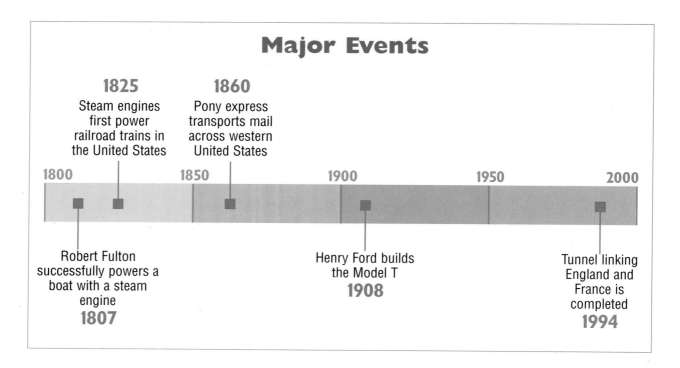

Major Events

1825
Steam engines first power railroad trains in the United States

1860
Pony express transports mail across western United States

1800   1850   1900   1950   2000

Robert Fulton successfully powers a boat with a steam engine
1807

Henry Ford builds the Model T
1908

Tunnel linking England and France is completed
1994

THINKING ABOUT VOCABULARY

Number a sheet of paper from 1 to 5. Write the word or words that best complete each sentence in the paragraph below.

Channel   satellites
communication   telegraph
pony express

Various means of transportation and ___1___ have developed over time. In 1844, the ___2___ first sent messages over wires. Later, in 1860 the ___3___ delivered mail across the western U.S. In the 1960s ___4___ enabled people to communicate around the world in seconds. And in the 1990s some high-speed trains travel below the English ___5___.

THINKING ABOUT FACTS

1. What types of transportation were available before 1800? Name several types of transportation developed since then. Which do you think influenced people's lives the most? Why?

2. What environmental problem is partly caused by modern transportation? What is one way to help prevent this problem?

3. What was the pony express? What invention replaced it?

4. What are four ways people communicate today? Which of these ways were not available to people before 1800?

5. How has the English Channel Tunnel changed the lives of people in England and France?

THINK AND WRITE

WRITING A JOURNAL ENTRY

Suppose you are Robert Fulton or one of the Wright brothers. Write a journal entry about the first time your invention worked.

WRITING TO CONVINCE

Write a letter to convince people that they need the wireless telegraph. Explain why this invention is needed when people can already send messages over telegraph wires.

WRITING A RADIO REPORT

Write a radio report about the English Channel Tunnel. Explain what it is, why it is important, and why people like or dislike it.

APPLYING GEOGRAPHY SKILLS

READING TRANSPORTATION MAPS

Answer the following questions about the map on page 249 to practice your skill of reading transportation maps.

1. What do transportation maps show?

2. What types of transportation are shown on the map key?

3. What kind of transportation can you use to get from Chicago to St. Louis?

4. Which cities are not on a railroad line? How could you travel there?

5. How are transportation maps different from grid maps? How are they alike?

Summing Up the Chapter

The chart below shows major changes in transportation and communication since 1800. Complete a copy of the chart by listing the missing development or person most responsible for it. How have we benefited by these changes in transportation and communication?

Person	Development
Robert Fulton	
	telegraph
Alexander Graham Bell	
	wireless telegraph
	Model T automobile
Wright Brothers	
Eduardo San Juan	"moon buggy"
French and English (1994)	

UNIT 4 REVIEW

THINKING ABOUT VOCABULARY

Number a sheet of paper from 1 to 10. Beside each number write the word or words from the list below that best completes each sentence.

channel   oath
diary   oral history
fuel   pioneers
immigrants   pony express
migration   prairie

1. Much of our pollution is caused by burning _____ .

2. Many _____ traveled west in wagon trains on the Oregon Trail.

3. By reading a _____ , we can learn about someone's personal life.

4. When people become citizens of the United States they must take an _____ of allegiance.

5. Many _____ came to the United States hoping to begin new lives.

6. The _____ north of African Americans began around 1900.

7. Some bodies of water are connected by a _____ .

8. By listening to _____ , we can learn what life was like in the past.

9. It was difficult for the _____ riders to cross the western United States to deliver mail.

10. Flat or rolling land covered with tall grasses is known as a _____ .

THINK AND WRITE ◄═══▷

WRITING A JOURNAL ENTRY
Suppose that you are crossing the United States by wagon train with your family in the 1850s. Write a journal entry describing what life is like during your trip West.

WRITING AN ADVERTISEMENT
Choose one of the developments in communication or transportation discussed in Chapter 10. Then create an advertisement to convince people that this development will make their lives better.

WRITING ABOUT PERSPECTIVE
Write a paragraph about how your life might be different today if there were no buses, cars, airplanes, computers, or even telephones.

BUILDING SKILLS

1. **Classifying** What is the first step to take when classifying items?

2. **Classifying** Classify items in your classroom into three groups.

3. **Transportation Maps** Look at the map on page 257. What are two ways to get from London to Dover?

4. **Transportation Maps** Look at the map again. How can you travel from Calais to Lille?

5. **Transportation Maps** When might you or your family need to use a transportation map?

LOCAL *connection*

How did people travel in your community long ago? How can you find out about how they traveled? Create a transportation map for your community long ago. Share your map with students and other people in your community.

READING ON YOUR OWN

Here are some books you might find at the library to help you learn more.

THE FIRST RIDE: BLAZING THE TRAIL FOR THE PONY EXPRESS
by Jacqueline Geis
The story of the Pony Express and how it blazed a trail through dangerous territory.

THE GLORIOUS FLIGHT
by Alice and Martin Provensen
Louis Bleriot had a wish: He wants to fly. Read how he makes his dream come true.

GRANDFATHER'S JOURNEY
by Allen Say
A Japanese immigrant struggles with his love for both the United States and Japan.

UNIT REVIEW PROJECT

Make Travel Stamps

1. Think of three ways people traveled long ago.
2. Design one stamp for each kind of travel. Use different colored construction paper for each stamp.
3. Decorate your stamps to make them more exciting.
4. Glue each stamp onto a piece of cardboard.
5. Write a description of each stamp on the cardboard. Tell why this form of transportation was important long ago.
6. Share your stamps and descriptions with a partner.

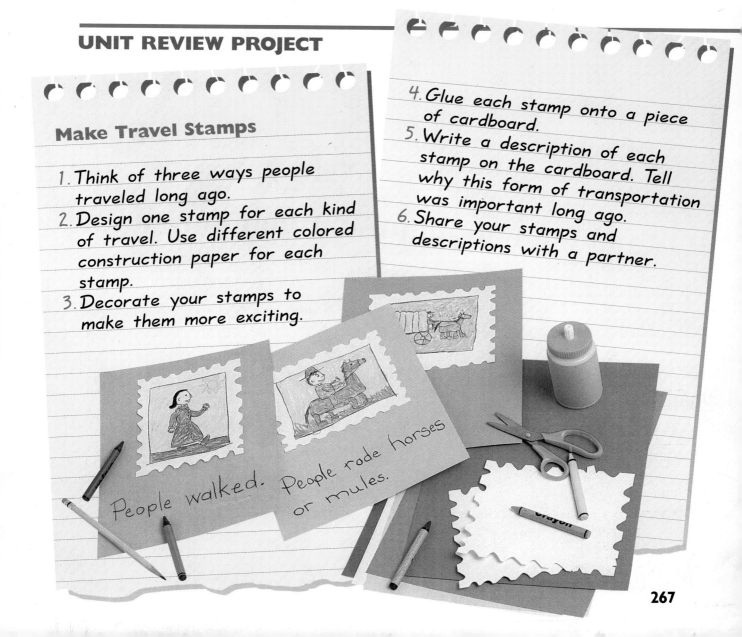

People walked. People rode horses or mules.

267

Working Together

Why Does it Matter?

As you know, people are an important resource in our country. The work that people do contributes to our country's growth. In this unit you will learn about the different types of jobs people have to make a living. You will also learn how people use money.

Some people help other people for a living. Still others turn natural resources into products that people can use. As you will see, most jobs require people to work together.

FIND OUT MORE!
Visit our website:
www.mhschool.com

*inter*NET
CONNECTION

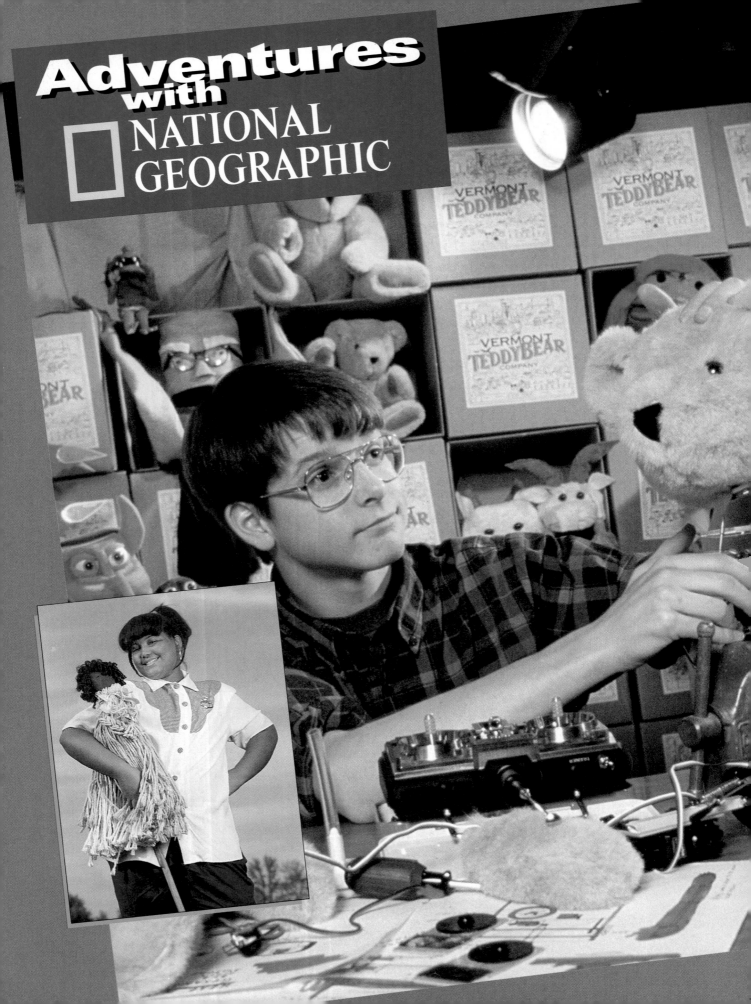

Kidz Biz

Being young didn't stand in Chris Webb's way when he created "Imagination Industries." This teenager from Vermont makes teddy bears that move—and he sells them. Other "businesskids" have also come up with great ideas. Casey Golden, of Colorado, makes biodegradable golf tees from grass seeds, apple sauce, and other materials. Brandi Champion, of Maryland, creates dolls out of mops. Celesly Shabi, of Arizona, weaves traditional Navajo rugs, a skill she learned from her mom. What business would you like to go into?

GEO JOURNAL

Write and draw an advertisement to sell a product you invent yourself.

Work and Money

THINKING ABOUT GEOGRAPHY AND ECONOMICS

Long ago people made or grew most things they needed. Today things have changed. Most people work at jobs to make money to buy things they need and want. In Chapter 11 you will see the many different jobs people have in communities around our country and in other countries too.

Fresno, California

Dallas, Texas

Tokyo, Japan

In Fresno, California, work around the house may include painting.

Basketball players in Dallas, Texas, have a difficult job, but onethat is fun and exciting.

Around the world there are many kinds of jobs, such as selling news-papers in Japan.

Jobs and Money

Focus Activity

READ TO LEARN

Why do people earn, save, and spend money?

VOCABULARY

- goods
- services
- employer
- interest
- consumer
- economy

PLACES

- Raleigh, North Carolina

Making a Living

Mr. Flythe has worked at the Flythe Cyclery shop in Raleigh (RAW lee), North Carolina for many years. His grandfather first opened the store back in the 1920s. What if his grandfather walked into the store today? He might be surprised at how it has changed. The style of bicycles has changed. And so have the prices. Bicycles are much more expensive today. But some things have remained the same. The sign on the front hasn't changed. There are still plenty of bicycles in the store. And, like his grandfather, Mr. Flythe provides goods for the people of Raleigh to buy. Goods are things that people make or grow. Mr. Flythe also offers a service by selling and repairing goods such as bicycles. A service is a job that helps others by providing something they need or want.

Why People Work

"I've been in this business ever since I was a little boy," says Mr. Flythe. "Whenever I was free, I was in the store with my grandfather. Then the business was my father's. Now it's mine. And one of my sons seems interested in joining the business. I've been warning him—it's a lot of hard work. But he still seems interested!"

Maybe Mr. Flythe's children will work in the bicycle shop. Or maybe they'll do some other work to earn money. Most people work to earn money. Then they use that money to pay for a place to live. They also use it to buy food, pay for visits to the doctor, and buy clothes and books. What are other reasons people need money?

Mr. Flythe does not work all by himself. He needs other people to help him sell and repair bicycles. So he hires other people to work for him. This means he is an employer. An employer is someone who hires and pays other people to work. There are six other people who work at Flythe Cyclery.

Raleigh, North Carolina

Like his grandfather long ago, Mr. Flythe provides a service by selling bicycles to people in Raleigh.

Saving Money

Elissa Zellinger is a 14-year-old girl who lives in Raleigh. She has visited Flythe Cyclery many times to look at the bicycles. "Looking at those bikes kept me going," says Elissa. Slowly, she has saved her allowance and money from jobs outside her home.

Elissa was saving her money in a piggy bank. Her parents had a better idea. They took her to a bank and helped her open an account. If you save money in a bank, the bank gives you extra money called interest. The interest is payment for lending money to the bank. "I need every extra penny of interest," says Elissa.

Mr. Flythe has used banks for his business too. He keeps the money the store earns in the bank. He has also borrowed money from the bank to help the business grow. He pays interest to the bank for his loan.

Elissa Zellinger worked at different jobs to earn money to buy a bicycle.

Being a Consumer

Finally Elissa saved enough money. She did some research to find out which bikes were the best buys. Elissa wanted to be a smart consumer. Consumers are people who buy goods and services. "I've worked hard to save money," says Elissa. "I want to make sure I don't throw it away!"

Mr. Flythe knows what Elissa means. "Children who have earned and saved their own money are my best consumers. I give a free workshop for children on bicycle safety and repair. Children who have saved their money are always the ones who take my class!"

Elissa loves her new bike. She even knows how to fix a tire or a slipped chain. She also knows she has to wear her helmet and be alert when she rides her bicycle. And she has also learned a lot about how our economy works. Economy is the making and consuming of goods and services.

Elissa is a smart consumer. She asked many questions before deciding which bicycle to buy.

WHY IT MATTERS

Flythe Cyclery is part of Raleigh's economy. Mr. Flythe and his employees provide a service and sell goods. They also earn money. They spend that money in their community. That money helps other businesses grow.

Some people do jobs that don't earn money. For example, some people work in their homes raising their families. That's an important job too. Everyone who works contributes something to a community and to its economy.

Elissa plays a role in her community's economy by earning money and buying goods.

✔️ Reviewing Facts and Ideas

MAIN IDEAS

- Goods are things people make or grow.
- A service is a job that helps other people by providing something they need or want.
- People who buy goods are called consumers.
- Interest is money paid for a loan.
- Economy is the making and consuming of goods and services.

THINK ABOUT IT

1. What is the difference between an employer and a consumer?
2. **FOCUS** Why do people earn, save, and spend money?
3. **THINKING SKILL** _Compare_ and _contrast_ Mr. Flythe's job with the job of a teacher or principal.
4. **WRITE** Suppose you want to earn money over the summer. Write a brochure advertising what services you can offer your neighbors. Make sure your brochure tells why people should hire you and what you will charge.

MAKING A DIFFERENCE

The Pencilmania Business

NEW YORK CITY, NEW YORK—Would you like a monster pencil holder, an eraser shaped like a clown, or a holiday bunch of lollipops and pencils? Jason Walder and José Rodriguez can help you. They are 12-year-old students at Public School 169 in New York City. They're in classes for students who have special learning needs. And they are "super salesmen" of a program called Pencilmania.

Pencilmania is a made-up word that means "crazy about pencils." Students in Pencilmania need not be crazy about pencils, but they are serious about learning to run a business. Every day at lunch, they sell pencils and gift items.

The students give some of the money they earn to the Make a Wish Foundation to help children who are very sick. The money also pays for class trips to museums and concerts.

"Selling the pencils is just one part of the business," Jason learned.

The students use catalogs and decide what and how many of each kind of pencil to order. When the pencils arrive, they make sure they have received everything they ordered. They advertise their goods with posters, fliers, and announcements over the school loudspeaker.

José enters the daily earnings on a computer. "I also help decide how much each item should sell for so we can make money. But what I like most is helping the customers decide what they want. And I like to count money. It helps me in math."

The hard work is rewarding. Jason explained, "I am proud I learned how to make good decisions." And José added, "We learned how to work together to get our job done."

Pencilmania

People at Work

Read Aloud

"When I was a child, I didn't think much about where textbooks came from. I didn't think about who wrote them or how they were printed. Now I think about textbooks a lot! Working on textbooks is how I make my living."

Where Did This Book Come From?

These are the words of Iris Kim. She works at the publishing company in New York City that made this book. Publishing companies make books, magazines, CD-ROMs, and other things people can read. Ms. Kim is an editor. An editor helps with all the steps involved in making a book.

Like Ms. Kim at your age, you may not have given thought to your textbooks. But many people work hard to make the books that appear on your desk at the start of each school year. For Ms. Kim and the people she works with, making textbooks is more than just a way to make a living. They hope that readers, like you, will learn from the books. In this lesson you will learn some of the steps involved in making a book like this one.

Planning a Book

One of the first steps in making a textbook is to decide what the book should be about. The authors and editors make this decision together. Ms. Kim does research to find interesting and important topics for the textbooks she helps plan. Textbook authors and editors also pay attention to what teachers want their students to learn. The authors and editors learn what people have liked about their books in the past. It is also important to find out what changes to the book people would like to see in the future.

As an editor Iris Kim must research information. She also discusses writing ideas with writers and other editors.

How Does It Read?

After the first version of the book is written, many changes are made. The editor reads each lesson and makes suggestions about how to improve them. "Then I try to make all the changes work," says Ms. Kim. "I used to do my work on a typewriter. Now I use computers and other new technologies. I can make many more changes in much less time. I try to make each lesson interesting for students to read!"

Sometimes more information is needed, so Ms. Kim does more research. Sometimes all the information will not fit in the lesson. Then Ms. Kim must decide what information to leave out. There are also pictures and maps. Deciding what is most important is the editor's job. Computers help editors keep track of what is on each page.

After Ms. Kim receives a page from a writer, she makes many corrections and changes.

The designer decides where the photos and drawings will go on each page (top). The pages are then sent to the printer and made into a book (bottom).

How Does It Look?

Next, designers look at the pages. Designers make sure that each page looks right. They use a computer to help them decide where pictures will fit. "I try to make these pages exciting to look at," says a designer of this book. "Learning should be fun, so I choose pictures and designs that I think children will enjoy and learn from."

Then there are people who make sure the book will be printed correctly. All in all, about 75 people have worked on the book you are holding in your hands right now! By making a textbook that will be used by consumers, Ms. Kim and others are producers. A producer is a maker of goods or services.

Infographic

interNET CONNECTION

Visit our website:
www.mhschool.com

At the Workplace

Look around you. Almost everything you see is the result of someone's job. People built your school building. People made your desk and your pencils. Read this Infographic. What are the different jobs in your community?

Dena Abergel

Ballet Dancer
New York City, New York

Dancing is what makes me most happy in the world. Not everybody gets to do what they love. I began to study dancing intensely at age 10. The most rewarding part is performing.

Denice Burnham

Veterinarian
Orofino, Idaho

I take care of dogs, cats, and other pets. I like working with children to teach them how to care for their pets because children are usually the ones who know their pets best.

Roberto Rodriguez

Fourth-Grade Teacher
Salinas, California

My job is to help my students learn. We use computers in our classroom. Students get very enthusiastic when they get to use the computer. I love seeing their faces when they learn something new. That's what makes the job so wonderful.

Leon Harris

Television Anchorperson
Stone Mountain, Georgia

I make news stories understandable. A story can happen and within minutes I'm talking about it. When I get nervous I just imagine I'm talking to my son.

Kim Guyette

Furniture Maker and Woodworker
Waterbury Center, Vermont

I build tables from start to finish. Working with wood is challenging because you don't know exactly how each piece will come out.

285

I Like My Job!

For people to do a good job, it's important that they enjoy their work. Read the story below about a man who loves his job.

UNCLE JED'S BARBERSHOP

Story by Margaree King Mitchell, 1993.

Jedediah Johnson was my granddaddy's brother. Everybody has their favorite relative. Well, Uncle Jedediah was mine.

He used to come by our house every Wednesday night with his clippers. He was the only black barber in the county. Daddy said that before Uncle Jed started cutting hair, he and Granddaddy used to have to go thirty miles to get a haircut.

After Uncle Jed cut my daddy's hair, he **lathered** a short brush with soap and spread it over my daddy's face and shaved him. Then he started over on my granddaddy.

I always asked Uncle Jed to cut my hair, but Mama wouldn't let him. So he would run the clippers on the back of my neck and just pretend to cut my hair. He even spread lotion on my neck. I would smell wonderful all day.

---

lathered: filled with soap

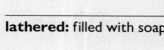

286

WHY IT MATTERS

In this lesson you have met people doing different things to earn a living. All of these people depend on other people to do their jobs. "I wouldn't be able to do my job by myself," says Ms. Kim. "Authors, designers, artists, and other editors all work on books with me. And the most important people of all are the students who read them. Without them, I wouldn't be able to work on books like this one at all!"

Ms. Kim and many other people have worked together to make this textbook.

✓ Reviewing Facts and Ideas

MAIN IDEAS

- Publishing companies make books. Authors, editors, and designers are some of the people who work on books.

- Technology has changed the way editors and designers do their jobs.

- A producer is a maker of goods and services.

- There are many different ways to make a living. People need to work together to do their jobs.

THINK ABOUT IT

1. What is a producer?

2. **FOCUS** What are some different ways a person can make a living?

3. **THINKING SKILL** Look around your classroom. List some jobs needed to produce the things you observe. _Classify_ the jobs into at least three groups. What do these groups tell you about making a living?

4. **WRITE** Write a letter to the editor of this book telling what you like and don't like about the book.

Legacy

Working AT Home

Museum of the City of New York

Working at home is a legacy that goes back long ago. People often lived above their shop or business or had a workshop in their backyard.

Today many people still work at home. As in the past some people work at home to care for their family and home. Still others work at home using computers and other high-tech machines to help run a business.

Cooking, cleaning and managing expenses are some of the many tasks homemakers do.

288

A pioneer family in the 1800s worked together for food and shelter. Water comes from the well behind the brown horse pictured here.

Modern technology like telephones, computers, and faxes enable people to keep in touch with businesses from home.

Craftmakers often work at home. Dressed as a colonist, a woman shows how candles were made (left). Today, an Arapaho woman sews quilts (below).

Thinking Skills

Identifying Cause and Effect

VOCABULARY

cause   effect

WHY THE SKILL MATTERS

In the last lesson you read about how technology has changed publishing. It is now easier for authors, editors, and designers to do their jobs. People can work all over the country, using fax machines and computers to send their work in.

New technology is one cause of these changes. A cause is something that makes something else happen. Some of the changes are effects of the new technology. An effect is what happens as a result of something else.

Understanding cause and effect connections helps you to make good decisions. For example, you know that opening your window on a cold day will cause cold air to come into the room. That will have the effect of making the room colder. You can then decide if you want to open the window or not. Look at the Helping Yourself box for some tips on how to find causes and effects as you read.

USING THE SKILL

One way to understand the connections between events is to look for clues as you read. Some words and phrases that may show you a cause are *because of*, *as a result of*, and *since*. Some that indicate effects are *as a result*, *so*, and *therefore*. As you read the story that follows, look for words to help you identify causes and effects.

> *Lisa Groome just took a new job. Since she is still learning how to do her new job, Lisa has to work late.*
>
> *Lisa is more excited about her work than she was at her old job. It is more rewarding. As a result, Lisa is happier.*

In the first paragraph, the word *since* connects two ideas. One idea is that Lisa is learning her new job. The other idea is that she is working late. *Since* shows you that Lisa's learning the job is the cause of her working late. Working late is an effect of learning the job.

Read the second paragraph again. Notice the phrase *as a result*, which indicates an effect. *As a result* shows that Lisa's happiness is an effect of her new job being more rewarding. The rewarding job is the cause of her happiness.

TRYING THE SKILL

Suppose that your mother or father is going to take a new job. Since the new job pays more money, your family will be able to save money for an exciting vacation. But the new job is located in another town, so you and your family will have to move.

What is the cause of your family being able to take a vacation? What is the effect of the job being in another town? How can you tell?

REVIEWING THE SKILL

1. What is a cause? What is an effect?

2. What can you do to tell if something is a cause or an effect?

3. As a result of technology, editors can change what is written more easily. Is the technology a cause or an effect? How do you know?

4. Why is it helpful to think about cause and effect when making a decision or solving a problem?

Focus Activity

READ TO LEARN

How do people live and work in Japan?

VOCABULARY

- journalist
- high-tech

PLACES

- Tokyo
- Japan

Life in Japan

Read Aloud

It is early Monday morning in Tokyo, Japan. Tokyo is one of the largest cities in the world. The subway platform is crowded. A train pulls into the station, silent and fast. The doors open and people start moving into the cars. Then the "pusher" comes along. He gently pushes people into the train to pack it more tightly. In Tokyo, the work day has begun.

A Growing Country

Tokyo (TOH kee yoh) is the capital of Japan. Japan is a small country in terms of land. Japan is a large country in terms of population. About 125 million people live in Japan. That number is about half the number of people living in the United States of America. To understand how crowded Japan is, picture half the people in our country moving to Montana!

Japan has been called "the land of the rising sun" because it is in the most eastern part of the continent of Asia. People there are among the first in the world to see the sun rise each day. Today "the land of the rising sun" has another meaning. The Japanese have worked hard to build up their country. So, they might see their country as a rising sun growing every day.

On the Job in Japan

Tsutomu Yamaguchi (tsew TOH mew yah mah GEW chee) is a journalist. A journalist writes for a newspaper, a magazine, or for a television news program. Mr. Yamaguchi lives in Japan and writes for a newspaper called the *Yomiuri Shimbun* (yoh mee ur ree SHIM bewn). "Working as a journalist is very challenging and exciting," says Mr. Yamaguchi. "I like finding stories and responding quickly to the news."

Mr. Yamaguchi also finds his job to be very hard at times. "The news is endless," he says. "And it is difficult to work on sad stories."

Just as Ms. Kim's job as an editor in the United States has changed because of technology, so has Mr. Yamaguchi's job. "We are very proud of our technology. We can get news stories and information faster than ever before. There is more information to understand," says Mr. Yamaguchi. "But it is still people who write the stories and make the decisions."

Mr. Yamaguchi is a journalist **who has worked in Japan and around the world.**

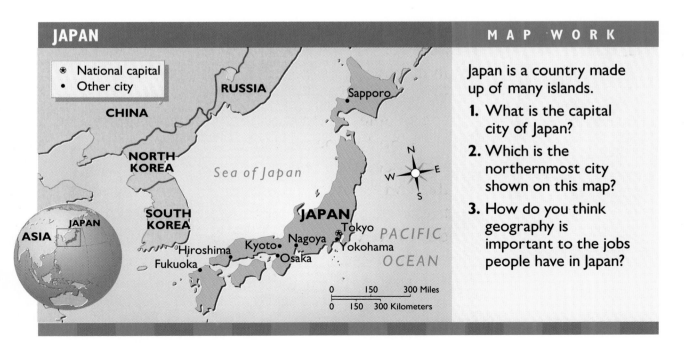

JAPAN

* National capital
• Other city

RUSSIA
CHINA
Sapporo
NORTH KOREA
Sea of Japan
SOUTH KOREA
JAPAN
ASIA JAPAN
Hiroshima
Kyoto Nagoya
Fukuoka Osaka
Tokyo PACIFIC
Yokohama OCEAN

0   150   300 Miles
0   150   300 Kilometers

MAP WORK

Japan is a country made up of many islands.

1. What is the capital city of Japan?
2. Which is the northernmost city shown on this map?
3. How do you think geography is important to the jobs people have in Japan?

Old and New

If you look around your home, the chances are you'll find something made in Japan. Like American companies, Japanese companies are also known for making **high-tech** products. High-tech is the use of the latest technology to make electronic and other goods. Japan makes cars, televisions, computers, video and recording machines, and other high-tech goods.

Japan has changed as quickly as technology has changed. It has kept much of its old culture as well. Look at the pictures on this page. They show some parts of Japanese culture. In his free time Mr. Yamaguchi likes to take part in a kind of theater called *Noh.* Actors in Noh theater wear masks that have been part of Japanese culture for hundreds of years. Mr. Yamaguchi also likes to make pottery. "In recent years, though, I haven't had time. I work long hours," says Mr. Yamaguchi. "When I have free time, I like to spend it with my family."

Kabuki theater, like Noh theater, is a very old tradition that is still popular in Japan.

Many people read the *Yomiuri Shimbun* (left). Baseball is popular in Japan.

A Changing Country

"In some ways, Japan is becoming more and more like other countries," says Mr. Yamaguchi. "My son is fifteen years old and his favorite music is American. But in other ways, Japan will always be different. For one thing, no other country speaks Japanese. It is a difficult language."

WHY IT MATTERS

You have read about some people who work for an American publishing company. You have also read about someone working for a Japanese newspaper company. What are some of the differences? Some things are very similar. Both work places have been changed by technology. And in both countries, as everywhere, people are the most important resource.

Japanese traditions like this style of house remain strong today, but Japan is changing as contact with other countries continues.

✓ Reviewing Facts and Ideas

MAIN IDEAS

- Japan is a small country with a large population.
- Journalists write for newspapers, magazines, or television news programs.
- Japan is known for making high-tech products.
- Japan has kept much of its traditional culture.

THINK ABOUT IT

1. What does a journalist do for a living?

2. **FOCUS** How do people live and work in Japan?

3. **THINKING SKILL** What is the _cause_ of Mr. Yamaguchi's being able to receive information more quickly? What are the _effects_ of technology on his job?

4. **WRITE** Write a two-paragraph newspaper article about something that happened at your school this week.

CHAPTER 11 REVIEW

THINKING ABOUT VOCABULARY

Number a sheet of paper from 1 to 10. Beside each number write the word or term from the list below that best completes each sentence.

consumer   high-tech
designer   interest
economy   journalist
employer   producers
goods   service

1. A good _____ makes sure that all the information in a news story is correct.

2. Some _____ products include fax machines and CD-ROMs.

3. People who produce and consume goods and services help our _____ to grow.

4. An _____ is someone who hires and pays other people to work.

5. A savings account in a bank earns extra money called _____.

6. When you buy something you are acting as a _____.

7. A _____ makes sure pages in a book look good.

8. _____ make things that consumers buy.

9. Books, cars, and sneakers are all examples of _____ people buy.

10. A doctor provides a _____ by helping people stay healthy.

THINKING ABOUT FACTS

1. Why do most people work?

2. What is the difference between goods and services?

3. What does it mean to be a smart consumer?

4. Why are people the most important resource in any economy?

5. Describe two ways in which Japan has kept its traditional culture.

THINK AND WRITE

WRITING A HOW-TO PARAGRAPH
Write a paragraph describing the steps involved in making a textbook such as this one.

WRITING A RESUME
A resume is a list of the jobs people had, with a description of each job. Write a short resume about yourself. Describe the different jobs or responsibilities you have.

WRITING ABOUT HOME
Look at the Legacy lesson on pages 288-289. Write a paragraph describing how working at home is different today than long ago.

APPLYING THINKING SKILLS

IDENTIFYING CAUSE AND EFFECT
Read the paragraph below and answer the questions that follow.

Twinkles Sports Shop was losing business because a huge new discount store was selling products at a lower price. It seemed that everyone was buying balls, bats, and skateboards there. Fortunately, the owner of Twinkles had an idea. She invited Muscles Malone, a famous football hero, to sign autographs and give tips on kicking and catching. As a result, Twinkles is full of customers now and sales are better than ever.

1. Define cause and effect.
2. What caused Twinkles Sports Shop to lose business?
3. What was the effect of Muscles Malone coming to Twinkles?
4. What do you think might be the effect of two stores selling the same products?
5. Why is it important to be able to tell the difference between causes and effects?

Summing Up the Chapter

Read the headings on the diagram below. Then review the chapter to find at least two pieces of information to include under each heading. When you have filled in a copy of the diagram, use it to write a sentence or two about how our economy works.

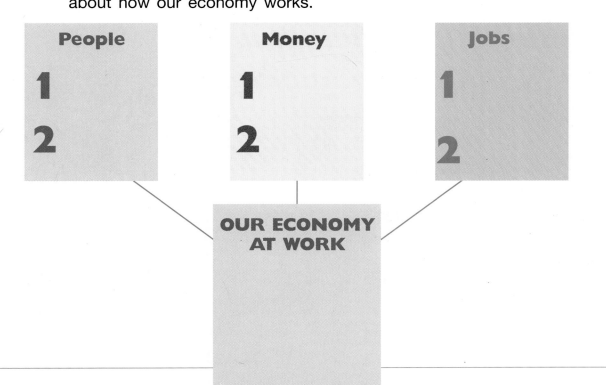

People	Money	Jobs
1 2	1 2	1 2

OUR ECONOMY AT WORK

Producing Goods

THINKING ABOUT
GEOGRAPHY AND ECONOMICS

Many things that people need are made from natural
resources. The availability of these resources influences
what can be produced. So, caring for our resources is
important not only to people who work with them but to
all of us. In Chapter 12 you will see how people today work
to turn resources into many different types of products.

Amsterdam, Netherlands

Port Arthur,
Texas

Saõ Paulo,
Brazil

**The United States exports
computers to countries
around the world.**

Automobiles are imported to the Netherlands.

Oil is produced in the United States.

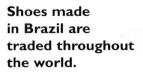
Shoes made in Brazil are traded throughout the world.

On the Farm

Read Aloud

"Sometimes my job is hard on my children. I come home tired and dirty. But the children bring me lunch and help in the fields. They see me working with the land, growing things. They learn a lot about nature, the economy, and hard work. I think they're proud of me.

Jon Lofgreen is a farmer. Across our country, there are many different kinds of farming. In this lesson you will see what life on one farm in Kansas is like.

Focus Activity

READ TO LEARN

How is wheat produced on farms?

VOCABULARY

- agriculture
- harvest
- fertilizer
- product map
- process

PLACES

- Norton, Kansas

A Farm in Kansas

Sometimes Jon Lofgreen just likes to stand in the middle of his wheat farm near Norton, Kansas. Kansas has good soil and a good climate for growing crops. Mr. Lofgreen looks around and sees his land surrounding him in all directions. Crops such as wheat and alfalfa grow on that land. Four hundred cows also graze on that land. This land has supported the Lofgreen family for over 100 years. But sometimes when Mr. Lofgreen stands and looks across his farm, he's not thinking about that. He's just looking at the beauty of the wheat blowing in the wind, covering the rolling hills.

Busy All Year

Of course, agriculture doesn't leave much time for gazing or standing around. Agriculture is the business of growing crops and raising animals. "We do several different kinds of farming here," says Mr. Lofgreen. "But most of the land is used for growing wheat. The harvest is gathered in about ten days at the end of June. But the rest of the year is spent getting ready for those ten days!"

The harvest is the ripe crops that are gathered. It takes planning, hard work, and help from nature to produce a good harvest. "Toward the end of September, we plant the crop in the brown soil. We use machines to plant the wheat and spread fertilizer," says Mr. Lofgreen. Fertilizers are chemicals that are used to help plants grow.

In the winter the wheat freezes. The fields turn brown again, but the plants are still working. They are producing seeds. In the spring the plants begin to turn dark green.

There are many jobs to do on a farm. Seth Lofgreen feeds a calf (below). Mr. Lofgreen loads wheat stored in a silo (bottom).

301

Farm Products

By mid–June, the wheat has turned from dark green to light green, and then to a golden color. The wheat is ready to be gathered. Farmers use a machine called a combine to cut the wheat, clean it, and put it in a holding tank. From there, trucks haul the wheat to storage tanks. Finally it is sold to companies that grind the wheat into flour. The flour is then made into bread, cakes, pasta, and other foods. These foods are then sold all over the world.

Wheat is just one of many crops grown in our country. Look at the product map below. A product map shows the places where goods are made or grown. This map shows crops that are grown in the United States.

Wheat is used to make many products you might eat, such as breads and cereals.

UNITED STATES FARM PRODUCTS

Corn
Cotton
Fruits and Vegetables
Dairy
Wheat

MAP WORK

Farmers throughout the United States supply many different types of products.

1. What are some of the different crops grown in the United States?

2. What products are from California?

3. In what ways do you think states in our country rely on each other for food products?

From milking cows to growing cranberries, farmers rely on technology to help make their work easier and faster.

New Ways of Farming

Sometimes Mr. Lofgreen is out in the fields, riding the combine or giving directions to workers. Other times he sits at a computer to do his farming. Here's what he says about how farmers today depend on technology to make a living. "I look at my computer and I can know in a second that wheat is selling for $3.69 a bushel. My computer helps me make decisions about when and where to sell my crop. I can see what's happening with other crops, in other parts of the world."

Look at the pictures on this page. Some farmers raise cows. Others grow cranberries. Many farmers are now using new technology like computers and high-tech combines to help raise their crops and animals.

Links to HEALTH

Why Eat Wheat?

Many breakfast cereals contain grains such as wheat. Grains are the seeds of cereal plants. Wheat and other grains give you important vitamins and minerals. They help your muscles, blood, nerves, bones, and teeth stay healthy.

Look at the nutrition labels on the containers and packaging of foods you eat. Which foods list wheat as one of the first three ingredients?

Throughout the history of our country, the harvest has been important to people. Some people celebrate the harvest with dancing and singing. Read the following song. Have you ever planted any of these crops?

Harvest

Georgia Folk Song

1. Time to gath-er har-vest. __ Oh, Em-ma, oh! ____
2. Dig-ging sweet_ po-ta-toes. __ Oh, Em-ma, oh! ____
3. Dig-ging ru-ta-bagas. __ Oh, Em-ma, oh! ____
4. Dig-ging big_ fat par-snips. __ Oh, Em-ma, oh! ____

You turn a-round, dig a hole in the ground, __

Oh, Em - ma, oh!

To Your Table

Farmers rely on each other. "The alfalfa I grow helps feed cattle on someone else's farm," points out Mr. Lofgreen. "The food on my table comes from another farm."

Many people other than farmers help make the food you see at your table. Some people process the food. To process is to change something into a different form. People process wheat to make bread and oranges to make orange juice. People at factories put the food into packages. Truckers drive the packages to stores. Stores sell the products to consumers.

WHY IT MATTERS

Native Americans farmed corn and other crops hundreds of years ago. Today Mr. Lofgreen makes a living from farming, as his great-great grandparents did. Farming is one of the important ways people make a living in our country.

Milk from cows is processed to make cheese and other dairy products.

✓ Reviewing Facts and Ideas

MAIN IDEAS

- Agriculture is the business of growing and raising crops. One example of agriculture is wheat farming.

- There are many different kinds of farming in our country.

- There are many different jobs involved in getting food from the farm to your table.

THINK ABOUT IT

1. What are two ways people earn their living in agriculture?

2. **FOCUS** How is wheat produced on farms?

3. **THINKING SKILL** What do you think might *cause* a bad harvest? What *effect* would this have on farming?

4. **GEOGRAPHY** Look at the product map on page 302. What kinds of farming are done in California?

Study Skills

Reading Flow Charts

VOCABULARY
flow chart

WHY THE SKILL MATTERS

For ten busy days in June, wheat is harvested on Jon Lofgreen's farm. But he and the other workers are busy the rest of the year too. As you have read, more than one step is involved in growing wheat. The order in which these steps are taken is important. A flow chart can be used to show the sequence of steps that are followed to produce a final product. Flow charts show the steps of an activity in order. Look at the Helping Yourself box for some tips on how to read flow charts.

USING THE SKILL

Suppose you want to see the sequence of steps in growing wheat. Look at how the flow chart below shows these steps and their order.

To read the flow chart, first look at its title. What is this flow chart about? Next notice that each step has a picture and a label. How many steps are shown in this flow chart?

The steps of an activity are shown in order in a flow chart. As you can see here, the first step in growing wheat is plowing the field. An arrow leads you to the next step—which is planting the wheat. The steps that follow are harvesting the wheat and finally selling it.

It is very important to follow the steps in order. If you plow the field after planting the wheat, you will not end up with much wheat to harvest!

GROWING WHEAT

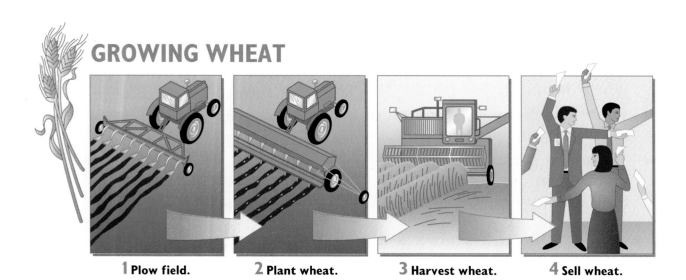

1 Plow field.   2 Plant wheat.   3 Harvest wheat.   4 Sell wheat.

TRYING THE SKILL

You have learned about some of the steps followed by wheat farmers. Farmers grow wheat in order to sell it. One wheat product is pasta. The flow chart on this page shows some of the steps in making pasta.

What is the first step in making pasta? What happens after flour is emptied into a bin? What happens after dough is formed into big sheets?

REVIEWING THE SKILL

1. What is a flow chart?

2. Look at the flow chart for making pasta. What is the last step shown?

3. Suppose you are making a flow chart of the steps you follow in making a sandwich. What would you show as the first step?

4. When is it helpful to read a flow chart?

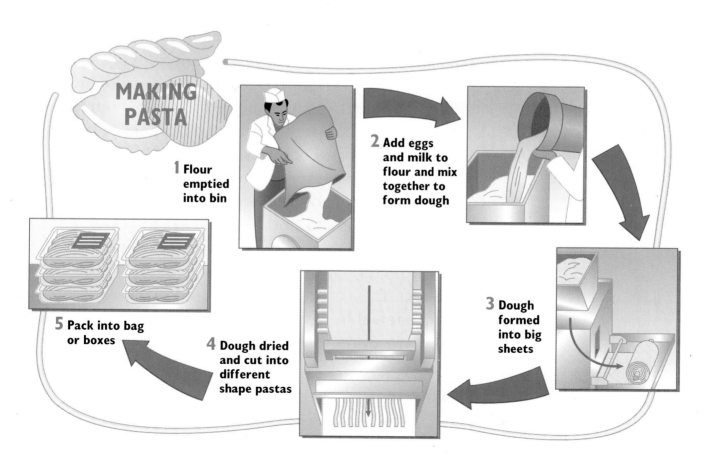

MAKING PASTA

1 Flour emptied into bin

2 Add eggs and milk to flour and mix together to form dough

3 Dough formed into big sheets

4 Dough dried and cut into different shape pastas

5 Pack into bag or boxes

Mining the Land

Read Aloud

Every state has certain symbols. For example, you may know the name of your state bird or state tree. Did you know that some states also have a state mineral? In this lesson you will read about why minerals are so important to people in our country.

Focus Activity

READ TO LEARN

What are some ways we get and use mineral resources?

VOCABULARY

- renewable resource
- nonrenewable resource
- public property
- private property

An Important Resource

Look at the pictures at the bottom of page 309. They show some everyday objects. Can you guess what these objects have in common? They all are made from the same mineral, copper.

Like farmers, miners also make their living from the land. They remove minerals from the land. There is one important difference, though. Many of the resources that farmers use are renewable resources. A renewable resource is one that can be replaced by nature, if used carefully. The soil and water used to grow wheat are renewable resources. Minerals are nonrenewable resources. That means they cannot be replaced. Once nonrenewable resources are used up they are gone forever.

Working in a Mine

Andy Romero knows a lot about the importance of natural resources. He is a copper miner in a community in Arizona. From the picture here you can see that Mr. Romero drives a truck in an open-pit mine. Copper that lies close to Earth's surface is removed by open-pit mining. "Natural resources like copper help keep our company in business and are important in making products people need," Mr. Romero says.

There are also other ways to mine copper. Some companies send miners deep down below the surface to dig for copper. Look at the chart on the next page to see what happens after copper is mined.

Andy Romero (top) drives a big truck at a mine. He is one of the many people who make copper available for all types of products (bottom). Copper is one of several minerals used to make a penny.

World of Resources

Copper is just one resource that people remove from Earth. Iron, gold, silver, limestone, coal, and oil are also mined. Our country is very rich in natural resources.

Some resources are on public property. Public property is land that has been set aside for all people to use. National parks and forests are public property.

Other resources are on private property. Private property is land that is owned by people or companies. Some people own land to build homes on it. Mining companies have bought a lot of land in order to mine it.

Minerals include (clockwise from top) gold, iron pyrite, and forms of copper.

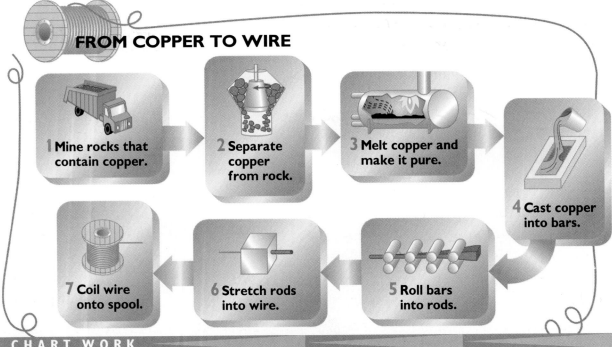

FROM COPPER TO WIRE

1 Mine rocks that contain copper.

2 Separate copper from rock.

3 Melt copper and make it pure.

4 Cast copper into bars.

5 Roll bars into rods.

6 Stretch rods into wire.

7 Coil wire onto spool.

CHART WORK

There are several steps involved before copper is made into wire.

1. What is the first step in the process of making copper wire?

2. What happens after the copper is made pure?

3. What are two questions you could ask to learn more about making copper products?

Boom Town to Ghost Town

Earth's resources provide jobs for many people. Sometimes "boom towns" grow when a resource is discovered. Many people move quickly to these towns to try to make money mining gold, oil, or other resources. Once the resource runs out, the jobs disappear.

People cannot make natural resources. But some companies make products that are like those found in nature. For example, plastic is sometimes used instead of metal.

WHY IT MATTERS

There are many mining jobs. People have to find the minerals. Some people are in charge of safety in the mines. Other people change minerals into forms people can use.

We use natural resources in different ways. But we must use them carefully to be sure that they will be here for a long, long time.

This ghost town in California was once a busy community. People hoped to get rich by finding valuable minerals.

Reviewing Facts and Ideas

MAIN IDEAS

- Mining is the removing of minerals from the earth.
- Renewable resources can be replaced by nature. Once nonrenewable resources are used, they are gone forever.
- Public property is land that has been set aside for all people to use. Private property is land that is owned by people or companies.

THINK ABOUT IT

1. Give an example of public property in your community. Give an example of private property.

2. **FOCUS** What are some ways we get and use mineral resources?

3. **THINKING SKILL** Suppose oil was discovered near your town. What might be some of the *effects* of this discovery?

4. **WRITE** Write a paragraph describing the process of making wire.

On the Assembly Line

Focus Activity

READ TO LEARN

How do factories work?

VOCABULARY

- manufacturing
- factory
- assembly line
- robot
- mill

PLACES

- Detroit, Michigan

Read Aloud

Suppose your class is making teddy bears to sell at a fair. Instead of each person making a complete bear, everyone has a special job. For example, one person will cut the fabric. Another will sew on the faces. Your class has just discovered a smart way to make a product. In this lesson you will read more about smart ways companies make things.

A Factory in Detroit

Whether you're making teddy bears or cars, you are manufacturing. Manufacturing is the business of making things. Manufacturing used to be done mostly by hand in factories. A factory is a place where things are manufactured. Today manufacturing is often done by people as well as by high-tech machines in factories.

Marge Gendron works in manufacturing at an automobile company in Detroit, Michigan. Most cars are built on assembly lines in factories like hers. An assembly line is a line of workers and machines all working together to make a final product. Different tasks are done at each stop along the way.

Assembly Lines Long Ago

The cars that roll off the assembly line today look very different from the first cars in our country. The assembly line is not a new idea for the automobile industry. In fact, assembly lines got their start in the early 1900s as a way to make cars.

At first only a few people could afford to buy cars. Cars took so much time to build that they were very expensive. But Henry Ford knew that many people would want to buy cars if they were less expensive. He started one of the first assembly lines. Soon it took less time to make cars. Then the price of cars went down and people rushed to buy them. In 1924 a Model T cost $290.

From filling bottles (top) to making automobiles (bottom), people had different jobs on assembly lines long ago.

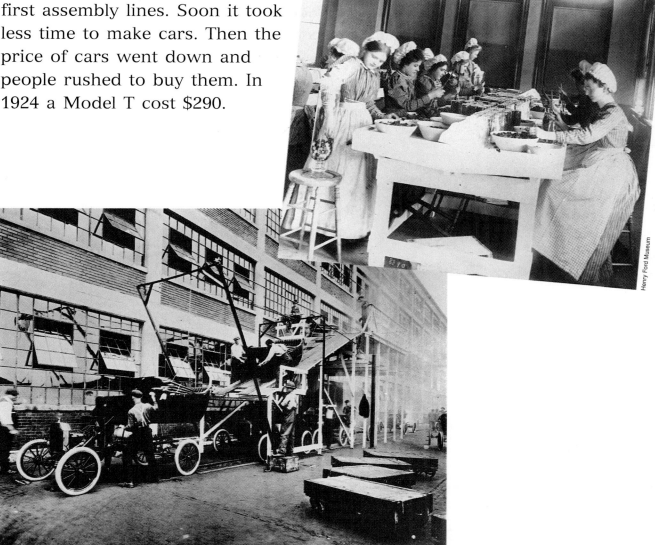

Henry Ford Museum

Making a Car Today

The assembly line Marge Gendron works on today is different from the one Henry Ford first used. Today's assembly lines use robots. Robots are machines made to do tasks. Marge feels lucky that her job is still done by people. "Otherwise," she says, "I'd be out of work!"

From the chart below you can see that a car has many parts. Ms. Gendron works at the "bumper station." There she checks that the bumpers are safely made. She also makes sure the bumpers have no scratches or paint marks. If she finds a problem, it is also her job to fix the bumper. One hour after she checks the bumper, it is attached to a finished car.

Marge Gendron works in a factory where she checks automobile bumpers.

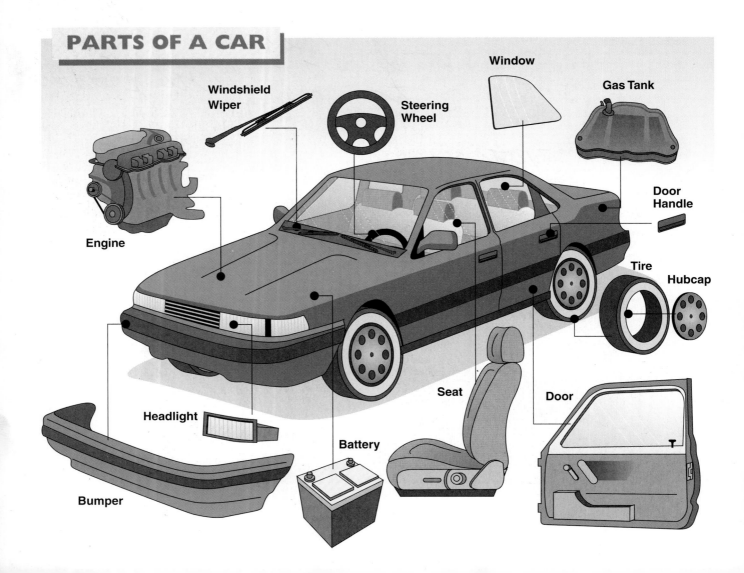

PARTS OF A CAR

Windshield Wiper

Window

Gas Tank

Steering Wheel

Engine

Door Handle

Tire

Hubcap

Headlight

Seat

Door

Battery

Bumper

Proud of a Product

Marge Gendron has been working at the same company for almost 30 years. "Sometimes it's been rough to do the same job day after day," she says. "Each bumper weighs about 30 pounds. That's a lot of bending and lifting. I feel proud when I see people driving our cars. I like to think that we do a good job. My best friend works next to me. I also like to hear people say we make beautiful cars."

Look at the pictures on this page. What do they tell you about how manufacturing is changing the jobs people like Marge Gendron do?

Robots do many jobs on assembly lines, including welding (top) and safety testing (bottom).

Manufacturing Today

Cars are just one of the many products manufactured in our country. Many companies are in the manufacturing business. Manufacturing is one of the biggest kinds of business in our country. Millions of people work in manufacturing. They make thousands of different products. Some of the most important products are transportation equipment, such as trains, cars, and buses. Chemicals, machines, medicines, food, toys, computers, and books are some other examples.

Not all things are manufactured on assembly lines. Can you think of something in your school that was not manufactured on an assembly line? How about your school building? It was most likely built by workers using tools, not on an assembly line. Or perhaps the blanket in your bedroom was made by hand by someone in your family.

Not all products are made in a factory. The house you live in and baked goods you eat were most likely made by hand.

A Manufacturing Town

The jobs people have are not only important to them, but they are also important to their family and community. The story below is about a steel **mill** in West Virginia. A mill is a place where people use machines to make natural resources into finished products. How do you think the jobs that people do at this steel mill influence the community?

MANY VOICES
LITERATURE

No Star Nights

Excerpt from the story by Anna Egan Smucker, 1989.

We went to school across from the mill. The smokestacks towered above us and the smoke billowed out in great puffy clouds of red, orange, and yellow, but mostly the color of rust. Everything—houses, hedges, old cars—was a rusty red color. Everything but the little bits of **graphite**, and they glinted like silver in the dust. At recess when the wind whirled these sharp, shiny metal pieces around, we girls would crouch so that our skirts touched the ground and kept our bare legs from being stung.

We would squint our eyes when the wind blew to keep the graphite out. Once a piece got caught in my eye, and no matter how much I blinked or how much my eye watered it wouldn't come out. When the eye doctor finally took it out and showed it to me, I was amazed that a speck that small could feel so big.

---

graphite: soft, black mineral

Using Resources

In manufacturing products, people need to use natural resources. Trees are used to make paper. Sand is used to make glass. Iron is used to make steel. Coal and oil are used to make the energy that runs the factories. So in manufacturing, people must also be sure to use resources carefully.

WHY IT MATTERS

A factory hires people like Marge Gendron to make products. It also creates jobs for even more people outside of the company. Suppose a company makes computers. Other people are hired to ship the computers. Still other people are needed to sell the computers. And someone else may design programs to be used on the computer. As you can see, most of the jobs in your community and around our country are connected to each other in many ways.

Nuts and bolts are manufactured from natural resources like iron.

✓// Reviewing Facts and Ideas

MAIN IDEAS

- Manufacturing is the business of making things.
- Many factories use assembly lines to make things faster and less expensively. On an assembly line different steps are done in order to make a finished product.
- Manufacturing is one of the most important types of businesses in our country today.

THINK ABOUT IT

1. List ten different things manufactured in our country today.
2. **FOCUS** How do factories work?
3. **THINKING SKILL** *Classify* these items—books, water, coal, cars, trees, computers, copper. Are they manufactured, or are they natural resources?
4. **GEOGRAPHY** Many types of manufacturing companies are located near big cities. Why do you think this is so?

MAKING A DIFFERENCE

Inventor and Friend

HOUSTON, TEXAS— One day Josh Parsons, age 10, made a close friend. It started with baseball. Josh's father coached Josh's Little League team, the Mustangs.

One day just before the season started, Mr. Parsons told Josh about a boy named David Potter. David wanted to try out for the Mustangs. He was a very good hitter and catcher. "This was unusual," Josh says, "because he has arms only to the elbows." When David was 4 years old, he lost his hands and lower arms in an accident.

Like Josh, David loved baseball. On his own he learned to swing a bat. He also taught himself to catch a ball. He used a glove attached to his elbow. But David could not find a way to throw a ball.

"I had an idea," says Josh. "I thought of making something to help him throw. It could be shaped like a scoop. I told my idea to my Dad. We made a model of it."

Josh and his father went to David's house. They wanted to show him the invention. "I didn't know

him. He didn't know me. At first he was shocked. Then he tried the throwing arm on. It fit perfectly over his elbow. We went into his yard and my dad threw the ball to him. He threw it back. The arm worked!"

With his new throwing arm, David tried out for and won a place on the Mustang team. Today both boys are still playing baseball. And Josh is still inventing. He made another throwing arm for a boy in Montana. "This one," says Josh "is good for throwing snowballs in the winter and baseballs in the summer."

"I thought of making something to help him . . ."

Josh Parsons

319

Focus Activity

READ TO LEARN

Why is trade important?

VOCABULARY

- trade
- domestic trade
- import
- export
- international trade

PLACES

- Canada

Partners in Trade

Read Aloud

You've read a lot in this book about how important our natural resources are. People in communities work together to share them and to make the most of them. People are also working to protect natural resources. In this lesson you will learn about another way in which people rely on each other around the world.

Not Only Baseball Cards

What do you think of when you hear the word trade? Perhaps you think about swapping sandwiches with a friend. Or you may think about trading baseball cards. For businesses and governments, trade means something a little different. Trade is the buying and selling of goods and services. In some ways, though, trade is not that different from exchanging things in the lunchroom or in the schoolyard. People and countries trade for the same reasons. They trade because each side has something the other wants.

Trade Across Borders

Earlier in this chapter you read that Kansas has good soil and a good climate for agriculture. But it does not have many big cities with manufacturing. Detroit, Michigan has a lot of automobile factories. But it does not grow much wheat. So people in Kansas buy cars made in Detroit. People in Detroit eat bread made from wheat grown in Kansas. This exchange is called domestic trade, or trade within one country.

Most countries can't produce everything they need. Instead they import goods that are made or grown in another country. To import is to buy goods from another country. Then often they export what they've made or grown to other countries. To export is to sell and ship goods to another country.

One of our country's biggest trading partners is Canada, our neighbor to the north. We import fish, wood, and other products from Canada. We export computers, fruits, and other products to Canada.

The United States imports products like fish and wood from Canada and exports products including computers and automobiles.

Infographic

inter**NET**
CONNECTION
Visit our website:
www.mhschool.com

U.S. Trade Around the World

International trade is the importing and exporting of goods between countries. Look at this Infographic to see some of the products the United States trades with other countries of the world.

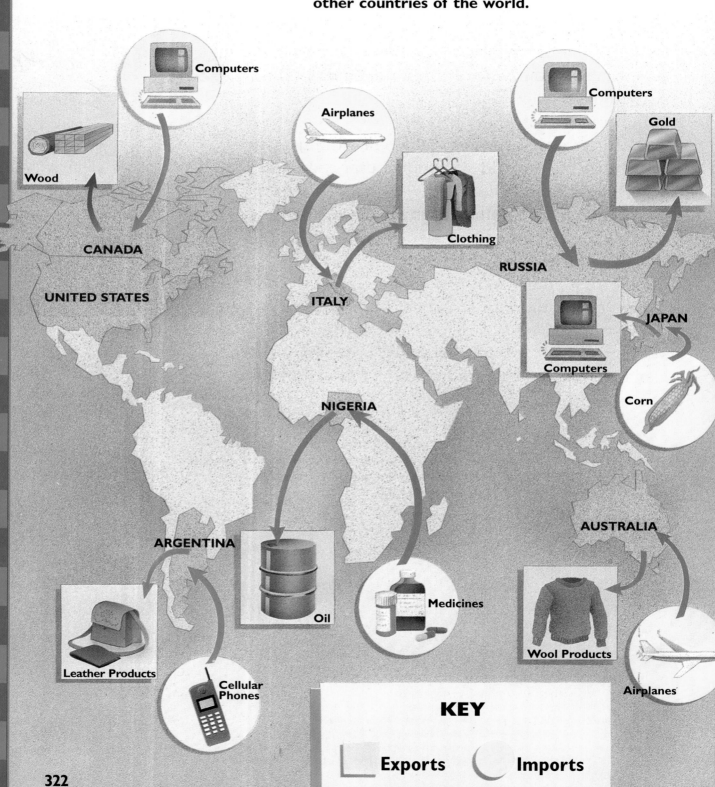

Computers

Airplanes

Computers

Gold

Wood

Clothing

CANADA

RUSSIA

JAPAN

UNITED STATES

ITALY

Computers

Corn

NIGERIA

AUSTRALIA

ARGENTINA

Oil

Medicines

Wool Products

Leather Products

Cellular Phones

Airplanes

KEY

Exports   Imports

322

The World at Home

Look at the picture on this page. If you visited a port, you might see many different products being imported and exported from around the world. Sugar might come from sugarcane grown in the Philippines or India. Coffee probably comes from beans grown in Colombia in South America. The wheat being loaded might be headed for Japan or Russia.

WHY IT MATTERS

People in communities in the United States and around the world depend on each other in many ways. One of these ways is trade. By working with each other in the years ahead, people in all communities can continue to make our planet a better place to live and work.

The port of Los Angeles handles **trade** between the United States and other countries.

Reviewing Facts and Ideas

MAIN IDEAS

- Trade is the business of buying and selling goods and services.
- To export is to sell goods to another country. To import is to buy goods from another country.
- The United States trades with Canada and other countries all over the world.
- Domestic trade is trade within one country.
- International trade is importing and exporting of goods between countries.

THINK ABOUT IT

1. What is the difference between imports and exports?

2. **FOCUS** Why is trade important?

3. **THINKING SKILL** Suppose the United States could not trade with other countries. What are some *effects* this might have on life in our country?

4. **GEOGRAPHY** Look at the map on page R10. What ocean would a ship carrying coffee have to cross to get from Colombia to the western United States?

CHAPTER 12 REVIEW

THINKING ABOUT VOCABULARY

Number a sheet of paper from 1 to 10. Beside each number write the word or term from the list below that matches the statement.

agriculture   import

assembly line   manufacturing

factory   process

fertilizer   robot

harvest   trade

1. The buying and selling of goods and services
2. A place where things are manufactured
3. The business of making things
4. The ripe crops that are gathered
5. The business of growing crops and raising animals
6. Chemicals used to help plants grow
7. To change into a different form
8. Machine made to do tasks instead of people
9. To buy goods from another country
10. A line of workers and machines all working together to make a final product

THINKING ABOUT FACTS

Number a sheet of paper from 1 to 5. Write **T** if a statement is true. If it is false, rewrite it to make it true.

1. In Kansas the wheat harvest is usually ready during the summer.
2. Today many farmers in the United States make use of computers and high-tech combines to help grow their crops.
3. Minerals like copper are examples of renewable resources.
4. The use of assembly lines lowers the cost of making products such as cars and trucks.
5. Domestic trade is trade between countries.

THINK AND WRITE

WRITING ABOUT A FARM

Write a story in which you describe what it might be like to live and work on a Kansas wheat farm.

WRITING ABOUT BUSINESS

Write a paragraph explaining why the assembly line helped reduce the cost of making automobiles.

WRITING A SHORT STORY

Write a story about a young boy or girl who lives near a copper mine. Describe how the mine and the people who work there are important to their community. You can refer to "Many Voices" on page 317 for help.

APPLYING STUDY SKILLS

READING FLOW CHARTS

Answer the following questions about the chart on page 310 to practice your skill of reading flow charts.

1. Explain how to read a flow chart.
2. What is the first step shown on the flow chart? What is the last step?
3. What happens right after the copper is separated from rock?
4. What happens just before the melted copper is rolled into rods?
5. Why is a flow chart a good way to explain how wire is made?

Summing Up the Chapter

Review the chapter to find information about each type of work shown in the theme diagram below. Next fill in a copy of the diagram with a main idea about each type of work. Then write a short paragraph describing one way in which goods are produced from natural resources.

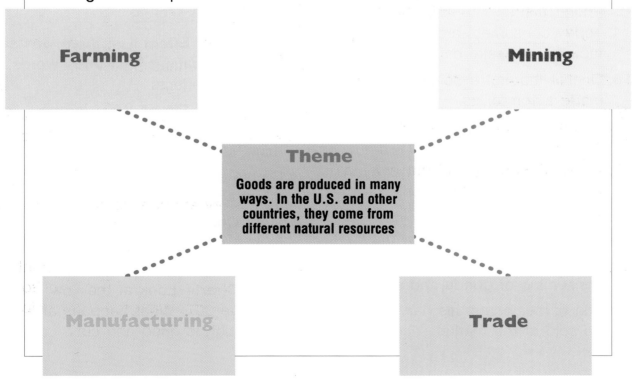

Farming

Mining

Theme

Goods are produced in many ways. In the U.S. and other countries, they come from different natural resources

Manufacturing

Trade

UNIT 5 REVIEW

THINKING ABOUT VOCABULARY

consumers   imports
designer   product map
employer   public property
export   robots
fertilizer   services

Number a sheet of paper from 1 to 10. Beside each number write **C** if the underlined word is used correctly. If it is not, choose the word or term from the list above that correctly completes the sentence.

1. During a sale, Andy's Bike Shop is always filled with <u>employers</u>.

2. The more money you save in a bank, the more <u>interest</u> you earn.

3. We enjoy camping on <u>private property</u> such as national parks.

4. Today <u>consumers</u> are used in factories to make cars and trucks.

5. One of the first <u>assembly lines</u> made automobiles.

6. The United States <u>imports</u> computers and cars from Japan.

7. A <u>journalist</u> makes sure that every page in a book looks good.

8. A <u>flow chart</u> shows the places where goods are made or grown.

9. The <u>economy</u> is the making and consuming of goods and services.

10. The farmer brings his <u>harvest</u> to be sold at the market.

THINK AND WRITE

WRITING ABOUT JOBS
In this unit you read about a variety of jobs. Write a paragraph explaining why you might choose to have any one of these jobs.

WRITING A PARAGRAPH
Suppose that you lived long ago, before the use of money. Write a paragraph describing how farmers might have obtained goods and services.

WRITING ABOUT WORKING TOGETHER
You have seen how people work together in many ways. Write a paragraph describing how the United States trades with other countries.

BUILDING SKILLS

1. **Cause and Effect** List three words that show causes. List three words that show effects.

2. **Cause and Effect** What is one effect of saving your money in a bank?

3. **Cause and Effect** What is one effect of using an assembly line?

4. **Flow Charts** Why is a flow chart a good way to learn about how things are made?

5. **Flow Charts** Look at the flow chart on page 307. What happens after the dough is dried and cut?

LOCAL *connection*

How have businesses in your community changed over time? Make a model village of your community long ago. Then make another model village of your community today. Use the two models to show how businesses and locations have changed in your community over time.

READING ON YOUR OWN

Here are some books you might find at the library to help you learn more.

AUNT LILLY'S LAUNDROMAT
by Melanie Hope Greenberg
Step into Aunt Lilly's laundromat and learn about working hard and keeping dreams alive.

COWS IN THE PARLOR
by Cynthia McFarland
Where does milk come from? Visit Clear Creek farm and learn about dairy farming.

IF YOU MADE A MILLION
by David Schwartz
Here's your chance to learn about making and spending a lot of money.

UNIT REVIEW PROJECT

Have a Career Fair

1. Have each group member choose one career they would like to research.
2. Write several facts and draw pictures for each career on a piece of cardboard.
3. Make a display showing the different careers in your group.

4. Share displays in a Class Career Fair. Have group members describe why they chose each career.

SPECIAL SECTION
EXPLORING YOUR
COMMUNITY

Welcome to Echo Park, an urban community in Los Angeles, California! It's the end of the year for Mrs. Stavert's third-grade class at Rosemont Elementary School. This year her class has studied and explored communities. Now the class wants to do something very special.

Each year new citizens move to Echo Park. So Mrs. Stavert's class decided to make a Community Welcome Center. It will be on display in the new Echo Park Public Library. Making the Welcome Center will be a fun way for the class to learn about their community. The Welcome Center will also be very useful to many other people in Echo Park.

As you will see, this is a very interesting community. And do you know what? So is your community. So, you too can use the resources in your community to make a Welcome Center. Turn the page and you will see how!

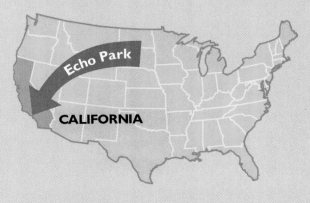

Echo Park

CALIFORNIA

The Geography of Echo Park

Down by Echo Park Lake. Up through Hollywood Hills. Samantha and Steven just moved to Echo Park and wanted to ride their bikes around the community with their parents. But learning to get around their community can be tricky, and tiring.

To learn more about the land around their area they found some maps of Echo Park and Los Angeles in their school library. Then they decided to make a community map and a clay terrain model of Los Angeles and Echo Park. Their terrain model is like a map with landforms that you can touch. It shows some of the area's important land features. Now they can try to avoid all the big hills and find all the fun places around Echo Park and Los Angeles. What places would you include in a map and terrain model of your community?

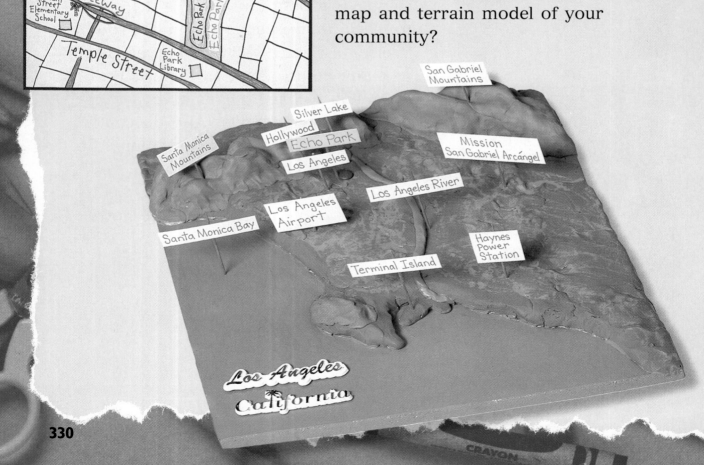

Helping Our Environment

The terrain model helped Mrs. Stavert's class to see that the environment is a very important part of any community. All communities need clean air, water, and land. That is why Mark, Jammie, and Andy wanted the Welcome Center to include a poster about protecting their environment.

First they researched information about the environment. Then they spoke with people at the Southern California Air Quality District office. They learned that the way people treat the environment today will affect, for good or bad, the lives of people in years to come. Look at their poster below. What does it say about air pollution in Echo Park? What would you say in a pollution poster about your community?

A Video Look at Our History

Why is Echo Park called Echo Park? Stephanie wanted to know. So she called the Echo Park Historical Society. She learned that in 1894, some men were working around the lake. One man called to the workers on the other side of the lake. He called and called, but all he could hear was the echo of his own voice. Soon after, everyone began calling the park "Echo Park."

At the library, Stephanie had an idea to make a video of a class play about the history of Echo Park. So she and her classmates researched the lives of people who lived in Echo Park. They found out about the conflicts people had. They also learned about the different clothes people wore. Then the class even made costumes to use in their play. Here you can read what they had to say. Enjoy the show!

"I am a Native American who lived here in a village with about 300 other members of my tribe in the 1600s."

"I am an explorer who came to this area in 1769," when my ship landed here after a long journey from Mexico.

"Like many Mexicans, I came to California in the 1940s to pick fruits and vegetables on farms around California."

"My family were pioneers who moved to the area of Echo Park in the 1880s."

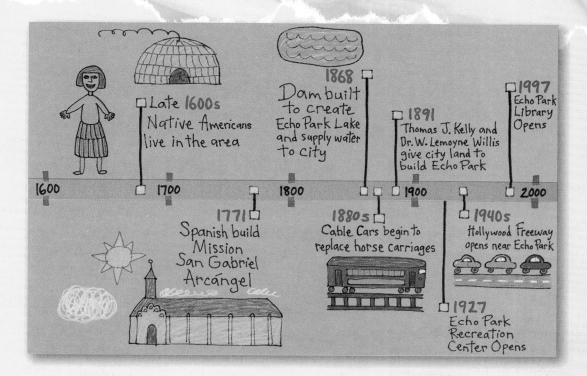

Echo Park Timeline

One day Andy met an interesting woman in the library. She happily told him stories of life in Echo Park long ago. Her name is Mrs. Delomes. She has lived in Echo Park for almost 70 years. She talked so much about so many interesting things, that Andy decided to make a time line about the events in Echo Park's past.

He read books. He saw old pictures that Mrs. Delomes had saved. He asked her even more questions. Her oral history gave him lots of answers. With the help of his classmates, Andy then used this information to make a history time line. What events would you put in a time line of your community? Whom could you speak to about your community long ago?

Photo of Echo Park taken around 1897

Working in Echo Park

Rebecca knew that many people come to Echo Park to find jobs and make a living. With the help of her parents and Mrs. Stavert, she spoke to different people who work in Echo Park. She was surprised and excited about what she found out. She then decided to take their pictures and put them in a special book. She called her book, "Working in Echo Park." Take a look at some of the people in Rebecca's book. What are the different jobs people have in your community?

Irma Gonzalez
Restaurant Worker

"I have been working at Barrangan's Restaurant for 31 years. I am the cashier. When people finish their meals, they come up to the cash register to pay for their meals. The rest of the time, I answer the telephone and take reservations for tables."

Joseph Santarromana
Website Designer

"I teach other people how to design and create their own websites on the Internet. The Internet could be a tool an artist could use to create new kinds of art."

Ed Slattery
Electric Company Mechanic

"My job is to make sure that our electrical system is safe and to restore electrical service as quickly as possible when it goes out during an emergency. I like helping people. It makes me happy when their house lights up again."

Services in Our Community

What would happen if your community ran out of water and electricity? You might not have any showers or lights! Whom would you call for help? These services are very important to a community.

So Juan and Jahaira (yah HĪ ruh) decided to use a computer to make a community services emergency telephone list. To make this list, they spoke to people who provide important community services. As you can see below, they put many important phone numbers in their list. What services would you put in a telephone list for your community?

OUR COMMUNITY SERVICES

, Ambulance, Fire Department . . 911
al 555-1234

member Susan Goldberg 555-2345
member Mike Hernandez 555-3456
. . . . 555-4567

Hotline . . . .
Center 555-5678
artment 555-6789
mpany 555-7890
. . . . 555-9876

hool 555-8765
. . . . 555-7654
nent . . . .
reation Center 555-6543
. . . . 555-5432

. . . . 555-4321

. . . . 555-3210
. . . . 555-3425

Our Local Government

This year, Mrs. Stavert's class learned about government and citizenship. So Trevor volunteered to make a chart that shows how local government works in Echo Park.

Trevor read the community newspapers. He learned that Echo Park is part of the Los Angeles city government. With the help of Mrs. Stavert, he called community leaders. They told him how people work together in government to solve problems. He even visited City Hall.

Then he decided to make the chart below to show how local government works. What would you do to learn about how your local government works?

Trevor also decided to speak to people who make a difference in Echo Park. He knew of an exciting art project that caught his attention. On the next page you will read what Trevor learned.

Mayor

City Council

Parks and Recreation

Police

Housing

Water and Power

Other Departments

MAKING A DIFFERENCE

A Wall of Many Colors

Trevor interviewed two volunteers in the community. One was an artist named Theresa Powers. The other was a nine year-old student named Sabrina Aguilar. Trevor met them when he noticed that they were painting a very colorful wall mural on a run-down building in the community. A mural is a picture painted on a wall. The mural is a project done by volunteers in a local program that helps to improve Echo Park.

Q: Why did you get involved in the program?

Ms. Powers: I live in Echo Park and I was looking for a way to get involved in the community. I was interested in helping to make the community beautiful.

Sabrina: I thought it would be fun to do something with my sisters and cousins and friends. I wanted to help make the neighborhood pretty.

Q: How did you make the mural?

Ms. Powers: First we talked to neighborhood families about how they wanted it to look. We made an outline on the wall, then the children started painting.

Sabrina: Before we did the mural, the wall was an ugly mess. It had spray paint all over it. But we covered that over.

Q: How do you feel like you are helping the community with this project?

Ms. Powers: It makes the people in the neighborhood feel proud and it has caused lots of other good things to happen. We ended up repainting the front of the store the mural is on. Other community groups got involved in cleaning up other parts of the community.

Sabrina: I had fun working together to make the community better. And the mural came out really, really colorful.

The Lotus Festival

Community Calendar of Events

Season	Event
Spring	Fishing Day at Echo Lake
	Baseball Season Opens
	Cuban Cultural Festival
Summer	Lotus Festival
	July 4th Celebration
	T Ball Clinic
Fall	Harvest Festival
	Halloween Carnival
	Echo Park Artists Festival
Winter	Holiday Show
	Festival of Lights
	Christmas Parade

Fun All Year!

Winter, spring, summer, or fall—there are many ways people have fun in Echo Park. Gideon decided to make a calendar of fun things to do in the community. He read newspapers and magazines. He spoke with his classmates and neighbors. Soon he had plenty of information to put in his calendar.

Have a look at Gideon's Community Calendar above. How are these events the same as those in your community? How are they different? What events would you want to put in your Community Calendar?

Communities Are Special

This year in social studies, Mrs. Stavert's class learned a lot about communities in our country and around the world. They learned that communities grow and change. They also learned that people's actions and decisions today will make a difference to the lives of others who will live in the community in years to come.

By making the Welcome Center that you see below, Mrs. Stavert's class learned that Echo Park is a very special community. When you explore your own community, you will learn that it too is special. Happy exploring!

Communities Celebrate Holidays

HOW MANY DIFFERENT HOLIDAYS CAN YOU THINK OF? WHICH OF THESE DO PEOPLE IN YOUR COMMUNITY CELEBRATE?

Portland OREGON

Durango COLORADO

San Francisco CALIFORNIA

San Diego CALIFORNIA

San Antonio TEXAS

ELECTION DAY

NEW YEAR'S DAY

HANUKKAH

CHRISTMAS

CINCO de MAYO

During the year, people in communities around our country come together to celebrate holidays that are important to them. Most holidays help us remember and celebrate important events of the past. Other holidays give people the time to do important things like voting.

Many holidays have their own symbols. A turkey is often thought of as a symbol of Thanksgiving. What other holiday symbols can you think of?

In this lesson you will read about many different holidays. You will also see how people in communities all across our country celebrate holidays.

KWANZAA

THANKSGIVING

EID AL FITR

PRESIDENTS' DAY

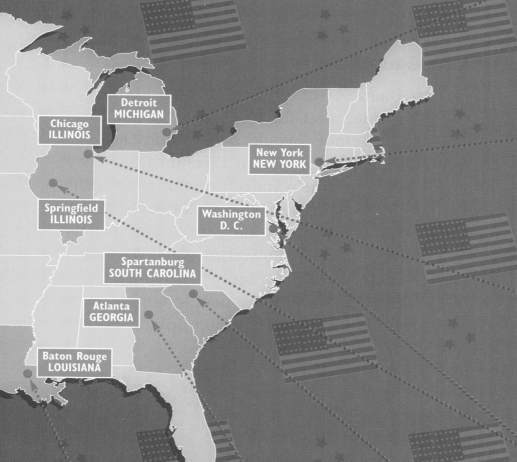
Detroit MICHIGAN
Chicago ILLINOIS
New York NEW YORK
Springfield ILLINOIS
Washington D. C.
Spartanburg SOUTH CAROLINA
Atlanta GEORGIA
Baton Rouge LOUISIANA

INDEPENDENCE DAY

MARTIN LUTHER KING, JR. DAY

MEMORIAL DAY

Election Day

It is important that people vote for their leaders. In Portland a firehouse is used as a place for voting (top). Another place to vote is at a booth in the street (bottom).

PORTLAND, OREGON—In 1845 the United States Congress decided that the Tuesday after the first Monday in November would be Election Day. People in our country vote on Election Day. They choose leaders and help make decisions for their community and country. Sometimes people also vote on other days during the year. Most citizens over the age of 18 are allowed to vote. The right to vote is one of our most important rights.

In Portland, Oregon, many people vote on Election Day. They vote at a polling place. Polling means "voting." These places can be schools, churches, or firehouses. Where do people vote in your community?

Thanksgiving Day

NEW YORK, NEW YORK—Pass the turkey, please! In 1621 a Thanksgiving celebration was held in Plymouth, Massachusetts. The Pilgrims wanted to give thanks for their rich harvest. They also wanted to thank the Wampanoag for helping them to grow their crops. Together, they held a special "Thanksgiving" meal.

Volunteers with America Sings! celebrate Thanksgiving at a parade (left). Afterwards they might enjoy a meal of turkey and vegetables (bottom).

Today, a Thanksgiving meal is a tradition for Americans. But for some people, Thanksgiving is also a time to say thanks by helping others. Every year, a group called "America Sings!" invites children from around the country to sing in New York's Thanksgiving Day parade. They bring toys and clothing for families in need. They also make meals for people who do not have food on Thanksgiving. For the children in "America Sings!", Thanksgiving means fun at the parade and helping others. Of course, it also means eating turkey.

Hanukkah

Hanukkah (HAH noo kah) is a holiday that is celebrated by Jewish people in communities in our country and around the world. This holiday is eight days long and often comes in December. It is a celebration of freedom for Jews.

Having fun on Hanukkah could mean enjoying a fun game called dreidel (top) or acting in a community play (bottom).

On each night of Hanukkah, people light candles on a menorah (meh NOH rah). A menorah is a candlestick with eight branches. It is a symbol of Hanukkah.

In San Diego, California, many people celebrate with a community party called a "Hanukkah Happening." They sing songs and light the menorah candles. They eat potato pancakes, a traditional Hanukkah dish. For children, there are also fun games to play.

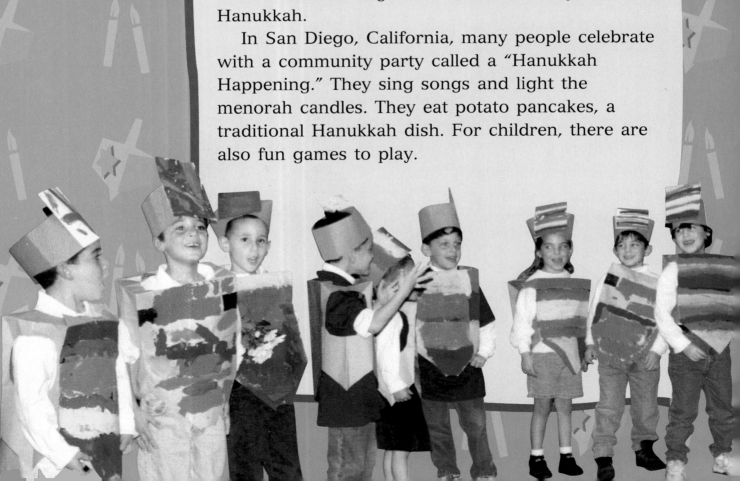

Christmas

A white Christmas in Durango includes snowy streets and colorful Christmas lights (top). At home people stay warm and celebrate by sharing gifts (bottom).

DURANGO, COLORADO—Christmas is a religious holiday that is celebrated on December 25th. Christmas celebrates the birth of Jesus Christ.

On Christmas Day people gather around the Christmas tree. They give each other gifts. People also like to celebrate by singing Christmas carols.

In some communities like Durango, Colorado, Christmas celebrations go on for a whole month. If you visit Durango in December, you will see the main street lit up with Christmas lights. You can drink hot cider and join in a Christmas carol sing-along. And do not forget to get in line for the community toy-and-cookie exchange!

Kwanzaa

Kwanzaa includes traditions like enjoying meals with friends and family that include chicken, rice, beans, yams and green vegetables (top) and lighting the kinara (bottom).

DETROIT, MICHIGAN—Kwanzaa (KWAHNZ uh) is a holiday celebrated by many African Americans today. The name "Kwanzaa" comes from the African language of Swahili (swah HEE lee). It means "first fruits." During Kwanzaa, people gather to honor their past and celebrate values like working together and helping each other.

Kwanzaa lasts for seven days, from December 26 to January 1. In communities like Detroit, Michigan, people gather each night of this week to celebrate and share food. They also light candles on the kinara (kee NAH rah), a candle holder. On a straw mat, they also put symbols of Kwanzaa like an ear of corn. It is a symbol of children. One ear of corn is often placed on the mat for each child in the family.

New Year's Day

SAN FRANCISCO, CALIFORNIA— Happy New Year! Did you know that New Year's celebrations are thousands of years old? People have always celebrated the coming of the New Year. Long ago people celebrated the New Year at harvest time. Later, people changed their calendar to begin the year on January 1.

In our country people often welcome in the New Year with parties. Some people also like to make New Year's promises to break bad habits or start good ones for the coming new year.

Some culture groups also have their own New Year's celebrations. For example, the Chinese New Year often takes place early in February, at the start of the full moon. In cities like San Francisco, this celebration lasts for about two weeks.

In California, people celebrate New Year's Day with parade floats made from roses (top). Chinese-Americans celebrate with a dragon, a sign of good luck (bottom).

Martin Luther King, Jr. Day

Dr. Martin Luther King, Jr. was born in this house in Atlanta in 1929 (bottom, right). Dr. King worked to make schools open to all people (bottom, left).

ATLANTA, GEORGIA—Dr. Martin Luther King, Jr., was born in Atlanta, Georgia, on January 15, 1929. During the 1950s and 1960s, he worked to make sure all people were treated fairly. In 1963 he made an important speech in Washington, D.C. He said "I have a dream" about black and white Americans living together as friends.

Dr. King was killed in 1968. Later, his birthday became a holiday. Today, in Atlanta his birthday is called a "Day of Service." Many children in Atlanta spend the day volunteering in their communities. They clean playgrounds and do other helpful activities. By working together for their community, they are trying to make Dr. Martin Luther King, Jr.'s, dream come true.

Presidents' Day

The man in the picture looks like Abraham Lincoln (top). On Presidents' Day he tells people about Lincoln's life. At the Washington Monument people gather to honor George Washington (below).

WASHINGTON, D. C.—Happy Birthday George and Abraham! Though their birthdays are on different days of the month and years apart, we celebrate George Washington's and Abraham Lincoln's birthdays on the same day. It is the third Monday in February. This holiday is called Presidents' Day.

George Washington was our country's first President. His birthday is celebrated every year at the Washington Monument in Washington, D.C.

Abraham Lincoln was President of our country during the Civil War. He was killed after the war in 1865. Every year people meet in Springfield, Illinois, to celebrate his birthday. Springfield was where Lincoln lived. How do you celebrate Presidents' Day?

Eid al Fitr

Children have fun by performing a play about the celebration of Eid al Fitr (top).

CHICAGO, ILLINOIS—If you lived in a Muslim community you would say "Eid Mubarak" (eed moo BAHR ak), on a holiday called Eid al Fitr (eed ahl FIHT er). These words mean "May your holiday be blessed."

Eid al Fitr takes place every year after the end of a month called Ramadan (rah mah DAHN). During this month, Muslims do not eat or drink during the day. It helps them try to become better people. In communities like Chicago, Illinois, families and friends celebrate Eid al Fitr with an early morning prayer.

Children dress in new clothes and get presents. Later, families and friends join together for a fun meal. Sweet foods made with dates and honey are a favorite treat. As part of the celebration, each family gives food or money to help others.

Cinco de Mayo

SAN ANTONIO, TEXAS—Have you ever heard someone say, "Viva la libertad!" (vee VAH lah lee bihr tahd)? It means, "long live liberty," in Spanish. In communities like San Antonio, Texas, these words are often said during a holiday called Cinco de Mayo (SEEN ko deh MĪ yoh). This holiday celebrates a Mexican army win over the French army on May 5, 1862 in Mexico. They fought because Mexico wanted liberty, to be free, from France.

Enjoying a parade (top) and dancing in traditional clothes (bottom) are two ways Mexican-Americans celebrate Cinco de Mayo.

Cinco de Mayo means "fifth of May" in Spanish. On this day, Mexican Americans in San Antonio and other communities celebrate with an all-day party. They give speeches. They sing and dance. The Mexican flag and the United States flag are often waved side by side. This is a symbol that both countries are friendly toward each other.

Memorial Day

SPARTANBURG, SOUTH CAROLINA—Not all holidays honor leaders and other well known people in our country's past. On a holiday called Memorial Day, Americans remember soldiers who have died fighting in our country's wars.

Memorial Day is on the last Monday in May. People celebrate Memorial Day in different ways. In Spartanburg, South Carolina, soldiers and citizens gather at the war memorial at Duncan Park. They say the Pledge of Allegiance. Then they place flowers on the memorial to honor the 633 people from Spartanburg who have died in wars since 1900. How is Memorial Day celebrated by people in your community?

At Duncan Park, speeches are given and wreaths are placed in honor of people who have died fighting wars in our country's past.

Independence Day

BATON ROUGE, LOUISIANA—Summer is a special time across our country. For many people summer fun starts only after a very well-known holiday. Can you guess the holiday? Well, if you said "July 4th," or "Independence Day," Happy holiday to you! This day marks the celebration of our country's birthday on July 4, 1776. It reminds us of our country's independence from England.

How do you like to celebrate Independence Day? In Baton Rouge (BAT uhn roohz), Louisiana, people gather for a big party along the Mississippi River. They dance and eat fun foods. And when night comes, look out. Here come the colorful fireworks!

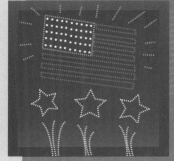

Pop!, Bang!, Wiz! That's the sound of fireworks exploding on Independence Day in communities like Baton Rouge, along the Mississippi River.

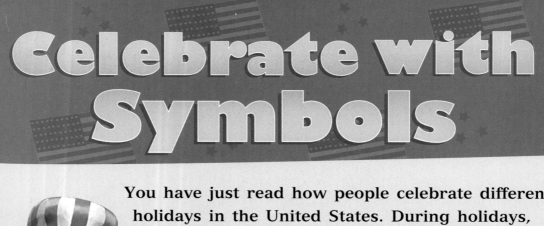

You have just read how people celebrate different holidays in the United States. During holidays, people come together to celebrate things that are important to them. Holidays help people feel that they are a part of their community and their country.

Symbols also help people to feel that they are a part of their community and country. A symbol is something that stands for something else. Some symbols help us remember people and ideas from the past that are important today. For many people our flag is a symbol that we are one country made up of fifty states. What symbols are important to people in your community?

Here's Uncle Sam. He is the popular symbol of our country. His Initials, "U.S.", are the same as the United States. Have you ever seen him?

These little leaguers are standing at attention during "The Star-Spangled Banner." It is a song that honors our flag as a symbol of our country.

The Statue of Liberty in New York Harbor has greeted millions of immigrants who came seeking better lives in our country. The Statue is a symbol of freedom and opportunity for people.

▲

Look up above. It is a bald eagle, a high flying symbol of our country being strong and free.

Our United States flag is a symbol of our country's past and future. Its 13 stripes are a symbol of the thirteen colonies. Its 50 stars are a symbol of our 50 states.

REFERENCE SECTION

The Reference Section has many parts, each with a different type of information. Use this section to look up people, places, and events as you study.

R4   Atlas

An atlas is a collection of maps. An atlas can be a book or a separate section within a book. This Atlas is a separate section with maps to help you study the geography in this book.

NORTH AMERICA: Political

EUROPE

ASIA

ICELAND

ARCTIC OCEAN

Chukchi Sea

Bering Sea

Bering Strait

Ellesmere Island

Queen Elizabeth Islands

GREENLAND (DEN.)

ALASKA (U.S.)

Yukon River

Beaufort Sea

Banks Island

Parry Islands

Baffin Bay

Fairbanks

Anchorage

Victoria Island

Baffin Island

Nuuk

Gulf of Alaska

Mackenzie River

Great Bear Lake

Iqaluit

Davis Strait

Juneau

Yellowknife

Great Slave Lake

Hudson Bay

Labrador Sea

Lake Athabasca

PACIFIC OCEAN

Edmonton

Saskatchewan River

CANADA

Newfoundland

Vancouver Island

Columbia R.

Lake Winnipeg

Gulf of St. Lawrence

Vancouver

Lake Manitoba

Quebec

Seattle

Winnipeg

Lake Superior

Montreal

Portland

Snake River

Ottawa

Lake Huron

Toronto

Boston

Salt Lake City

Minneapolis

Lake Michigan

Detroit

Lake Ontario

New York

Great Salt Lake

Chicago

Lake Erie

Philadelphia

San Francisco

Platte River

Missouri River

Washington, D.C.

ATLANTIC OCEAN

Denver

Arkansas River

St. Louis

Ohio River

Colorado River

UNITED STATES

Los Angeles

Phoenix

Atlanta

BERMUDA (U.K.)

Dallas

Mississippi River

Ciudad Juárez

Houston

Rio Grande

New Orleans

Miami

ANTIGUA AND BARBUDA

THE BAHAMAS

St. John's

Gulf of California

Monterrey

Gulf of Mexico

Nassau

ST. KITTS AND NEVIS

PUERTO RICO (U.S.)

MEXICO

Havana

CUBA

DOMINICAN REPUBLIC

San Juan

Guadalajara

HAITI

Roseau

Mexico City

JAMAICA

Port-au-Prince

Santo Domingo

DOMINICA

Kingston

ST. LUCIA

ST. VINCENT AND THE GRENADINES

BELIZE

Belmopan

GRENADA

Caribbean Sea

TRINIDAD AND TOBAGO

GUATEMALA

HONDURAS

Guatemala City

Tegucigalpa

San Salvador

NICARAGUA

EL SALVADOR

Managua

Panama City

COSTA RICA

San José

PANAMA

SOUTH AMERICA

⊛ National capital   • Other city

| 0 | 500 | 1,000 Miles |
| 0 | 500 | 1,000 Kilometers |

N
W E
S

Caribbean Sea

Barranquilla
Maracaibo
Valencia •Caracas
Lake Maracaibo

CENTRAL AMERICA

Gulf of Panama

Orinoco River

VENEZUELA

Georgetown
Paramaribo
Cayenne

GUYANA

SURINAME

FRENCH GUIANA (FR.)

Medellín
Bogotá

COLOMBIA

Cali

Negro River

Quito
ECUADOR
Guayaquil

Iquitos

Manaus

Amazon River

River

Belém

PERU

Trujillo

Madeira River

Tapajóz River

Xingu River

Recife

Callao •Lima

Cuzco

Lake Titicaca

Arequipa

La Paz

BOLIVIA

Sucre

BRAZIL

São Francisco River

Brasília

Salvador (Bahía)

PACIFIC OCEAN

Antofagasta

Tucumán

PARAGUAY

Paraguay River

Asunción

Paraná River

São Paulo

Belo Horizonte

Rio de Janeiro

CHILE

Córdoba

Rosario

Uruguay River

Pôrto Alegre

ATLANTIC OCEAN

Valparaíso
Santiago

Buenos Aires

URUGUAY

Montevideo

Rio de la Plata

ARGENTINA

Concepción

Colorado River

N
W E
S

⊛ National capital   • Other city

0   250   500 Miles
0   250   500 Kilometers

FALKLAND ISLANDS (U.K.)

Strait of Magellan

Punta Arenas

SOUTH GEORGIA (U.K.)

R5

RUSSIA

ALASKA

ARCTIC OCEAN

CANADA

Nome

Fairbanks

Yukon River

Anchorage

Juneau

PACIFIC OCEAN

0   250   500 Miles
0   250   500 Kilometers

N
W   E
S

CANADA

Seattle
Spokane
WASHINGTON
Olympia

River

Great Falls
Helena
MONTANA
Billings

Columbia

Portland
Salem
Eugene
OREGON

IDAHO
Boise

Snake River

Missouri River

WYOMING
Pocatello
Casper
Cheyenne

Ogden
Great Salt Lake
Salt Lake City
Provo
COLORADO

Reno
NEVADA
Carson City

San Francisco
Sacramento
Oakland
San Jose

UTAH

Denver
Colorado Springs
Pueblo

CALIFORNIA

Las Vegas

River

Los Angeles
Long Beach

San Diego

Colorado

ARIZONA

Phoenix

Tucson

Albuquerque
Santa Fe
NEW MEXICO

El Paso

Rio Grande

PACIFIC OCEAN

N
W   E
S

MEXICO

PACIFIC OCEAN

Kauai
Niihau
Oahu
Honolulu
Molokai
Lanai
Maui
Kahoolawe
HAWAII   Hawaii   Hilo

N
W   E
S

0   100   200 Miles
0   100   200 Kilometers

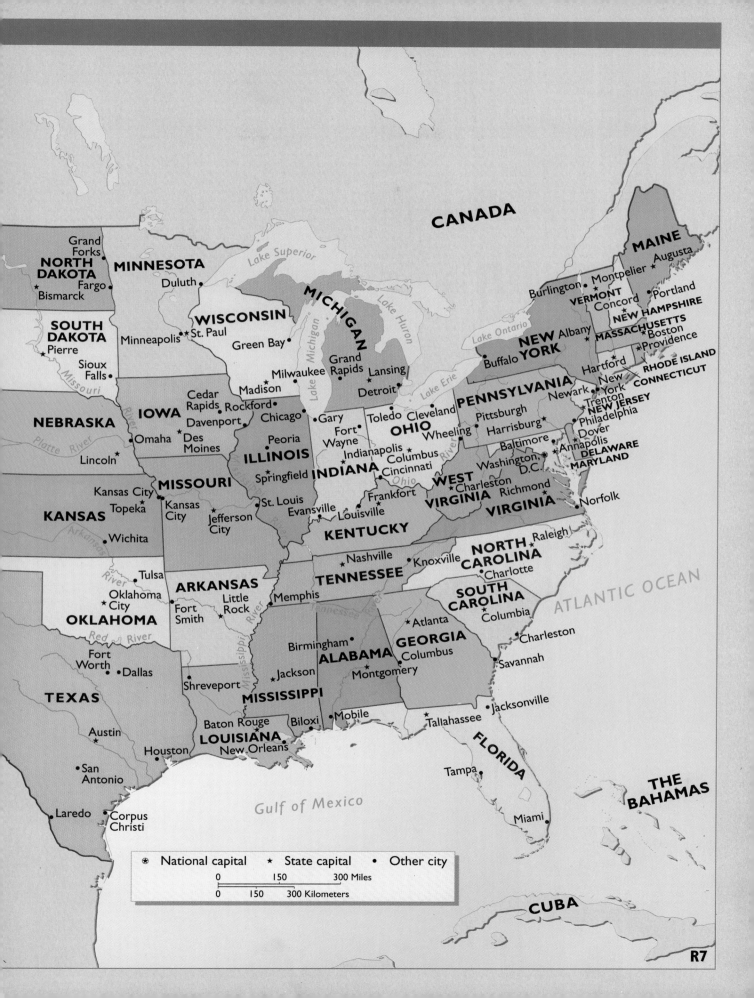

CANADA

Grand Forks
NORTH DAKOTA
★ Bismarck
Fargo

MINNESOTA
Duluth
Lake Superior

MICHIGAN

Lake Huron

MAINE
Augusta
Burlington • Montpelier • Portland
VERMONT ★ Concord
NEW HAMPSHIRE

SOUTH DAKOTA
★ Pierre
Sioux Falls

WISCONSIN
Minneapolis ★ St. Paul
Green Bay

Lake Michigan

Grand Rapids
Lansing
Detroit

Lake Ontario
NEW York
Albany
Buffalo

MASSACHUSETTS
Boston
★ Providence
RHODE ISLAND

NEBRASKA

IOWA
Cedar Rapids
Rockford
Davenport
Omaha
★ Des Moines

Chicago
Gary
Fort Wayne
Peoria

Toledo Cleveland
OHIO
Wheeling
Indianapolis
Columbus
Springfield INDIANA
Cincinnati

Lake Erie
PENNSYLVANIA
Pittsburgh
Harrisburg
Baltimore

Hartford
New
York
Newark
Trenton
NEW JERSEY
Philadelphia
Dover
Annapolis
DELAWARE
MARYLAND

CONNECTICUT

Lincoln
ILLINOIS

Madison
Milwaukee

St. Louis
Evansville
Louisville
KENTUCKY
Frankfort
Washington, D.C.

Ohio River

WEST
VIRGINIA
Charleston
Richmond
VIRGINIA
Norfolk

KANSAS
Kansas City
Topeka ★
Wichita

MISSOURI
Kansas City
Jefferson City

Nashville
Knoxville
NORTH CAROLINA
Raleigh
Charlotte

Tulsa
OKLAHOMA
Oklahoma City
Fort Smith

ARKANSAS
Little Rock
Memphis
TENNESSEE

SOUTH CAROLINA
Columbia
Charleston

ATLANTIC OCEAN

Fort Worth
Dallas

TEXAS

Shreveport
MISSISSIPPI
Birmingham
Jackson
ALABAMA
Montgomery

Atlanta
GEORGIA
Columbus
Savannah

Austin
Houston
San Antonio

LOUISIANA
Baton Rouge
New Orleans
Biloxi
Mobile

Tallahassee
Jacksonville

FLORIDA

Laredo
Corpus Christi

Gulf of Mexico

Tampa
Miami

THE BAHAMAS

⊛ National capital   ★ State capital   • Other city

0   150   300 Miles
0   150   300 Kilometers

CUBA

R7

Alaska Inset

RUSSIA

ARCTIC OCEAN

BROOKS RANGE

ALASKA

CANADA

Yukon River

ALASKA RANGE
▲ Mt. McKinley
20,320 ft.
(6,194 m)

Bering Sea

Bering Strait

0   250   500 Miles
0   250   500 Kilometers

Main Map

CANADA

Missouri   River

ROCKY MOUNTAINS

Yellowstone River

Granite Peak
12,799 ft.
(3,900 m)

BLACK HILLS

GREAT PLAINS

Puget Sound

Mt. Rainier
14,410 ft.
(4,391 m)

Mt. St. Helens
8,366 ft.
(2,550 m)

Columbia River

Mt. Hood
11,235 ft.
(3,424 m)

COLUMBIA PLATEAU

Snake River

TETON RANGE

COAST RANGES

CASCADE RANGE

Cape Mendocino

Mt. Shasta
14,162 ft.
(4,316 m)

Great Salt Lake

GREAT SALT LAKE DESERT

WASATCH RANGE

Kings Peak
13,528 ft.
(4,123 m)

Mt. Elbert
14,433 ft.
(4,398 m)

Pikes Peak
14,107 ft.
(4,301 m)

Sacramento River

SIERRA NEVADA

CENTRAL VALLEY

Lake Tahoe

GREAT BASIN

San Francisco Bay

COAST RANGES

San Joaquin River

Mt. Whitney
14,491 ft.
(4,418 m)

DEATH VALLEY

Lake Mead

COLORADO PLATEAU

Colorado River

Wheeler Peak
13,065 ft.
(3,982 m)

PACIFIC OCEAN

MOJAVE DESERT

Humphreys Peak
12,633 ft.
(3,850 m)

Salton Sea

SONORA DESERT

Gila   River

Pecos River

Guadalupe Peak
8,751 ft.
(2,667 m)

Rio Grande

Gulf of California

MEXICO

Hawaii Inset

PACIFIC OCEAN

Kauai

Oahu

Maui

HAWAII

Hawaii

Mauna Kea
13,796 ft.
(4,205 m)

0   100   200 Miles
0   100   200 Kilometers

CANADA

Lake of the Woods

MESABI RANGE

Lake Superior

GREAT LAKES

Lake Huron

Lake Michigan

St. Lawrence River

WHITE MTS.

Mt. Washington
6,288 ft.
(1,917 m)

GREEN MTS.

ADIRONDACK MTS.

Lake Ontario

Cape Cod

Hudson River

Mississippi River

CENTRAL PLAINS

Lake Erie

ALLEGHENY PLATEAU

APPALACHIAN MOUNTAINS

Susquehanna River

Long Island

Platte River

Missouri River

Wabash River

Ohio River

ALLEGHENY MOUNTAINS

Potomac River

ATLANTIC COASTAL PLAIN

Delaware Bay

Chesapeake Bay

Arkansas River

INTERIOR PLAINS

OZARK PLATEAU

Mississippi River

Tennessee River

Mt. Mitchell
6,684 ft.
(2,037 m)

PIEDMONT

Cape Hatteras

OUACHITA MOUNTAINS

Savannah River

ATLANTIC OCEAN

Red River

Brazos River

Alabama River

Chattahoochee River

Colorado River

GULF COASTAL PLAIN

Mobile Bay

Mississippi Delta

Galveston Bay

Gulf of Mexico

Lake Okeechobee

Bahama Islands

Florida Keys

Straits of Florida

N
W E
S

| 0 | 150 | 300 Miles |
| 0 | 150 | 300 Kilometers |

ARCTIC OCEAN

GREENLAND
(DENMARK)

ALASKA (U.S.)

CANADA

NORTH

AMERICA

UNITED STATES

BERMUDA
(U.K.)

ATLANTIC
OCEAN

MIDWAY ISLANDS
(U.S.)

MEXICO

See inset below

HAWAII (U.S.)

Caribbean Sea

VENEZUELA   GUYANA
SURINAME

COLOMBIA

FRENCH GUIANA
(FRANCE)

PACIFIC OCEAN

0° — Equator

GALÁPAGOS ISLANDS
(ECUADOR)

ECUADOR

SOUTH
AMERICA

SAMOA

AMERICAN SAMOA
(U.S.)

FRENCH POLYNESIA
(FRANCE)

PERU

BRAZIL

TONGA

BOLIVIA

PARAGUAY

URUGUAY

CHILE   ARGENTINA

FALKLAND ISLANDS
(U.K.)

ANTARCTICA

Central America
and West Indies

Gulf of Mexico

FLORIDA
(U.S.)

THE
BAHAMAS

TURKS AND
CAICOS IS. (U.K.)

ATLANTIC OCEAN

CUBA

CAYMAN ISLANDS
(U.K.)

JAMAICA

HAITI DOMINICAN
REPUBLIC

VIRGIN ISLANDS
(U.K.)

ST. KITTS
AND NEVIS

MEXICO

BELIZE

PUERTO RICO
(U.S.)

VIRGIN ISLANDS
(U.S.)

ANTIGUA AND
BARBUDA

GUADELOUPE
(FRANCE)

GUATEMALA

HONDURAS

Caribbean Sea

MARTINIQUE
(FRANCE)

DOMINICA

ST. LUCIA

EL SALVADOR

N

W   E

S

NICARAGUA

ARUBA
(NETHERLANDS)

NETHERLANDS
ANTILLES
(NETHERLANDS)

ST. VINCENT AND
THE GRENADINES

BARBADOS

GRENADA

PACIFIC
OCEAN

COSTA
RICA

PANAMA

TRINIDAD AND
TOBAGO

0   250   500 Miles

0   250   500 Kilometers

COLOMBIA

VENEZUELA

GUYANA

ARCTIC OCEAN

SPITSBERGEN
(NORWAY)   SVALBARD IS.
                  (NORWAY)

ICELAND

See inset below

RUSSIA   ASIA

North
Sea

EUROPE   KAZAKHSTAN   MONGOLIA

AZORES IS.   GEORGIA
(PORTUGAL)   ARMENIA   UZBEKISTAN   KYRGYZSTAN   NORTH
                TURKEY   TURKMENISTAN TAJIKISTAN   KOREA   JAPAN
MOROCCO   TUNISIA LEBANON SYRIA   AZERBAIJAN AFGHANISTAN   CHINA   SOUTH
                        ISRAEL IRAQ   KOREA   PACIFIC OCEAN
CANARY IS.   JORDAN IRAN   PAKISTAN   HONG KONG
(SPAIN)   ALGERIA   LIBYA   EGYPT   KUWAIT   BAHRAIN   INDIA NEPAL BHUTAN   TAIWAN
WESTERN SAHARA   QATAR   MACAU
(MOROCCO)   SAUDI   UNITED   WAKE ISLAND
                                    ARABIA   ARAB   OMAN   MYANMAR   (U.S.)
MAURITANIA   NIGER CHAD SUDAN   EMIRATES   BANGLADESH (BURMA) LAOS   NORTHERN   MARSHALL ISLANDS
CAPE VERDE   MALI   ERITREA   THAILAND VIETNAM MARIANA IS. (U.S.)
SENEGAL   AFRICA   YEMEN   GUAM (U.S.)
AMBIA   BURKINA   DJIBOUTI   SRI   PHILIPPINES PALAU   FEDERATED STATES
GUINEA- FASO NIGERIA   ETHIOPIA   LANKA   CAMBODIA   OF MICRONESIA
BISSAU   BENIN   CENTRAL   BRUNEI
SIERRA LEONE GHANA   AFRICAN REP.   MALAYSIA   KIRIBATI
LIBERIA TOGO   CAMEROON   UGANDA SOMALIA   MALDIVES SINGAPORE   Equator   NAURU   0°
SÃO TOMÉ AND PRÍNCIPE   GABON   KENYA   INDONESIA PAPUA   SOLOMON
EQUATORIAL GUINEA   RWANDA   NEW   ISLANDS
                CONGO   BURUNDI   INDONESIA GUINEA TUVALU
ATLANTIC   CONGO   TANZANIA SEYCHELLES   INDIAN   VANUATU   FIJI
OCEAN   REPUBLIC   COMOROS   OCEAN   NEW
                ANGOLA MALAWI   CALEDONIA
                    ZAMBIA MOZAMBIQUE   AUSTRALIA   (FRANCE)
            NAMIBIA ZIMBABWE MADAGASCAR
                BOTSWANA   MAURITIUS

N
W   E   SOUTH   SWAZILAND
S   AFRICA LESOTHO   NEW
                                                                                    ZEALAND

0   1,000   2,000 Miles

0   1,000   2,000 Kilometers

Scale accurate at Equator

ANTARCTICA

Europe

FINLAND

NORWAY   SWEDEN
                        ESTONIA
UNITED   North   LATVIA
IRELAND KINGDOM Sea DENMARK Baltic
                            Sea   LITHUANIA   RUSSIA
                    NETHERLANDS   RUSSIA
ATLANTIC   BELGIUM GERMANY POLAND   BELARUS
OCEAN   LUXEMBOURG
                FRANCE LIECHTENSTEIN CZECH
                        REPUBLIC SLOVAKIA   UKRAINE
                    SWITZERLAND   AUSTRIA HUNGARY MOLDOVA
                            SLOVENIA   N
PORTUGAL ANDORRA MONACO   CROATIA ROMANIA   W   E
        SPAIN   SAN BOSNIA AND   Black Sea S
                        MARINO HERZEGOVINA YUGOSLAVIA   GEORGIA
    GIBRALTAR (U.K.) CORSICA   ITALY ALBANIA BULGARIA
                    (FR.)   MACEDONIA
        BALEARIC IS.   TURKEY
        (SP.)   SARDINIA   GREECE   ASIA
        Mediterranean (IT.)
        Sea   SICILY
0   250   500 Miles   (IT.)   CYPRUS SYRIA
                MALTA   CRETE (GR.)   LEBANON
0 250 500 Kilometers

R11

Dictionary of GEOGRAPHIC TERMS

HILL (hil) Rounded, raised landform; not as high as a mountain.

GULF (gulf) Body of water partly surrounded by land; larger than a bay.

PENINSULA (pə nin′sə lə) Land that has water on all sides but one.

MESA (mā′sə) Landform that looks like a high, flat table.

LAKE (lāk) Body of water completely surrounded by land.

PLAIN (plān) Large area of flat land.

PORT (pôrt) Place where ships load and unload goods.

CANAL (kə nal′) Waterway dug across the land to connect two bodies of water.

BAY (bā) Body of water partly surrounded by land.

HARBOR (här′bər) Protected place by an ocean or river where ships can safely stay.

BEACH (bēch) Land covered with sand or pebbles next to an ocean or lake.

ISLAND (ī′lənd) Land that is surrounded on all sides by water.

MOUNTAIN (moun′tən) High landform with steep sides; higher than a hill.

CANYON (kan′yən) Deep river valley with steep sides.

VALLEY (val′ē) Area of low land between hills or mountains.

RIVER (ri′vər) Long stream of water that empties into another body of water.

PLATEAU (pla tō′) High flat area that rises steeply above the surrounding land.

COAST (kōst) Land next to an ocean.

CLIFF (klif) High steep face of rock.

OCEAN (ō′shən) A large body of salt water.

Gazetteer

This Gazetteer is a geographical dictionary that will help you to pronounce and locate the places discussed in this book. The page numbers tell you where each place appears on a map (m.) or in the text (t.).

A

Africa (af′ri kə) A continent located in the Eastern and Southern hemispheres. (m. G5, t. 59)

Antarctica (ant ärk′ti kə) A continent in the Southern Hemisphere. (m. G5)

Arctic Ocean (ärk′tik ō′shən) A large body of water located in the Northern Hemisphere. (m. G5)

Argentina (är jən tē′nə) A country in southern South America. (m. 322, t. 322)

Asia (ā′zhə) A continent in the Eastern and Northern hemispheres. (m. G5, t. 292)

Atlantic Ocean (at lan′tik ō′shən) A large body of water located to the east of North and South America. (m. G5, t. 37)

Australia (ôs trāl′yə) An island continent in the Southern Hemisphere between the Pacific and Indian oceans. (m. G5, t. 322)

B

Baltimore (bôl′tə môr) Port city on the Chesapeake Bay in the state of Maryland. (m. 243, t. 252)

Belgium (bel′jəm) A country in Western Europe on the North Sea. (m. 257)

Bothell (bäth′əl) A suburban community near Seattle, Washington. (t. 18)

C

Calais (ka lā) City that is the connecting point for the English Channel Tunnel in France. (m. 257)

Canada (kan′ə də) A very large country located in the northern part of North America, bordering the United States. (m. 211, t. 321)

Capitol (kap′i təl) The building in Washington, D.C., where Congress meets. (m. 171, t. 171)

Chesapeake Bay (ches′ə pēk bā) A bay, partly enclosed by Maryland and Virginia. (m. 99, t. 99)

Chicago (shi kä′gō) A port city in northeastern Illinois. It is the largest city in the state. (m. 23, t. 227)

Chinatown (chī′nə toun) A large Chinese-American community in San Francisco, California. Many Chinese first came to this area during the Gold Rush in 1849. (m. 118, t. 129)

Colombia (kə ləm′bē ə) A country in the northwestern part of South America. (m. R5, t. 323)

Cuajimalpa (kwä hē mäl′pə) A suburban community near Mexico City, Mexico. (t. 25)

pronunciation key

a	at	ī	ice	u	up	th	thin
ā	ape	îr	pierce	ū	use	th	this
ä	far	o	hot	ü	rule	zh	measure
âr	care	ō	old	ù	pull	ə	about, taken,
e	end	ô	fork	ûr	turn		pencil, lemon,
ē	me	oi	oil	hw	white		circus
i	it	ou	out	ng	song		

Cumberland (kəm′bər lənd) The most eastern city on the National Road. It is located in Maryland. (m. 243, t. 248)

D

Dakar (dä kär′) The capital and largest city in the country of Senegal. (m. 179, t. 178)

Detroit (di troit′) The largest city in Michigan. It is an important automobile manufacturing center. (m. 23, t. 312)

E

Eastern Hemisphere (ēs′tərn hem′is fîr) The half of Earth east of the Atlantic Ocean that includes Europe, Africa, Asia, and Australia. (m. 58, t. 58)

Echo Park (ek′ō pärk) An urban community in Los Angeles, California. (m. 329, t. 329)

Ellis Island (el′is ī′lənd) A small island located near New York City. It was the first stop for millions of immigrants who came to the United States from 1892 to 1954. (t. 219)

England (ing′glənd) Part of the United Kingdom, an island country off the continent of Europe. (m. 257, t. 256)

English Channel (ing′glish chan′əl) A narrow waterway between England and France. It connects the Atlantic Ocean and the North Sea. (m. 257, t. 256)

Equator (i kwā′tər) An imaginary line around the middle of Earth between the Northern Hemisphere and the Southern Hemisphere. (m. G4, t. G4)

Erie Canal (îr′ē kə nal′) A narrow waterway located in New York State connecting the Hudson River with Lake Erie. (m. 249, t. 248)

Europe (yůr əp) The smallest of Earth's seven continents. (m. G5, t. 256)

F

Folkestone (fōk′stən) City that is the connecting point for the English Channel Tunnel in England. (m. 257)

Four Corners (fôr kôr′nərz) The only place in the United States where four states meet. The states are Arizona, New Mexico, Utah, and Colorado. (m. 79, t. 78)

France (frans) A country in western Europe on the Atlantic Ocean and the Mediterranean Sea. (m. 257, t. 256)

G

Golden Gate National Recreation Area (gōl′dən gāt nash′ə nəl rek rē ā′shən âr ē ə) A large park located in San Francisco, California, and an area north of the city along the Pacific Coast. (m. 118, t. 118)

H

Hudson River (hud′ sən riv′ər) A river that flows in the eastern part of New York State. (m. 249, t. 243)

I

Independence (in di pen′dəns) A community in Missouri that marked the beginning of the Oregon Trail in the 1840s. (m. 211, t. 211)

India (in′dē ə) A country located in South Asia. (R11, t. 234)

Indian Ocean (in′dē ən ō′shən) A large body of water located east of Africa. (m. G5)

Italy (it′ə lē) A country in southern Europe. (m. 322, t. 322)

J

Jamestown (jāmz′toun) A community in southeastern Virginia along the James River.

Settled in 1607, it was the first permanent English colony established in North America. (m. 99, t. 98)

Jamestown Settlement (jāmz′toun set′əl mənt) A living history museum showing how the English colonists and the Powhatan lived in the 1600s. (t. 108)

Japan (jə pan′) A country of islands in the Pacific Ocean off the eastern coast of Asia. (m. 293, t. 292)

Jefferson Memorial (jef′ər sən mə môr′ē əl) A building in Washington, D.C., dedicated to the memory of President Thomas Jefferson. It was completed in 1943. (t. 172)

L

Lafayette Park (läf ē et′ pärk) A public park located near the White House in Washington, D.C. (m. 176, t. 174)

Lake Erie (lāk îr′ē) The most southern of the five Great Lakes. It is located on the border between Canada and the United States. (m. 41, t. 248)

Lake Huron (lāk hyür′ən) The second largest of the five Great Lakes. It is located on the border between Canada and the United States. (m. 41)

Lake Michigan (lāk mish′ə gən) The third largest of the five Great Lakes. It is located between the states of Michigan and Wisconsin. (m. 41)

Lake Ontario (lāk on târ′ē ō) The smallest of the five Great Lakes. It is located on the border between Canada and the United States. (m. 41)

Lake Superior (lāk sə pîr′ē ər) The largest of the five Great Lakes. It is located on the border between Canada and the United States. (m. 41)

Lincoln Memorial (ling′kən mə môr′ē əl) A building in Washington, D.C., that honors President Abraham Lincoln. (m. 176, t. 173)

M

Mesa Verde (mā′sə vûr′dē) The ruins of an Anasazi community built into the side of a cliff and located in the southwestern part of the state of Colorado (m. 79, t. 80)

Mesa Verde National Park (mā′sə vûr′dē nash′ə nəl pärk) A national park in the state of Colorado that was an Anasazi community long ago. (m. 89, t. 88)

Mexico (mek′si kō) A country in North America that borders the southern United States. (m. 25, t. 24)

Mexico City (mek′si kō sit′ē) The capital of Mexico. (m. 25, t. 25)

Mission Dolores (mish′ən dōl lô′rəs) Former Spanish mission built in San Francisco, California, in 1776. Today it is a church and museum visited by many people. (m. 118, t. 123)

Mississippi River (mis ə sip′ē riv′ər) One of the longest rivers in North America. It flows south from northern Minnesota into the Gulf of Mexico. (m. 40–41, t. 37)

N

National Mall (nash′ə nəl môl) An area in Washington, D.C. where many monuments, memorial, museums, and government buildings are located. (m. 176-177, t. 176)

National Road (nash′ə nəl rōd) A highway built in the 1800s that ran from Cumberland, Maryland to Vandalia, Illinois. It opened the way for people to move west. (m. 243, t. 243)

New England (nü ing′glənd) The northeastern part of the United States. It includes Maine, Vermont, New Hampshire, Massachusetts, Connecticut, and Rhode Island. (m. 187, t. 187)

New Orleans (nü ôr′lē ənz) The largest city in the state of Louisiana. It is an important Mississippi River port. (m. R7, t. 17)

New York City (nü yôrk sit′ē) The largest city in the United States, located in southeastern New York. (m. 249, t. 218)

Nigeria (nī jîr′ ē ə) A country in West Africa. (m. 322, t. 234)

North America (nôrth ə mer′i kə) A continent in the Northern and Western hemispheres. (m. G5, t. 59)

Northern Hemisphere (nôr′thərn hem′i sfîr) The half of Earth north of the equator. (m. 59, t. 58)

North Pole (nôrth pōl) The place farthest north on Earth. (m. G5)

Norton (nôr′tən) A farming community in northern Kansas. (m. 302, t. 300)

Oakland (ōk′lənd) A port city in western California. It is on San Francisco Bay directly opposite the city of San Francisco. (m. R6, t. 195)

Oregon City (ôr′i gən sit′ē) A city located in the northwestern part of Oregon. In the 1840s it marked the end of the Oregon Trail. (m. 211, t. 214)

Oregon Trail (ôr′i gən trāl) A route that pioneers used in their move west in the 1840s. It ran from Independence, Missouri to Oregon City, Oregon. (m. 211, t. 211)

P

Pacific Ocean (pə sif′ik ō′shən) A large body of salt water bordering the west side of the United States. (m. G5, t. 37)

Paracas (pə räk′əs) A fishing community located in the country of Peru in South America. (m. 53, t. 52)

Peru (pə rü′) A country on the western coast of South America. (m. 53, t. 52)

Philadelphia (fil ə del′fē ə) A port city in southeastern Pennsylvania. It is the largest city in the state. (m. 147, t. 146)

Phillipines (fil′ə pēnz) An island country located in Southeast Asia, separated from the mainland by the South China Sea. (m. R11, t. 323)

Poland (pō′lənd) A country in Eastern Europe on the Baltic Sea. (m. R11, t. 234)

Portland (pôrt′lənd) A port city in northwestern Oregon on the Columbia River. (m. R6, t. 194)

R

Raleigh (rô′lē) The capital city of the state of North Carolina. (m. 275, t. 274)

Rochester (räch′ə stər) A rural farming community located in northern Indiana. (m. 23, t. 19)

Rocky Mountains (rok′ē moun′tənz) The longest mountain range in North America. It stretches from Alaska into Mexico. (m. 40, t. 38)

Russia (rush′ə) A country in Eastern Europe and Northern Asia. (m. 322, t. 322)

pronunciation key

a at; ā ape; ä far; âr care; e end; ē me; i it; ī ice; îr pierce; o hot; ō old; ô fork; oi oil; ou out; u up; ū use; ü rule; ù pull; ûr turn; hw white; ng song; th thin; th this; zh measure; ə about, taken, pencil, lemon, circus

S

Sacramento (sak rə men′tō) The capital of the state of California. It also served as the westernmost stop on the route of the pony express. (m. 10, t. 8)

St. Joseph (sānt jō′zef) A city in Missouri that was the easternmost stop on the route of the pony express. (m. 251, t. 251)

San Diego (san dē ā′gō) A port city in southern California. (m. 126, t. 232)

San Francisco (san frən sis′ kō) A diverse port city located in California along the Pacific Ocean. (m. 118, t. 118)

San Francisco Bay (san frən sis′kō bā) A bay that is located next to the city of San Francisco, California, and is connected to the Pacific Ocean by the Golden Gate. (m. 118, t. 118)

Senegal (sen′i gôl) A country in western Africa. (m. 179, t. 178)

Shapleigh (shap′lē) A rural community in the state of Maine. (m. 187, t. 187)

South America (south ə mer′i kə) A continent in the Southern and Western hemispheres. (m. G5, t. 52)

Southern Hemisphere (suth′ərn hem′i sfîr) The half of Earth south of the equator. (m. 59, t. 58)

South Pole (south pōl) The place farthest south on Earth. (m. G5)

T

Tampa (tam′pə) A port city in west-central Florida on the Gulf of Mexico. (m. R7, t. 193)

Tokyo (tō′kyō) The capital of Japan and its largest city. (m. 293, t. 292)

V

Vandalia (vân dal′ē ə) The western-most city on the National Road. It is located in the state of Illinois. (m. 243, t. 248)

Veracruz (ver ə krüz′) A port city on the eastern coast of Mexico. (t. 232)

Vietnam Veterans Memorial (vē et näm′ vet′ər ənz mə môr′ē əl) A place in Washington, D.C., that has the names of more than 58,000 Americans who died in the Vietnam War. (m. 176, t. 173)

Virginia (vər jin′yə) A southern state on the Atlantic Ocean. It was one of the original 13 colonies. (m. 99, t. 98)

W

Washington, D.C. (wô′shing tən) Capital city of the United States. (m. 171, t. 168)

Washington Monument (wô′shing tən mon′yə mənt) A tall tower in Washington, D.C., that honors President George Washington. (m. 176, t. 172)

Western Hemisphere (wes′tərn hem′i sfîr) The half of Earth that includes North and South America. (m. 58, t. 58)

White House (hwīt hous) The home of the President of the United States, located in Washington, D.C. (m. 171, t. 166)

Biographical Dictionary

The Biographical Dictionary tells you about the people you have learned about in this book. The Pronunciation Key tells you how to say their names. The page numbers let you see where each person first appears in the text.

Adams, Abigail (ad′əmz), 1744–1818 Wife of President John Adams and mother of another president, John Quincy Adams. (p. 166)

Bell, Alexander Graham (bel, al ig zân′dər grā′əm), 1847–1922 Inventor who built the first working telephone in 1876. (p. 252)

Adams, John (ad′əmz), 1735–1826 The second President of the United States, 1797-1801. He was the first President to live in the White House. (p. 166)

Cooper, Peter (kü′pər), 1791–1883 Inventor who built the *Tom Thumb* in 1830, one of the first railroad steam engines. (p. 244)

Banneker, Benjamin (ban′i kər), 1731–1806 Surveyor who helped to draw plans for designing the city of Washington, D.C. in 1791. (p. 168)

Earhart, Amelia (âr′härt, â mēl yuh), 1898–1937 First woman to fly alone across the Atlantic and Pacific oceans. (p. 246)

pronunciation key

a	at	ī	ice	u	up	th	thin
ā	ape	îr	pierce	ū	use	th	this
ä	far	o	hot	ü	rule	zh	measure
âr	care	ō	old	ù	pull	ə	about, taken,
e	end	ô	fork	ûr	turn		pencil, lemon,
ē	me	oi	oil	hw	white		circus
i	it	ou	out	ng	song		

Ford, Henry (fôrd), 1863–1947 Maker of the Model T car in 1908. He made his cars so that many people could afford them. (p. 245)

Jemison, Mae (jem'ə sən, mā), 1956– In 1992 she became the first African American woman to travel in space. (p. 246)

Franklin, Benjamin (frang'klin), 1706–1790 American colonial leader, writer, and scientist. (p. 147)

King, Martin Luther, Jr. (king), 1929–1968 Leader who worked to make laws fair for all people. (p. 229)

Fulton, Robert (ful'tən), 1765–1815 Inventor who built the *Clermont,* one of the first steamboats, in 1807. (p. 243)

L' Enfant, Pierre (län fän', pē'yâr), 1754–1825 Builder who drew up the plans for Washington, D.C. in 1791. (p. 167)

Jefferson, Thomas (jef'ər sən), 1743–1826 Colonial leader who wrote the Declaration of Independence and was third President of the United States. (p. 150)

Lawrence, Jacob (lôr'əns), 1917– Artist who made a series of paintings about the Great Migration in 1941. (p. 224)

Lin, Maya Ying (lin, mīʹə ying), 1959– Artist who designed the Vietnam Veterans memorial in Washington, D.C. (p. 174)

Lincoln, Abraham (lingʹkən), 1809–1865 The sixteenth President of the United States, 1861–1865. He led the North during the Civil War and wanted to end slavery. (p. 225)

Lyons, Oren (līʹənz, ôrʹən), 1931– A teacher and leader of the Iroquois people. (p. 74)

Madison, James (madʹə sən), 1751–1836 The fourth President of the United States, 1809–1817. In 1787, he made a plan for three different parts of government. (p. 157)

Marconi, Guglielmo (mär kōʹnē, gül yêlʹmō), 1874–1937 Inventor of the wireless telegraph in 1895. (p. 253)

Morse, Samuel (môrs), 1791–1872 Inventor who built one of the earliest telegraphs in 1844. (p. 252)

Otis, Elisha (ōtʹəs, e līʹshə), 1811–1861 He invented an automatic safety clamp in 1852 that led to the first elevators. (p. 246)

Pocahontas (pō kə honʹtəs), 1595?–1617 Daughter of Chief Powhatan who helped the English colony of Jamestown to survive. (p. 105)

pronunciation key

a at; ā ape; ä far; âr care; e end; ē me; i it; ī ice; îr pierce; o hot; ō old; ô fork; oi oil; ou out; u up; ū use; ü rule, u̇ pull; ûr turn; hw white; ng song; th thin; th this; zh measure; ə about, taken, pencil, lemon, circus

Biographical Dictionary

Powhatan (pou ə tan'), 1550?–1618 Chief of the Powhatan who lived on Chesapeake Bay near the English settlement at Jamestown. (p. 102)

Rolfe, John (rälf), 1585–1622 Leader of Jamestown colony who grew a new kind of tobacco that could be sold for a lot of money. (p. 105)

San Juan, Eduardo (san hwän', əd währ'dō), 1925–1988 Designer of the vehicle that astronauts drove on the moon in 1971 and 1972. (p. 246)

Serra, Junípero (ser ə, h ū nē pe rō) 1713–1784 Spanish missionary who founded the first mission in present-day California in 1769. In 1776 he also established present-day Mission Dolores in San Francisco. (p. 123)

Smith, John (smith), 1580?–1631 English colonial leader in Virginia who helped the Jamestown settlement to survive during hard times. (p. 102)

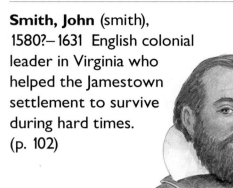

Washington, George (wô'shing tən) 1732–1799 The first President of the United States, 1789–1797. During the American Revolution he led the colonial army. (p. 154)

Wright, Orville (rīt), 1871–1948 With his brother Wilbur, he built the world's first successful airplane. (p. 245)

Wright, Wilbur (rīt), 1867–1912 With his brother Orville, he built the world's first successful airplane. (p. 245)

Glossary

This Glossary will help you to pronounce and understand the meanings of the vocabulary in this book. The page number at the end of the definition tells where the word first appears.

A

agriculture (ag′ri kul chər) The business of growing crops and raising animals for food. Farmers are an important part of the **agriculture** business. (p. 301)

almanac (ôl′mə nak) A book that comes out every year with information on many different subjects. *Poor Richard's* **Almanac** was popular long ago. (p. 148)

ambassador (am bas′ə dər) A person who is sent to represent his or her country in another country. The **ambassador** studies the different cultures of the countries she visits. (p. 178)

American Revolution (ə mer′i kən rev ə lü′shən) The war fought by the American colonies to end English rule, 1775-1783. The American colonies defeated the English in the **American Revolution**. (p. 150)

artifact (är′tə fakt) A human-made object left behind by a group of people who lived long ago. The Anasazi left behind many **artifacts** at Mesa Verde. (p. 87)

assembly line (ə sem′blē līn) A line of workers and machines all working together to make a final product. Airplanes and televisions are two products made on an **assembly line**. (p. 312)

author (ô′thər) The writer of a book or other printed work. An **author** does research before writing a book. (p. 191)

B

bar graph (bär graf) A graph that uses bars of different heights to show amounts of things. The **bar graph** showed the population of three cities in Florida. (p. 134)

bay (bā) A part of a sea or lake that is partly surrounded by land. The English sailed in ships over the Chesapeake **Bay** to get to Jamestown. (p. 99)

Bill of Rights (bil uv rīts) A list of our country's most important rights and freedoms that was added to the Constitution in 1791. The **Bill of Rights** includes the right to free speech and the right to practice religion freely. (p. 159)

C

cable car (kā bəl kär) A small car that runs on a track and is pulled by a cable. Many people in San Francisco travel on **cable cars**. (p. 129)

canyon (can′yən) A deep valley with steep sides. The river ran a few miles through the **canyon**. (p. 80)

pronunciation key

a	at	ī	ice	u	up	th	thin
ā	ape	îr	pierce	ū	use	th	this
ä	far	o	hot	ü	rule	zh	measure
âr	care	ō	old	u̇	pull	ə	about, taken,
e	end	ô	fork	ûr	turn		pencil, lemon,
ē	me	oi	oil	hw	white		circus
i	it	ou	out	ng	song		

Capitol (kap′i təl) The building in Washington, D.C., where Congress meets to make laws. Both the House of Representatives and the Senate meet in the **Capitol**. (p. 171)

cardinal directions (kär′dən əl di rek′shenz) Cardinal directions are north, south, east, and west. The airplane pilot used the compass rose to find the **cardinal directions** on the map. (p. G8)

cause (kôz) Something that makes something else happen. The **cause** of the sunburn was too much sun. (p. 290)

channel (chan′əl) A narrow waterway between two larger bodies of water. The ships sailed through the **channel** before reaching the ocean. (p. 256)

citizen (sit′ə zən) A member of a community or country. Communities need **citizens** to work together to solve problems. (p. 11)

city council (sit′ē koun′səl). Group of elected people who make the laws for a city. The **city council** meets in the town hall on Main Street. (p. 186)

Civil War (siv′əl wôr) The war between the North and the South, 1861-1865. After the **Civil War**, African Americans were free from slavery. (p. 225)

classifying (klas′ə fī ing) The grouping together of similar things. The movers **classified** the furniture into two groups: heavy pieces and light pieces. (p. 216)

cliff (klif) The high, steep face of a mountain or rock. The Anasazi lived in homes built into the **cliffs**. (p. 80)

climate (klī′mit) The weather a place has over a long period of time. Alaska has a cold **climate**. (p. 39)

coast (kōst) The land next to an ocean. There are many beaches and ports along the California **coast**. (p. 52)

coastal plain (kōs′təl plān) The flat land along a coast. The settlers built farms along the **coastal plain**. (p. 100)

colonist (kol′ə nist) Someone who lives in a colony. The **colonists** built a community at Jamestown. (p. 103)

colony (kol′ə nē) A place that is ruled by another, distant country. The King of England hoped that the **colony** at Jamestown would provide great riches. (p. 103)

communicate (kə mū′ni kāt) To share ideas, thoughts, or information with someone. Telephones help people **communicate** quickly. (p. 250)

community (kə mū′ni tē) A place where people live, work, and have fun together. It is usually made up of several different neighborhoods. Many people in Michael's **community** have fun by going to the beach during the summer. (p. 8)

compare (kəm pâr′) To see how things are alike. The students will **compare** the different jobs people have in the community to understand how they are alike. (p. 160)

compass rose (kum′ pəs rōz) A guide to the cardinal directions on a map. Mary used the **compass rose** to find that the river was south of her community. (p. G8)

compromise (kom′prə mīz) To settle an argument by agreeing that each side will give up some of its demands. In making fair laws people often work together and **compromise**. (p. 157)

Congress (kong′ris) The part of the United States government that makes laws for our country. Members of **Congress** are elected by citizens. (p. 157)

Constitution (kon sti tü′shən) The plan of government for the United States that explains what the different parts of government are and outlines the most important laws. Today the **Constitution** is still important in helping people make laws in our country. (p. 156)

consumer (kən sü′mər) People who buy goods and services. **Consumers** buy the products that are made or grown by producers. (p. 277)

continent (kon′tə nent) A very large body of land. Canada and the United States are both located on the **continent** of North America. (p. G5)

contrast (kən trast′) To see how things are different. At the museum, the visitors saw the differences in Jacob Lawrence's paintings by **contrasting** them. (p. 160)

culture (kul′chər) The way of life of a group of people including that group's language, music, foods, holidays, and beliefs. The language the Iroquois speak and the dances they participate in are all part of their **culture**. (p. 25)

D

dam (dam) A wall built across a river to control the flow of water. The **dam** was built to help provide water to the city. (p. 121)

decision (di sizh′ən) The act of choosing one thing rather than another. When you choose what food to eat, you are making a **decision**. (p. 92)

Declaration of Independence (dek lə rā′shən uv in di pen′dəns) A document written by Thomas Jefferson in 1776 that explains why the colonies had decided to free themselves from England. On July 4th, Americans celebrate the signing of the **Declaration of Independence**. (p. 150)

desert (dez′ərt) A dry environment where little rain falls. A **desert** gets less than 10 inches of rainfall each year. (p. 78)

designer (di zī′nər) A person who plans how something will look. Book **designers** choose the photographs and illustrations to be used in books. (p. 283)

diary (dī′ə rē) A written record of what someone has seen, done, or thought. In her **diary** Sallie described her life. (p. 213)

domestic trade (də mes′tik trād) Trade within one country. **Domestic trade** may involve buying wheat in Kansas and selling airplanes in Washington. (p. 321)

E

economy (i kon′ə mē) The making and consuming of goods and services. Our country's **economy** needs people to buy and sell products. (p. 277)

editor (ed′i tər) Someone who works with authors and designers in all the steps involved in making a book. The **editor** decided to include a story in the book about Philadelphia. (p. 280)

effect (i fekt′) Something that happens as a result of a cause. The **effect** of the sunburn was that Jane's skin hurt. (p. 290)

elect (i lekt′) To choose by voting. George Washington was **elected** the first president of the United States in 1789. (p. 156)

pronunciation key

a at; ā ape; ä far; âr care; e end; ē me; i it; ī ice; îr pierce; o hot; ō old; ô fork; oi oil; ou out; u up; ū use; ü rule; ù pull; ûr turn; hw white; ng song; th thin; th this; zh measure; ə about, taken, pencil, lemon, circus

employer (em ploi′ər) Someone who hires and pays other people to work. The **employer** had seven people working in the office. (p. 275)

encyclopedia (en sī klə pē′dē ə) A book or set of books with facts about people, places, things, and past events. Catherine looked in the **encyclopedia** for information about Senegal. (p. 190)

endangered (en dān′jerd) Plants or animals that are in danger of dying out. The black rhinoceros is one of many **endangered** animals. (p. 30)

environment (en vī′rən mənt) All the air, water, land, and the living things surrounding people. People are working to save the **environment** and its many resources. (p. 48)

equator (i kwā′tər) An imaginary line around the middle of Earth. The **equator** divides Earth into the Northern Hemisphere and Southern Hemisphere. (p. G4)

export (ek′spôrt) To sell and ship goods to another place or country. Canada **exports** fish to the United States. (p. 321)

F

factory (fak′tə rē) A place where things are manufactured. Many of the products we use are made in **factories**. (p. 312)

fertilizer (fûr′tə li zər) Chemicals used to help plants grow. The farmer uses **fertilizers** for the crops. (p. 301)

fiction (fik′shən) Made-up stories of people, places, and events. *Alice in Wonderland* is Jill's favorite **fiction** book. (p. 190)

flow chart (flō′ chärt) A chart that shows the order of steps that are followed to make a final product. The scientist used a **flow chart** to show how the rocket would be built. (p. 306)

fuel (fū′əl) Something that is burned to provide heat, light, or power. Most cars use gasoline for **fuel**. (p. 247)

geography (jē og′rə fē) The study of Earth and the way people, plants, and animals live on and use it. Knowing **geography** helps people learn about the land and water in their community. (p. 36)

gold rush (gōld rush) A quick movement of people to a place where gold has been discovered. During the **Gold Rush** many people hoped to get rich in California. (p. 126)

goods (gůdz) The things for sale that people make or grow. Many **goods** are made in factories. (p. 274)

governor (guv′ər nər) An elected leader of a state's government. The **governor** chooses people to help run state government. (p. 186)

Great Migration (grāt′ mī grā′shən) In the early to mid 1900s, the journey of thousands of African Americans from the South to build new lives in the cities of the North. During the **Great Migration** many people traveled to large cities in the North by train. (p. 224)

grid map (grid map) A map with a set of crisscrossing lines used to find places on the map. The tour book has a **grid map** of Mexico City. (p. G11)

guide words (gīd wûrdz) The words that appear at the top of the page in many reference books. They tell the first and last subjects that appear on each page. Richard used the **guide words** in the dictionary to find the word he wanted to define. (p. 190)

H

harvest (här′vist) Ripe crops that are gathered. The **harvest** was loaded onto trucks at the end of the summer. (p. 301)

hemisphere (hem′i sfêr) Half of a sphere or globe. The United States is located in the Northern **Hemisphere**. (p. 58)

high-tech (hī′ tek′) The use of the latest technology to make electronic and other goods. Computers are **high-tech** products. (p. 294)

history (his′tə rē) The story of what happened in the past. At Jamestown Settlement, people learn about the **history** of the Powhatan and the English. (p. 70)

I

immigrant (im′i grənt) Someone who comes from one country or place to live in another. Many **immigrants** to the United States came through Ellis Island. (p. 218)

import (im′pôrt) To buy goods from another place or country. Russia **imports** wheat from the United States. (p. 321)

independence (in di pen′dəns) Freedom from others. Mexico won its **independence** from Spain in 1821. (p. 126)

index (in′deks) An alphabetical list that shows where information can be found. Peter looked at the **index** on the grid map to find the Washington Monument. (p. 176)

interest (in′trist) Money paid for the use of borrowing money. Joe paid **interest** on his loan from the bank. (p. 276)

intermediate directions (in tər mē′dē it di rek′shənz) A direction halfway between two cardinal directions. **Intermediate directions** are helpful in showing the relationship between two different places on a map. (p. 50)

international trade (in tər nash′ə nəl trād) The import and export of goods between countries. **International trade** is important to many countries around the world. (p. 322)

J

journalist (jûr′nə list) A writer for a newspaper, magazine, or television news program. The President explained his ideas to the **journalist**. (p. 293)

K

kiva (kē′və) A special room used for religious ceremonies by some Native Americans. The Pueblo people held the ceremony in a **kiva**. (p. 84)

L

landform (land′fôrm) One of the shapes of Earth's surface. Pioneers saw many different types of **landforms** while traveling on the Oregon Trail. (p. 38)

landform map (land′fôrm map) A map that shows the different kinds of land on Earth. Mountains and hills can be seen on a **landform map**. (p. G10)

legacy (leg′ə sē) A part of our past that we value in our lives today. Celebrating Thanksgiving is a **legacy** people share from long ago. (p. 14)

---

pronunciation key

a **at**; ā **ape**; ä **far**; âr **care**; e **end**; ē **me**; i **it**; ī **ice**; îr **pierce**; o **hot**; ō **old**; ô **fork**; oi **oil**; ou **out**; u **up**; ū **use**; ü **rule**; ù **pull**; ûr **turn**; hw **white**; ng **song**; th **thin**; th **this**; zh measure; ə **about**, tak**e**n, penc**i**l, lem**o**n, circ**u**s

Glossary

line graph (līn graf) A graph that uses the rising or falling of a line to show how something changes over time. The **line graph** shows the total number of cars manufactured in the United States between 1920 and 1960. (p. 134)

living history museum (liv'ing his'tə rē mū zē'əm) A place that shows what the past was like by having people dress, talk, and do things as people did long ago. At the **living history museum,** people can eat food like Native Americans did long ago. (p. 108)

local government (lō'kəl guv'ərn mənt) The people who run a city or community. **Local governments** are often led by a mayor. (p. 186)

locator (lō'kāt tər) A small map included on a bigger, or main, map. Jeff used the **locator** to find California. (p. G9)

M

manufacturing (man yə fak'chər ing) The business of making things. People who work in **manufacturing** make many different products like cars, clothes, foods, and books. (p. 312)

map key (map kē) Something that tells what the symbols on a map stand for. Jane used the **map key** to help find the airport on the map. (p. G7)

mayor (mā'ər) A person who is the head of a city government. The **mayor** makes sure that local laws are obeyed. (p. 179)

memorial (mə môr'ē əl) Anything, such as a monument or holiday, that is set aside to remember a person or event. The Jefferson **Memorial** in Washington, D.C. honors Thomas Jefferson. (p. 172)

mesa (mā'sə) A landform that looks like a high, flat table. Native Americans grew crops on the **mesa.** (p. 80)

migration (mī grā'shən) The movement of people or animals from one place or country to another. Each year people go to the park to watch the **migration** of birds to the south. (p. 224)

mill (mil) A place where people use machines to turn natural resources into finished products. Steel and paper are products made in a **mill.** (p. 317)

mineral (min'ər əl) Natural substance found in the earth that is not a plant or animal. Iron and diamonds are examples of **minerals.** (p. 47)

mission (mish'ən) Communities set up by Roman Catholic priests to teach their religion to others. Mission Delores was established as a **mission** in 1776. (p. 123)

missionary (mish'ə ner ē) A person sent by a church to spread its religion into a different country. Spanish **missionaries** taught Native Americans to speak and write in Spanish. (p. 123)

museum (mū zē'əm) A place where people can look at objects of art, science, or history. The students saw artifacts of colonial life at the **museum.** (p. 89)

N

national park (nash'ə nəl pärk) Land set aside by a government for all people to enjoy. The family was not allowed to build a house in the **national park.** (p. 28)

natural resource (nach'ər əl rē'sôrs) Something found in nature that people use. Water and soil are examples of **natural resources.** (p. 46)

nonfiction (non fik'shən) Information about real people, places, and events. A book about the life of George Washington would be located in the **nonfiction** section of the library. (p. 190)

nonrenewable resource (non ri nü′ə bəl rē′sôrs) Things found in nature that cannot be replaced, such as minerals. People are taking care to save **nonrenewable resources**. (p. 308)

North Pole (nôrth pōl) The place farthest north on Earth. Very few people live on the **North Pole**. (p. G4)

O

oath (ōth) A serious promise made in public. New immigrants take an **oath** of loyalty to our country when becoming citizens. (p. 235)

ocean (ō′shən) A very large body of salt water. People are finding new ways to work together to help fight pollution in **oceans** around the world. (p. G5)

oral history (ôr′əl his′tə rē) Recorded interviews with people who can tell firsthand what life was like in the past. The students listened to **oral histories** to learn more about Echo Park. (p. 219)

P

peninsula (pə nin′sə lə) Land that has water on all sides but one. Paracas is a community located on a **peninsula**. (p. 53)

pioneer (pī ə nîr′) A person who is among the first to explore an area not known to them. **Pioneers** traveled for many months on the Oregon Trail. (p. 210)

plain (plān) A large area of flat land. Long ago, many buffalo lived on the **plains** of our country. (p. 38)

plateau (pla tō′) A large area of high, flat land that is raised above surrounding land. The hikers climbed up the **plateau** and pitched their tents. (p. 38)

Pledge of Allegiance (plej uv ə lē′ jəns) An oath promising to be loyal and to support the government of the United States. In saying the **Pledge of Allegiance**, people are promising to be loyal to the United States. (p. 192)

pollution (pə lü′shən) Anything, such as a harmful chemical, that spoils land, water, or air. At the town meeting, people made laws to help fight **pollution**. (p. 11)

pony express (pō′nē ek spres′) A team of daring horseback riders who swiftly rode across the western United States to deliver mail. The **pony express** delivered mail from 1860 to 1861. (p. 251)

port (pôrt) A place, such as a harbor, where ships load and unload their goods. Francis liked to watch the boats being unloaded at the **port**. (p. 233)

prairie (prâr′ē) Flat or rolling land covered with tall grasses. The rich soil of the **prairie** makes it good for growing corn and other crops. (p. 210)

President (prez′i dənt) The leader of the United States government. People vote for **President** every four years. (p. 157)

private property (prī′vit prop′ər tē) Land that is owned by people or companies. The mall was built on **private property**. (p. 310)

process (pros′es) To change a product into a different form so that it can be sold. Corn and other grains are **processed** to make breakfast cereals. (p. 305)

pronunciation key

a **at**; ā **ape**; ä **far**; âr **care**; e **end**; ē **me**; i **it**; ī **ice**; îr **pierce**; o **hot**; ō **old**; ô **fork**; oi **oil**; ou **out**; u **up**; ū **use**; ü **rule**, u̇ **pull**; ûr **turn**; hw **white**; ng **song**; th **thin**; <u>th</u> **this**; zh **measure**; ə **about, taken, pencil, lemon, circus**

producer (prə dü′sər) Someone who makes goods or services. Farmers and car makers are two examples of **producers**. (p. 283)

product map (prod′ukt map) A map that shows the places where goods are made and crops are grown. Tanya used a **product map** to find different products that are grown in Texas. (p. 302)

public property (pub′lik prop′ər tē) Land that has been set aside for all people to use. Many parks are built on **public property**. (p. 310)

publishing (pub′lish ing) The making and selling of books, magazines, CD-ROMs, musical scores, or other informational material. This book was made by a **publishing** company. (p. 280)

R

recycling (rē sī′kling) Using something over again. Karen carried the bottles and cans to the bin for **recycling**. (p. 48)

reference (ref′ər əns) Type of book or other kind of stored information that contains facts on many different subjects. Susan looked at books in the **reference** section of the library for information on gardening. (p. 190)

renewable resource (ri nü′ə bəl rē′sôrs) Things found in nature that can be replaced. Water is a **renewable resource**. (p. 308)

research (ri sûrch′) To look for information. To do their class report, students **researched** facts at the library. (p. 190)

robot (rō′bot) Machine that does jobs instead of people. **Robots** are often used to make cars and other products. (p. 314)

rural (rür′əl) A community of farms or open country where distances are far between one place and another. Many fishing villages are located in **rural** communities. (p. 19)

S

satellite (sat′ə līt) A spacecraft that is used to connect radio, telephone, and television communications. Many of the TV programs we watch are sent by **satellites**. (p. 254)

scale (skāl) A ruler on a map that measures distance. It helps you to find out the larger, real distance on Earth. The pilot used a **scale** to measure the distance between two cities on a map. (p. 22)

services (sûr′vis əz) Work that helps others by providing something they need or want. Restaurants provide a **service** by making food for customers. (p. 274)

slavery (slā′və rē) The practice of one person owning another. President Abraham Lincoln wanted to end **slavery**. (p. 107)

South Pole (south pōl) The place farthest south on Earth. Explorers and scientists travel to the **South Pole**. (p. G4)

suburb (sub′ûrb) A community located near a city. People who live in **suburbs** often work in nearby cities. (p. 18)

Supreme Court (sə prēm′ kôrt) A part of the American government that makes sure laws follow the Constitution. There are nine judges on the **Supreme Court**. (p. 157)

symbol (sim′bəl) Anything that stands for something else. The Statue of Liberty is a **symbol** of freedom for many people. (p. G6)

T

tax (taks) Money people pay to support the government. The colonists did not want to pay **taxes** to England. (p. 150)

technology (tek nol'ə jē) The use of skills, ideas, and tools to meet people's needs. Computers are an example of a **technology** that some people use every day. (p. 81)

telegraph (tel'i graf) To send messages long distances over wires, using special codes. The ambassador sent a **telegraph** from the United States to Japan. (p. 252)

time line (tīm līn) A strip marked off evenly in periods of time that shows events in the same order as they happened. The **time line** shows important events in the history of Washington, D.C. (p. 112)

town meeting (toun mē'ting) A yearly gathering of town people to discuss and vote on community laws, rules, and other issues. At the **town meeting**, students introduced their plans for building a new park. (p. 187)

trade (trād) The buying and selling of goods and services. Different countries around the world **trade** many kinds of products with each other. (p. 320)

transportation (trans pər tā'shən) The moving of people or goods from one place to another. Buses and trains are important types of **transportation**. (p. 19)

transportation map (trans pər tā'shən map) A map that shows the routes people can use to travel from place to place. Gary used a **transportation map** to locate the subway stops in the city. (p. 248)

U

urban (ûr'bən) A community that includes the city and its surrounding areas. Many people in **urban** communities live in tall apartment buildings. (p. 17)

V

volunteer (vol ən tîr') Someone who does a job by choice, without pay. Communities need **volunteers** to deliver food to people who can't leave their homes. (p. 11)

W

wildlife (wīld'līf) The animals that live in an area. Birds and fish are two types of **wildlife**. (p. 54)

pronunciation key

a at; ā ape; ä far; âr care; e end; ē me; i it; ī ice; îr pierce; o hot; ō old; ô fork; oi oil; ou out; u up; ū use; ü rule, ủ pull; ûr turn; hw white; ng song; th thin; th this; zh measure; ə about, taken, pencil, lemon, circus

index

This Index lists many topics that appear in the book, along with the pages on which they are found. Page numbers after an *m* refer you to a map. Page numbers after a *p* indicate photographs, artwork, or charts.

CREDITS

Cover design by: MMSD

Maps: Geosystems

Charts and Graphs: MMSD

Illustrations: Mike Adams: pp 246, 260, 304; Hal Brooks: pp 149; Genevieve Claire: pp 11, 28, 39, 54, 83, 100, 130, 158, 174, 195, 212, 244, 252, 276, 303; Renee Daily: pp 73, 74; Michael Hampshire: pp 116-117, 124-125; Jim Hays: pp 164-165, 208-209; Robert Korta: pp 68-69, 82, 83, 84-85, 86, 240-241; Kelly Maddox: pp 42, 71; Karen Minot: pp 322; Paul Mirocha: pp 55; Hima Pamoedjo: pp 16-19, 22, 50; Rebecca Perry: pp 314, G7, G8, G11; Rodica Prato: pp 106, 112-113; James Ransome: pp 286; Margaret Sanfilipo: pp R19-R22; Rob Schuster: pp 6, 34, 68, 97, 117, 145, 165, 184, 209, 241, 272, 298; Nina Wallace: pp 306, 307, 310; David Wenzel: pp 96-97, 144-145; Lane Yerkes: pp 216-217, 235, 289

PHOTOGRAPHY CREDITS: All photographs are by the Macmillan/ McGraw-Hill School Division (MMSD) except as noted below:

iii: t. George Jones/Photo Researchers; b. Lawrence Migdale. iv: t. Richard T. Nowitz; m. Anne Nielson for MMSD. v: l. Richard T. Nowitz; r. Anne Nielson for MMSD. vi: b.m. Anne Nielson for MMSD; b. Jeff Greenberg/The Picture Cube; t. Chermayeff & Geismar/Metaform. vii: b. Deters/Monkmeyer; m. Gary Buss/FPG International; t. Chermayeff & Geismar/Metaform. G2: t.r. Mark Wagner/Tony Stone Images; b.l. Joseph Muench. G3: t.r. Greg Mellis; m.l. Nicholas DeVore III/Photographers/Aspen; b.r. Thomas Nebbia. G2-G3: Elizabeth Wolf. G6: J.A. Kraulis/MasterFile. **Chapter** 1 2: b.l. Bob Torrez/Tony Stone; m.r. Richard Palsey/Stock Boston; t. Liz Hymans/Tony Stone; r. Lawrence Migdale; m.l. Tim Davis/Photo Researchers. 3: b.Chromo Sohm/Photo Researchers; r. Wolfgang Kaehler. 4-5: Daniel R. Westergren. 6: Jim Schwabel/New England Stock Photo. 7: l. Jack Hoehn/Profiles West; r. Barry Durand/Odyssey; m. Bonnie Sue Rauch/Photo Researchers. 8: Ed Cooper/FPG International. 9: Jim Levin for MMSD. 10: Tom Myers. 11: t.b. Tom Myers. 14: b. Thomas T. Taber/Madison Public Library. 14-15: m. George Jones/Photo Researchers. 14: frame Jim Levin for MMSD. 15: b.r. Lawrence Migdale. 15: t.r. Matt Bradley/West Stock; b.l. Sobel/Klonsky, The Image Bank; 16: postcard borders Jim Levin for MMSD; b. Fulton County Historical Society; t. John Neubauer/West Stock, Inc.; m. Louis Beneze/Liaison International. 17: t. David Noble/FPG; b. Bob Krist/Black Star. 18: t. Tim Heneghan/West Stock; b. Louis Bencze/Liaison International. 19: t. Darryl Jones, Fulton County Historical Society; b. Joseph Nettis/Photo Researchers. 21: Bryan Peterson/West Stock. 24: Howard Breitrose for MMSD. 25: J. P. Courau/D. Donne Bryant Stock Photo. 26: t.l. Robert Frerck/Odyssey; b.r. Cameramann Int'l., Ltd. 27: Howard Breitrose for MMSD. 28: r. Howard Breitrose for MMSD; l. Jim Levin for MMSD. 29: Bob Thomason/Leo de Wys Inc., NY. 30: W. Hille/Leo de Wys Inc., NY. 31: t. courtesy of Khadashia King; m. George Lujan; b. Charlotte Moore. **Chapter** 2 35: l. Uniphoto; m. Wolfgang Kaehler; r. Gabe Palmer/The Stock Market. 36: Uniphoto. 37: m. courtesy Francis Akinsulie; t. Mulvehill/The Image Works; b. Joe Sohm/The Image Works. 38: l. Luis Garcia; r. David Hiser/Photographers Aspen. 39: r. Bryan & Cherry Alexander; l. Chuck Carlton/Black Star. 41: l. Barry L. Runk/Grant Heilman; b.m.r. Trevor Wood/The Image Bank; t.r. William H. Mullins/Photo Researchers; b.r. Harold Sund/The Image Bank; t.m.r. James Randkley/Tony Stone International. 43: Terry E. Eiler/Stock Boston; l. inset Jim Levin for MMSD. 44: l. Pierre Fabre. 44-45: m. Creda Axton. 45: m.r., b.l. Pierre Fabre; t. Bettmann Archives. 46: Peter Cole/Bruce Coleman, Inc. 47: t. Hans Wendler/The Image Bank; m.r. Dwight Kuhn/Bruce Coleman, Inc.; b.l. Gordon M. Kurzweil/Uniphoto Picture Agency; b.r. D.D. Morrison/The Picture Cube. 48: l. Peter Beck/The Stock Market; r. courtesy Tara Church. 49: b. Ken Kerbs for MMSD; t. Jim Levin for MMSD. 52: Alejandro Balaguer. 53: George Holton/Photo Researchers. 54: r. Alejandro Balaguer; l. Brian Parker/Tom Stack Associates. 56: Alejandro Balaguer. 57: Michael McDermott. 60: J.P.Meyers/Academy of Natural Sciences- Vireo. 63: Monica Stevenson for MMSD. 64: m. John Running; b. Laurence Parent; t.l. Tom Bean; t.r. Anne Nielson for MMSD. 65: t.r. Richard T. Nowitz; m.r. Anne Nielson for MMSD; b.l. Robert Llewellyn. 66: b.l. Michael Schwarz. 66-67: © Michael Philip Manheim. 67: t. Dorothy Littell Greco/Stock Boston; b. Cotton Coulson. **Chapter** 3 70: Richard Welch. 72: t.l. National Museum of the American Indian; b.l. David Heald/National Museum of the American Indian; b.r. Joslyn Art Museum. 74: Monty Roessel/TBS, Inc. 75: Lawrence Migdale. 76-77: Chris Roberts. 77: b.r. Michael Crummett; b.l. John Running; t. Edwin L. Wisherd/National Geographic Society. 78: David Muench. 79: b. David Muench; t. David Carriere/Tony Stone International. 80: b.l. Todd Powell/Profiles West; b.r. Rod Planck/Tony Stone International; t.l. Ann Trulove/Unicorn Stock Photos. 81: George H.H. Huey. 87: David Hiser/Photographers Aspen; bkgnd. Jim Levin for MMSD. 88: Steve Rudolph. 89: Jerry Jacka Photography. 90: l. David Hiser/Photographers Aspen; r. The Image Bank. 91: courtesy Steve Rudolph. **Chapter** 4 98: Bruce Roberts. 99: Fil Hunter. 100: The Granger Collection. 101: Llewellyn. 102: The Bettmann Archives. 103: b.r. Superstock;l. Archive Photos; t.r. The Granger Collection. 104: b. The Granger Collection. 105: r. Don Henley & Savage/Dominion Photosource; b.l. The Granger Collection. 107: The Bettmann Archives. 108: Jamestown Yorktown Foundation. 109: t. Jamestown Yorktown Foundation; b.l. Robert Llewellyn; b.r. Richard T. Nowitz/Photo Researchers. 110: b.r. Fil Hunter/Time Life Books, Inc.; t.l. Fil Hunter for MMSD. 111: Robert Llewellyn. **Chapter** 5 118: Brenda Mard/Photo Researchers. 119: Tom Myers. 120: t. Lawrence Migdale; m. San Francisco Public Library; b. FPG International. 121: California State Library. 122: Underwood Photo Archives. 123: b. Tony Freeman/Photo Edit. 126: t.b. Tom Myers. 127: Pete Baloutos/Stock Market. 128: Stock Imagery. 129: t. Wayne Newton/Photo Edit; b.l. Index Stock; b.r. Lawrence Migdale. 130: t.l. Lawrence Migdale; t.r. Ed Kashi. 132: David Weintraub/Stock Boston. 133: Courtesy of Terri Crisp. 139: Monica Stevenson for MMSD. 140: t.r. Santi Visalli/The Image Bank; b.r. Richard T. Nowitz; l. Anne Nielson for MMSD. 141: b.l. Anne Nielson for MMSD; r. Jeff Hunter/The Image Bank. 142: t.l. Stanley Tretick; b.l. Library of Congress. 142-143: bkgnd: Tony Stone Images. 143: t. The Bettmann Archive; b. Dennis Brack/Black Star. **Chapter** 6 146: The Bettmann Archives. 147: r. Cigna Museum & Art Collection; l. North Wind Picture Archives. 148: Joseph Boggs Beale/Modern Galleries Philadelphia, PA. 150-151: Superstock. 152-153: m. Doug Armand/Tony Stone Worldwide. 152: b.l. NASA. 153: t.l. North Wind Pictures; b. Archive Photos; m.r. Martin Rogers/Stock Boston. 154: FPG International. 155: b.l. Archive Photos; m., t. The Granger Collection. 156: t.r. National Geographic Photographer George F. Mobley/courtesy U.S. Capitol Historical Society; b.l. Superstock. 157: r. Ken Kerbs for MMSD; t. Superstock. 158: r. Ted Spiegel. 159: Harold M. Lambert. 160-161: The Granger Collection. (on page credit). 162: The Granger Collection. **Chapter** 7 166: c. White House Historical Association. Photo by National Geographic Society. 167: Photri. 168: The Granger Collection. 169: North Wind. 170: Mike Yamashita/Woodfin Camp & Associates. 171: courtesy: Ms. Bernadette Senn. 172: David Ball/The Picture Cube. 173: t. Tony Stone Images; b.l. Uniphoto Picture Agency; m. Andre Jenny/Stock South. 174: b.l. Richard T. Nowitz; r. Jim Pickerell/Stock Boston. 175: Dirick Halstead/Gamma-Liaison. 178: Nik Wheeler. 179: courtesy Dorothy Padilla. 180: b. Thierry Prat/Sygma; t. Superstock. 181: b. M & E Bernheim/Woodfin Camp. **Chapter** 8 185: b. William Whitehurst/The Stock Market; t.l. Richard Hutchings/Photo Researchers; t.r. Uniphoto; t.m. Andre Jenny/Stock South. 186: B. Howe/Photri. 187: Kevin A. Byron/ The Sanford News. 188: t. Jim Brown/Gilles Lavigne/Gino Romano; b., m. Jim Brown/Gilles Lavigne. 189: t. courtesy Wendy Wehmeyer; b. courtesy Adam Pierce. 192-193: Mark Pokemper/Tony Stone Worldwide. 193: t.r. courtesy Alberta Reid; b.r. Zigy Kaluzny/Tony Stone Images. 194: t. Ben Brink/The Oregonian; b. Ross Hamilton/The Oregonian. 195: Oakland City Council, courtesy John Russo. 196: bor. UPI/Bettmann. 197: r. Tony La Gruth/New England Stock Photography; l. Dimaggio Kalish/The Stock Market. 198: Russ Kinne/Comstock. 199: t. courtesy Suzanne Hee; m. courtesy Debbie Macon; b. courtesy Joel Rosch. 203: Robert Milazzo for MMSD. 204: t.m., t.l. Chermayeff & Geismar/Metaform; b. Jeff Greenberg/The Picture Cube; r. Andrea Pistolesi/The Image Bank; m. Anne Nielson for MMSD. 205: l. Anne Nielson for MMSD; r. Southern Stock/NASA, FL. 206: l. David Hiser/Photographers/Aspen. 206-207: bkgnd David Hiser. 207: David Hiser. **Chapter** 9 210: USDI Bureau of Land Management. 211: Oregon Historical Society. 212: The Corcoran Gallery of Art, gift of Mr and Mrs. Lansell K. Christie. 213: b.r. St. Louis Mercantile Library; m. Clackmas County Historical Society - Oregon City, Oregon; t. National Geographic Society. 214: b. Oregon Historical Society; t. The Granger Collection. 215: t. John Elk III/Stock Boston; b. Phyllis Picardi/Stock Boston. 218: Uniphoto. 219: t. Culver Pictures; b.l., b.r. Audrey Buchter. 220: b. The Jacob A. Riis Collection/Museum of the City of New York; t. Brown Brothers. 221: t. Brown Brothers; b. Lewis W. Hine/George Eastman House. 222: Nancy A. Potter/Bruce Coleman, Inc. 223: Superstock. 224: Florida State Archives. 225: Abraham Gardner/Photri. 226: t. National Geographic Society/Dr. Louis Fargo; b. National Geographic Society/Willard Price. 227: courtesy Donna Van Der Zee, photo by James Van Der Zee. 228: t. Discovery Channel/Spike Mafford; b. The Phillips Collection. 229: Superstock. 230-231: Sam Holland for MMSD. 232: Dolores Stivalet. 233: t. Victor Perez de Lara/Leo de Wys, Inc.; b. Bushnell/Soifer//Tony Stone Images. 234: t.l. Kumar S. Nochur; b.l. Nicolas Jawdosiuk; m.l. E. B. Wilson/Oyeyinka Oyelaran; r. John Ortner/Tony Stone International. 236: r. M. Mantel/SIPA Press; l. courtesy: Dept of Immigration. **Chapter** 10 242: Jeff Hunter/The Image Bank. 243: Brown Brothers. 244: The Bettman Archive. 245: t., b. Brown Brothers; m. Keith Marvin. 247: Norman Owen Tomalin/Bruce Coleman. 248-249: The Granger Collection. 250: The Bettman Archive. 251: Buffalo Bill Historical Center, Cody, WY. 252: l. Charles Harrington, Cornell University Photo; r. The Bettman Archive. 253: t. Leonard Lessin/Peter Arnold; b.r. Charmet/Science/Photo Library/Photo Researchers; b.l. Archive Photos. 254: NASA. 255: Lawrence Migdale/Stock Boston. 256: Archive/Imapress/N'Diaye. 257: John Lamb/Tony Stone. 258: t.l., t.r. Q A Photos; b. Monica Stevenson for MMSD. 259: b. Q A Photos; t. Terminus/Gamma Liaison. 260: m. Eurotunnel Education in collaboration w/ Kent Arts and Libraries. 262-263: Benn Mitchell/The Image Bank. 263: t.l. Culver Pictures; t.r. Lori Adamski Peek/Tony Stone; b.r. Bob Winsett/Tom Stack and Associates; b.l. Bob Daemmrich/Stock Boston. 267: Monica Stevenson for MMSD. 268: b. Deters/Monkmeyer Press; t.r. Gary Buss/FPG; t.l. National Museum of American Art, Smithsonian Institution, DC Art Resource - Thomas Hart Benton, Wheat 1967, Oil on wood, 20" x 21", Gift of Mr./Mrs. James A. Mitchell and Museum purchase. 269: b. Superstock. 270: l. Daniel R. Westergren.; bkgnd Richard T. Nowitz. 271: t. Steven Pumphrey; b. Jerry Jacka. **Chapter** 11 273: t. Orion Press; l. Anthony Boccacio/The Image Bank; r. Doug Milner/Uniphoto; m. Sylvain Grandadam/Photo Researchers. 274: Jim Stratford. 275: l. Jim Stratford; r. Skip Flythe. 276-278: Jim Stratford. 279: Joel Seigelman. 280-281: Robert Milazzo for MMSD. 283: t. Robert Milazzo; b. Blair Seitz/Photo Researchers. 284: t.m. Dena Abergel in A Midsummer Night's Dream; m.l. Steve Joester/FPG International; b.l. photo courtesy of Denice Burnham; b.r. Zack Burris Photography. 284-285: t. Bobbie Kingsley/Photo Researchers, Inc. 285: t. Courtesy Roberto Rodriguez. 285: t.r. photo courtesy of Alfredo Estrada; m. (television screen) Superstock; m. Eccles/Outline; b. photo courtesy of Kim Guyette; b.r. Henry Wolf/The Image Bank. 287: Anne Nielsen. 288-289: t. Currier & Ives/Museum of the City of New York. 288: b. Bob Daemmrich. 289: b.r. Eastcott/Momatiuk/The Image Works; t.r. R.L. Wolverto/Profiles West. 289: b.l. Robert Davis. 292: Ken Strait/The Stock Market. 293: courtesy Tsutomu Yamaguchi. 294: t. Richard Nowitz; b.r. Ronald D. Modra/Sports Illustrated/Time, Inc. 295: Michael S. Yamashita. **Chapter** 12 298: IBM. 299: r. Antonio Ribeiro/Gamma Liaison; m. McAllister of Denver/Uniphoto; l. Romilly Lockyer/The Image Bank. 300: Chester Peterson Jr. for MMSD. 301: b.l., t.r. Chester Peterson, Jr. for MMSD; b.r. John & Diane Harper/New England Stock Photo. 302: First Light (A.G.E. Fotostock). 303: m.l. David Overcash/Bruce Coleman; t.r. Chuck O'Rear/WestLight; b.l. Charlie Ott/Photo Researchers. 305: Michael Rosenfeld/Tony Stone Worldwide. 308: t. Alan Kearney/Viesti Assoc. 308-309: b. Peter Dreyer/The Picture Cube. 309: m.r. courtesy Andrew Romero; t.r. courtesy Dana Romero; b.m. Paul Lau/Gamma-Liaison International; b.r. Richard Treplow/Photo Researchers. 310: David E. Spaw/Midwestock. 311: Ron Sanford/F-Stop Pictures. 312: Steve Dunwell/The Image Bank. 313: t. from the collections of Henry Ford Museum & Greenfield Village; b. Brown Brothers. 314: Andy Sacks. 315: t. Frank Fisher/West Stock; b. John Riley/Southern Stock Photos. 316: l. David Ulmer/Stock Boston; r. Rob Crandall/Stock Boston. 317: Superstock. 318: H. Armstrong Roberts. 319: Marc Morrison. 320: Peter Vandermark/Stock Boston. 321: b.r. Grant V. Faint/The Image Bank; b.l. Greig Cranna/Stock Boston; t. James Kirby/Photri, Inc. 323: Uniphoto. 325: Paul Lau/Gamma Liaison International. 327: Robert Milazzo for MMSD. **Chapter** SS

(continued from page ii)

Acknowledgments
From **Ben Franklin of Old Philadelphia** by Margaret Cousins. Copyright 1952 by Margaret Cousins, renewed 1980. Random House. From **New Letters of Abigail Adams** edited w/an Introduction by Stewart Mitchell. Copyright 1947 by the American Antiquarian Society. Greenwood Press Publishers, a division of Williamhouse-Regency, Inc. **The Great Migration** . Copyright 1993 by the Museum of Modern Art, New York, and the Phillips Collection. "Harvest" from **Slave Songs of the Georgia Sea Islands.** "Georgia Folk Song", book by Lydia Parrish. Copyright 1942 by Lydia Parrish, renewed 1969 by Maxfield Parish, Jr. Reprinted by permission of Farrar, Straus & Giroux, Inc. From **"No Star Nights"** by Anna Egan Smucker. Text copyright 1989 by Anne Egan Smucker. Illustrations copyright 1989 by Steve Johnson. Reprinted by permission of Alfred A. Knopf. World Book Encyclopedia. Copyright © 1996 World Book, Inc. By permission of the publisher.

The Princeton Review
— Handbook of —
Test-Taking Strategies

STANDARDIZED TEST SUPPORT

READ QUESTIONS CAREFULLY

The most common mistake students make when they take a test is to answer the questions too quickly. Rushing through a test causes careless mistakes. Don't rush. Read each question carefully. Make sure you understand the question BEFORE you try to answer it.

THE HEMISPHERES

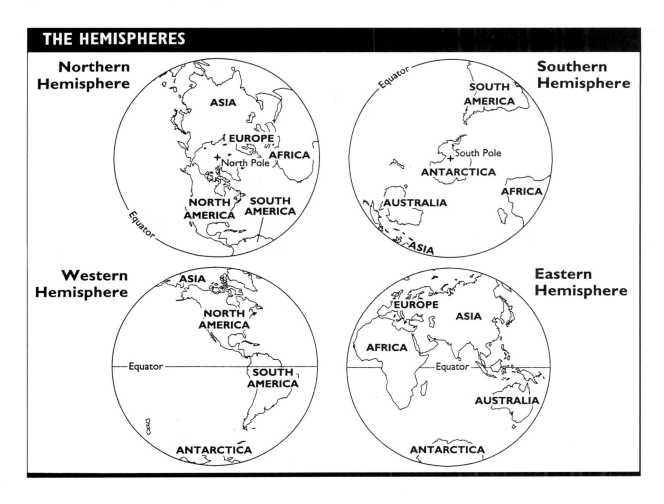

1 Australia lies in which two hemispheres?

○ Eastern Hemisphere
○ Southern Hemisphere
○ Southern Hemisphere and Eastern Hemisphere
○ Northern Hemisphere and Western Hemisphere

READING A MAP

Look carefully at all the parts of a map. Maps contain a lot of information. Whenever you see a map, you should ask yourself questions like these:

- What is the title of the map?
- Where is the map key?
- What symbols are on the map key? What do they stand for?
- Where is the compass rose? Is "North" toward the top of the page?

Make sure that you study this map and all its information BEFORE you try to answer the question below.

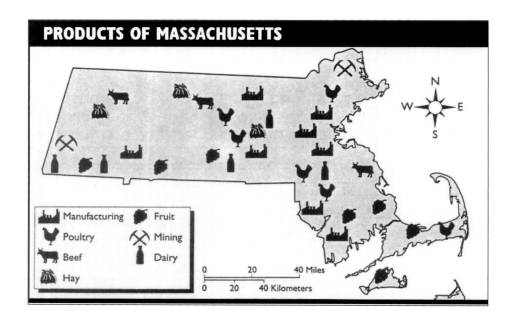

1 On the map, find the part of Massachusetts that is farthest to the east. What kind of product is produced there?

○ Manufacturing   ○ Poultry
○ Dairy   ○ Mining

Remember: Do not write in your textbook.

LOOK AT THE DETAILS BEFORE YOU START

Some test questions contain lots of details. These questions may use:

- charts
- graphs
- flow charts

- time lines
- word webs
- maps

Before you try to answer questions like these, take a few moments to study the information that the charts, graphs, maps, or other visuals contain.

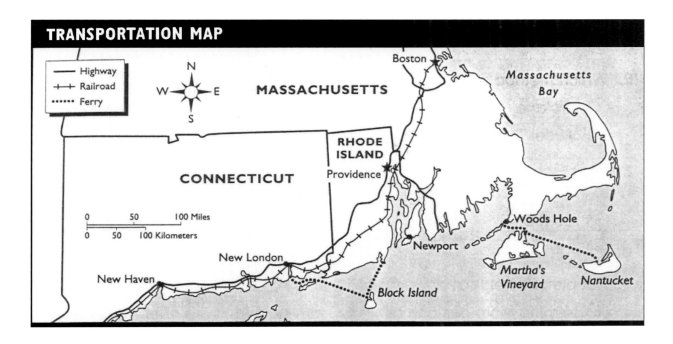

TRANSPORTATION MAP

1 Which two places are connected by a ferry?

○ Boston and New London
○ Nantucket and Woods Hole
○ Providence and New London
○ Martha's Vineyard and Block Island

READING A TIME LINE

A time line shows events in the order in which they happened. Time lines are usually read from left to right, like a sentence. If a time line is drawn vertically, it is usually read from top to bottom.

Use your finger to find information on a time line. For example, if a question asks you to find an event that occurred in 1785, look at the time line and put your finger on 1785. Putting your finger on a time line prevents careless mistakes.

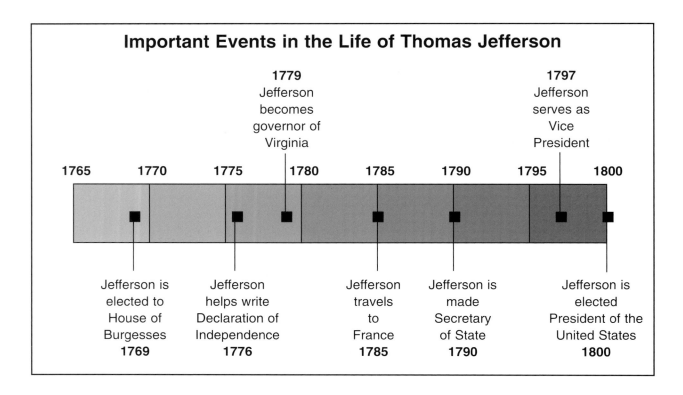

Important Events in the Life of Thomas Jefferson

1779 Jefferson becomes governor of Virginia

1797 Jefferson serves as Vice President

1765   1770   1775   1780   1785   1790   1795   1800

Jefferson is elected to House of Burgesses **1769**

Jefferson helps write Declaration of Independence **1776**

Jefferson travels to France **1785**

Jefferson is made Secretary of State **1790**

Jefferson is elected President of the United States **1800**

1 According to the time line, what important event happened in Thomas Jefferson's life in 1800?

○ He helped write the Declaration of Independence.

○ He became governor of Virginia.

○ He traveled to France.

○ He was elected President of the United States.

Remember: Do not write in your textbook.

READ DIRECTIONS CAREFULLY

Some questions begin with a set of directions. The directions contain important information. Don't skip over them! Read directions carefully.

DIRECTIONS: The time line below shows when different communities in North America were settled. Look at the time line, then answer the question.

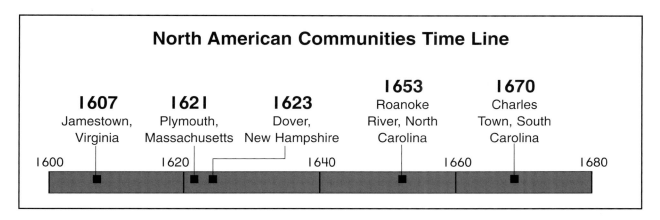

North American Communities Time Line

1607	1621	1623	1653	1670
Jamestown, Virginia	Plymouth, Massachusetts	Dover, New Hampshire	Roanoke River, North Carolina	Charles Town, South Carolina

1600   1620   1640   1660   1680

1 According to the time line, what happened in 1623?

○ Plymouth, Massachusetts, was destroyed.

○ Dover, New Hampshire, was destroyed.

○ Plymouth, Massachusetts, was settled.

○ Dover, New Hampshire, was settled.

READING A FLOW CHART

A flow chart shows the sequence of steps used to complete an activity and the order in which they happen. A flow chart usually uses arrows to show which step happens next.

The first thing to do when you look at a flow chart is to see if it has a title. The title will tell you what the flow chart is about. The next thing you should do is find the arrows. The arrows tell you the order for reading the chart. Try to find where the flow chart begins.

This flow chart shows how wool is made into yarn. Study the flow chart. Then answer Number 1.

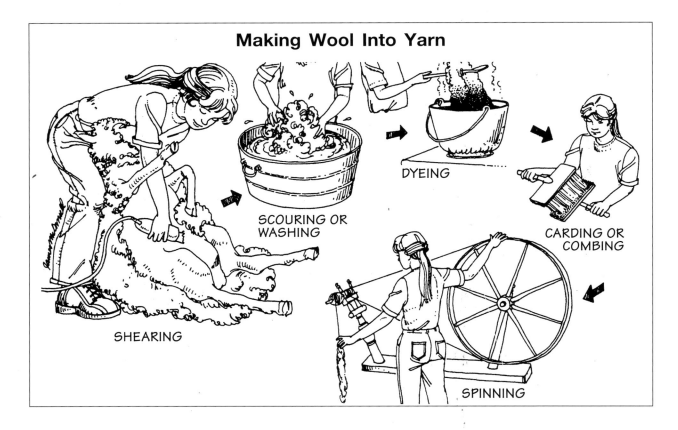

Making Wool Into Yarn

SHEARING

SCOURING OR WASHING

DYEING

CARDING OR COMBING

SPINNING

1 According to the flow chart, what happens after carding?

○ Shearing   ○ Dyeing

○ Scouring   ○ Spinning

Remember: Do not write in your textbook.

PROCESS OF ELIMINATION

Sometimes when you read a test question, you will not know the answer right away. If you don't know the answer, don't give up. Only one of the answer choices is the best answer. The others are wrong. Look at the choices and see if there are any that you know are wrong. If there are, you can ELIMINATE, or ignore, those answers. When you are finished eliminating wrong answers, choose one of the answers that is left over. Sometimes there will only be one left! That is probably the best answer.

1 The capital of Peru is

○ Boston   ○ London

○ San Francisco   ○ Lima

2 Which of these is an example of a person being a good citizen?

○ A driver throwing trash out the car window

○ A student helping the elderly by reading aloud at a retirement home

○ A person walking across the street when the sign says "Don't Walk"

○ A teenager forgetting to return a library book

Remember: Do not write in your textbook.

READING A BAR GRAPH

A bar graph uses bars of different heights or lengths to show amounts. Bar graphs are a good way to compare amounts.

A bar graph includes a lot of helpful information. It has a title that tells you what information is included. Labels tell you what the different bars represent. In the bar graph below, for example, each bar represents a different area of the world.

Look at the graph below. If you wanted to find out how many immigrants to the United States came from Asia in 1993, how would you do it? First, find the bar that represents Asia. Then, run your finger up the bar until you reach the top of the bar. Next, slide your finger to the left until you get to the numbers. About how many Asian immigrants came to the United States in 1993?

Study the graph. Then answer Number 1.

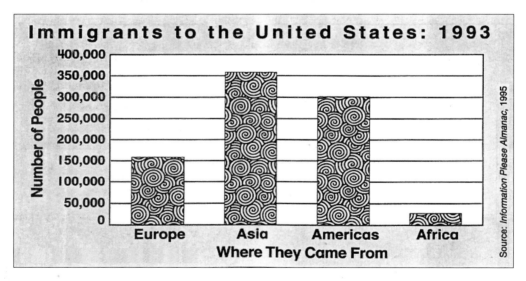

1 According to the bar graph, from which part of the world did the FEWEST immigrants to the United States come in 1993?

○ Europe   ○ Americas

○ Asia   ○ Africa

Remember: Do not write in your textbook.